Miniature Books

Comparative Research on Iconic and Performative Texts
Series Editor: James W. Watts, Syracuse University

While humanistic scholarship has focused on the semantic meaning of written, printed, and electronic texts, it has neglected how people perform texts mentally, orally and theatrically and manipulate the material text through aesthetic engagement, ritual display, and physical decoration. This series encourages the twenty-first-century trend of studying the performative and iconic uses of material texts, especially as encouraged by the activities of the Society for Comparative Research on Iconic and Performative Texts (SCRIPT).

Published

How and Why Books Matter: Essays on the Social Function of Iconic Texts
James W. Watts

Iconic Books and Texts
Edited by James W. Watts

Reframing Authority: The Role of Media and Materiality
Edited by Laura Feldt and Christian Høgel

Sensing Sacred Texts
Edited by James W. Watts

Forthcoming

Books as Bodies and as Sacred Beings
Edited by James W. Watts and Yohan Yoo

Miniature Books:
The Format and Function of Tiny Religious Texts

Edited by

Kristina Myrvold and Dorina Miller Parmenter

equinox

SHEFFIELD UK   BRISTOL CT

Published by Equinox Publishing Ltd.

UK: Office 415, The Workstation, 15 Paternoster Row, Sheffield, South Yorkshire S1 2BX

USA: ISD, 70 Enterprise Drive, Bristol, CT 06010

www.equinoxpub.com

Chapter 5 first published in this volume.
All other chapters first published in Volume 9.2-3 of the journal *Postscripts*.
© Equinox Publishing Ltd 2019.
First published in book form 2019

© Kristina Myrvold, Dorina Miller Parmenter and contributors 2019

British Library Cataloguing-in-Publication Data

A catalogue record for this book is available from the British Library.

ISBN-13 978 1 78179 860 7 (hardback)
         978 1 78179 861 4 (paperback)
         978 1 78179 862 1 (ePDF)

Library of Congress Cataloging-in-Publication Data

Names: Myrvold, Kristina, editor.
Title: Miniature books : the format and function of tiny religious texts /
   edited by Kristina Myrvold and Dorina Miller Parmenter.
Description: Bristol : Equinox Publishing Ltd., 2019. | Series: Comparative
   research on iconic and performative texts | Includes bibliographical
   references and index.
Identifiers: LCCN 2018058552 (print) | LCCN 2019006949 (ebook) | ISBN
   9781781798621 (ePDF) | ISBN 9781781798607 (hb) | ISBN 9781781798614 (pb)
Subjects: LCSH: Religious literature. | Miniature books.
Classification: LCC BL41 (ebook) | LCC BL41 .M55 2019 (print) | DDC 099--dc23
LC record available at https://lccn.loc.gov/2018058552

Typeset by CAUFIELD COPYEDITING AND TYPESETTING

Contents

LIST OF FIGURES

CONTENTS

LIST OF FIGURES

Religious Miniature Books:
Introduction and Overview

Kristina Myrvold and Dorina Miller Parmenter

Kristina Myrvold is Associate Professor of Religious Studies at Linnaeus University. She is the author and editor of numerous publications on Indian cultures, religions, and migration.

Dorina Miller Parmenter is Associate Professor of Religious Studies at Spalding University in Louisville, Kentucky. Her research interests include material uses of the Christian Bible.

Miniature books, handwritten or printed books in the smallest format, have fascinated religious people, printers, publishers, collectors, readers, and others throughout the centuries because of their unique physical features, and continue to do so today. The small lettering and the delicate pages, binding, and covers highlight the material form of texts and invite sensory engagement and appreciation. This book addresses miniature books with focus on religious books considered sacred in Jewish, Christian, Muslim, Hindu, and Buddhist traditions. The volume is a result of the interdisciplinary workshop "Miniature Books: Production, Print, and Practice" that was held at Linnaeus University in Sweden during October 2016 and included researchers working in religious studies, book history, and art history. The aim of the workshop was to discuss empirical and theoretical issues related to the production, use, and material properties of miniature books in historical and contemporary contexts by starting from a perspective that combined religious studies with book history and explored how religious interests intersect with technological developments.

The discussions from the 2016 workshop and the chapters collected in this volume reflect new perspectives on miniature religious books because until now, most of the available literature on miniatures has been written by book collectors. These collectors have contributed significantly to the understanding of the field with inventories of library holdings and catalogs of miniature books that identify and trace the histories of specific editions and present technical details of the books' physical formats (see for example: Adomeit 1980; Bromer and Edison 2007; Spielmann 1961; Welsh 1989). When discussing possible uses of miniature books, collectors have emphasized the practical function of texts that take up little space and can easily travel, lest we think that they exist only for humans' fascination with and appreciation for the craftsmanship required to produce tiny books (see for example: Bondy 1981, 3; Henderson 1933, 147; O'Donnell 1943, 177; Welsh 1987, 1). These contributions have opened up a niche for the chapters in this volume as well as continued research on miniature books in the scholarly framework of material culture and religion that focuses on the circulation, exchange, and practices of material objects and how "things" can bear significant values and actively shape human behaviors and relations in various cultural contexts (Meyer *et al.* 2010; Morgan 2010). From this perspective on material culture, books are not just conveyers or containers of knowledge but their physical forms are sites of meaning, believed to affect the content, use, and experience of them. As material objects, they are always products of human collaboration and agency. When books store religious texts they may also be attributed with various cultural understandings of textuality and sacredness and presented as having a durable life beyond human contexts and agencies. Religious people ritualize both the content and the material form of religious books, which may be perceived to evoke and mediate supernatural powers when the books are used and displayed, resulting in veneration or worship. Even if religious books are rendered as "de-contextualized" with a fixed status detached from a ritual setting, they are sharable across temporal and spatial borders and continually involved in re-contextualizing processes that create new interpretations and meanings (Myrvold 2007, 2010; Veidlinger 2006). When religious books are miniaturized to the smallest format, several questions arise related to the intricate relationships between the content and the material form of the books and the religious status and use of them.

The definitions and classifications of small books have varied over time, but characteristic for all are attempts to decide the maximum size of a miniature. In the language of modern publishers and book historians who refer to a codex-format, a miniature book is equal to a 64mo (sexagesimo-quarto) which is the smallest size of a book when a standard uncut single sheet of paper is folded to have sixty-four pages (Welsh 1987, 5). Although collectors of miniature books have not always agreed, many have identified 7.6 centimeters or three inches as the maximum size in height and width for a book to be termed a miniature (Bondy 1981, 1; Welsh 1987, 9). As Anne Bromer and Julian Edison explained their more pragmatic definition, "if a book can fit roughly in the palm of a hand it is a miniature" (Bromer and Edison 2007, 51). These definitions also imply that the smallness of miniature books is only restricted by the material limitation and can be exposed to continued experimentation when interacting with new technologies. The arrival of various printing methods (for example, typography and later lithography and photo-lithography) allowed for producing books in considerably reduced size, some of which became a celebration of new technological inventions, and nanotechnologies in the twenty-first century have extended the borders of smallness and the criteria for what can be included in definitions of miniature books. This emphasis on size as the defining criterion follows Western conventions since it presumes a norm of printed books on paper in codex format; however, many diminutive books in history and different parts of the world have used diverse materials and formats for producing texts, such as scrolls, tablets, palm leaves, bones, wood, silk, and even nutshells. From the perspective of book historians, the word "book" may rather be used broadly to signify "an object that records an idea in coded form" (Stam 2010, 26). A book is popularly associated with "codex" but, as a technical term, it may include various physical formats.

Throughout the history of books, texts of all kinds—religious (scriptures, prayer books, etc.) and secular (novels, dictionaries, almanacs, speeches, etc.)—have been created in miniature format. They have included luxury items crafted for people with power and prestige and mass-produced books sold for a shilling to common people. They have been produced for public display and admiration as well as for highly personal and private uses. Many of the diminutive books have been presented as tiny facsimiles, copies, or imitations of much larger original texts or they have included selected texts as a condensation of the original book and its semantic content. When reproducing small versions of authorized texts and presenting them in a similar, recognizable format to the larger prototypes, the miniature books can make appeals to traditions and authorities. As such, they become representations of the prototypical books that provide legitimacy to their owners and users. Yet by their smallness, the miniature books challenge the boundaries for legibility of texts and the users' access to the semantic content. The creation of clear and readable characters in the smallest handwriting or print often has been considered a sign of high quality of the books. Thus miniaturization simultaneously draws attention to material scale, the aesthetics of books, and the technologies and methods by which they are produced. The creation of books in the smallest format has involved experimentation and manipulation of the exterior forms and served as a demonstration of artistic skill among scribes, printers, and binders, expected to affect and impress potential users. In the case of religious texts, believed to be of otherworldly origin, it is especially important to reproduce exact and legible copies of the original texts that are accredited a sacred status, and the creation of these books in the smallest scale has even been considered an act of worship in itself.

The various production methods of both small and large religious books reveal how religious traditions adopt divergent stances to the media and technology that are used for creating and transmitting texts, which also shape cultural conventions for the aesthetics of books. While some traditions (like Christianity) espoused letterpress printing early, others (such as Islam) were more restrictive to typographical print since it was considered disrespectful to sacred words and instead favored handwritten manuscripts and later lithographic print which enabled a continuation of the manuscript culture. The use of letterpress printing followed, in a modified form, European typographic conventions for what constituted an aesthetically acceptable book, whereas lithography enabled appearances that provided legitimacy to printed books in cultures that valued scribal and calligraphic traditions (see for example: Myrvold 2017; Shaw 1994; Stark 2009; Yelle 2013). In many traditions, the norms guiding the aesthetics of larger books seem to have been followed on the smallest copies as well, sometimes by using complementary technologies. The introduction of photomechanical reproduction of texts in the nineteenth century could combine different technologies in the production and led to the increased popularity and mass-production of miniature books. The effects of these technological inventions transformed the books into commodities for the masses and altered the methods for their distribution, acquisition, and use.

Miniature books, and especially diminutive religious books, are often mentioned as interesting curiosities by collectors and practitioners alike, but have seldom been exposed to detailed research studies. The chapters in this volume serve to fill this gap and pay special attention to the purposes and functions of producing and using religious miniature books in shifting historical and cultural contexts. In many cases, there are very few sources available to researchers and little is known about the actual uses of or performances with the small books by those who have purchased or possessed them. Often the material properties of the books, such as their print, illustrations, and covers, stand as the only sources available for information. Producers have sometimes addressed the books' functions by adding specific paratextual features to them, like written instructions and images within the books that signal how readers should ideally approach them. As with larger books, conscious choices of the writing or print systems, orthographies, and paratextual features convey social meanings and, when specific forms of books become stipulated, the books may even represent collective identities, religions, and nations (Genette 1997; Jaffe *et al.* 2012). The books may further include different paraphernalia, like bookmarks, key or neck chains, and magnifying glasses, which indicate possible uses. Given the small scale, many explanations for their use frequently point to practicality of portability and textual intimacy, in the sense that the books may be brought for travels and can be carried close to the body. In the heyday of miniature books during the nine-teenth century, with the mass production of books and the availability of new kinds of travel through the railway system, practical explanations like these probably projected visions of a new modern and mobile lifestyle in company with one's favorite or most venerated book. Other explanations for the uses of miniature religious books refer to their apotropaic and amuletic functions to protect, bring luck, and ward off misfortunes.

Religious books, as both texts and material objects, do not have any intrin-sic quality, nature, or meaning outside of a social and relational context, but are attributed meanings and functions when humans are interacting with them. The efficiency and power that religious people ascribe to objects like religious books are often reinforced by means of ritual performances with and care of the objects. Within the religious traditions there usually exists a wide range of prescriptions and normative practices for the uses of religious books and it is often expected that the miniaturized versions should be given a treatment similar to their larger prototypes. Since miniaturization empha-sizes the material aspects of books, many chapters in this volume discuss the *iconic dimension* and how religious books are presented as material objects or artifacts. In an effort to further research on the social functions of books, James W. Watts has presented a theory about the ritualization of their seman-tic, performative, and iconic dimensions. According to Watts, religious books can be understood in terms of a ritualization that formalizes their uses. While the semantic dimension refers to different ways of interpreting the content that may create power and authority through ritualization, the performative dimension signifies different enactments of texts, ranging from recitation to dramatization, that can provide religious inspiration. The iconic dimension is expressed in the physical forms of books that convey religious significance and are used for legitimizing purposes. Religious scriptures are given spe-cial material properties that distinguish them from other books and can be manipulated in various social and political contexts to legitimize persons, institutions, and regimes by linking them to religious authority. Often all the three dimensions ritualized in culturally different ways, but printing tech-nologies have come to emphasize the iconic dimension: religious scriptures can act as powerful material symbols for cultures, religions, and nations, and give their users, owners, and patrons power and legitimacy (Watts 2006). From this theoretical framework, several chapters in this volume discuss how miniature books, as iconic material objects in the smallest format, may evoke sensual interaction when they are ritually displayed, create remembrance of the religious attitudes that should be given to their larger prototypes, and may function to structure and index social statuses, identities, and power relations when they are used and exchanged.

Overview of the chapters

This volume includes ten chapters that address the format and function of religious miniature books. In the opening chapter, James W. Watts suggests that the distinctive form of miniature books provides a concentrated emphasis on the ritualization of the iconic dimension of books. Starting from his theory on the three dimensions of scriptures, he argues that miniature books are not only read, interpreted, and performed (the semantic and performative dimensions), but a sustained attention to the size of these books invites people to engage with them as visual and material objects. This opens up different ways of ritualizing the iconic dimension which then invokes rhetoric related to the books as mass produced, personal texts. Miniature books thus represent distinctions between public and private spheres of power while also offering those with relative social disempowerment a sense of legitimacy and prestige in their personal practices.

Focusing on the functions of miniaturized religious books in Jewish traditions, Marianne Schleicher starts with a critical note on the predominant size criterion of miniature books since it privileges the codex format and printing technologies in the history of Western cultures. She provides examples from a broad history of books, from clay tablets in Mesopotamian and silk scrolls in China to typographic printing in Europe, in order to illustrate how a variety of small books have served to store cultural material. While presenting religious miniature books as both texts and artifacts, she presents theoretical reflections on how processes of miniaturization facilitate individualized religiosity when the large and complex is transformed to something small and easy to handle. Although miniaturized books in Jewish religion, such as community rules, Hebrew Bible codices, and Torah codices and scrolls, may serve many different functions, the artifactual properties of the books activate sensory responses and illusions of being close to what they metonymically represent, that is, the divine words or God. In times of exile the Jews have miniaturized their religious books partly because of the portability of small books.

Another type of miniature book that expands the understanding of different material formats are the carved wooden beads that depict events from the Christian story in the inner parts and were objects for devotion in late medieval Europe. These textual objects in the form of "prayer nuts" were used like rosaries and invited various sensory interactions. In her chapter, Lucy Razall explores how visual and verbal representations of the *Iliad* enclosed in a nutshell became widely popular in early modern England after Philemon Holland's English translation of Pliny's *Natural History* in 1601. As the chapter describes and analyzes, the image of *Iliad* in a nutshell became a popular motif in the literary culture that forced readers and viewers to an awareness of scale in visual and intellectual terms. The desire to condense larger works, such as the Bible, into miniature format reflected a wider anxiety about the intricate relationship between physical size and literary weightiness.

By approaching the Bible as an iconic book with attributed power and status related to its material properties, Dorina Miller Parmenter explores the genre of "thumb Bibles" that were intended for children and functioned as representations of Bibles that contained selections or summaries of the Bible texts. First produced in England starting in the seventeenth century, modified versions of them became popular in America during the nineteenth century. The latter were produced as representations of the Bible appropriate for children in their texts and illustrations that functioned as didactical tools to learn and venerate the book. When new technologies at the end of the nineteenth century allowed for the production of the whole Bible in miniature size, such as those produced by David Bryce in Glasgow, the popularity of thumb Bibles ended and the miniscule Bibles became iconic books for visual display with the physical relationship with the semantic dimension reduced. As the chapter argues, the thumb Bibles for children envisioned future Bible uses, while the iconic reductions of the Bible produced by Bryce relied on nostalgia and the memory of prior Bible uses. The consequence of size upon the parameters and practicalities of devotional use, technical execution, and the signification of overt or underlying ideologies is especially potent when contending with the extremes of scale expressed through miniaturized or gigantic proportions.

Heather Coffey examines in her chapter the Islamic manuscript tradition and specifically the manuscript Adomeit C12, which is a miniature Qur'an from the Safavid period in sixteenth century Persia that includes a *falnama*, a book of divination. An outline of the history of Qur'anic miniature codices and the possible reasons for producing them illustrate that the miniaturization of religious books was present throughout the formative centuries of Islamic manuscript traditions. The chapter provides a detailed description of the Adomeit C12 and how divination by means of a codex was performed and believed to evoke divine guidance and blessing. Arguing that miniaturization is relational in the sense that it implicitly refers to a larger object, the chapter demonstrates that the divinatory material found in codices of larger size were replicated in the miniature version. A contextualization of the Adomeit C12 and a comparison of it to *falnamas* contained in manuscript Qur'ans of larger size illustrates how miniature books were integrated in widespread divinatory practices that were characteristic of the Safavid period.

Focusing on the production of printed miniature Qur'ans in the late nineteenth and early twentieth century, Kristina Myrvold investigates how the influential publisher David Bryce in Scotland began printing and selling large quantities of diminutive Qur'ans intended for an Indian market. Although very few historical sources are available on the work and life of Bryce, preserved letters from his colleague Henry Frowde at Oxford University Press reveal how the two publishers cooperated with the production of miniature books over three decades and operated in transnational networks of book trade. Realizing the profitable business of religious books, Bryce took use of the latest printing technologies to mass-produce small facsimiles of sacred texts in the world religions for a global market. After an overview of religious approaches to printing technologies, the chapter describes how Bryce worked with the content, size, and appearance of miniature Qur'ans in the Arabic script. In literature of the twentieth century these mite Qur'ans became objects of fascination and were linked to Orientalist narratives of Arabs and Indian Muslim soldiers during the First World War that enmeshed the books in amuletic traditions of Islam.

Exploring the specific historical context of the First World War, Kristina Myrvold and Andreas Johansson further describe how miniature Qur'ans were distributed to Indian Muslim soldiers that served the British army in Europe. When the British entered the war in 1914 one third of their forces were Indians of the British Indian Army and many of these were Muslims from the northern part of India. The religious needs of the Indian soldiers became a concern for military and colonial authorities since religion was believed to affect the morale among soldiers stationed in Europe as well as influence the political opinion in India. British authorities tried to identify the soldiers' religious needs through various measures, including regular checks of the soldiers' letters that underwent military censorship and communicated requests for religious scriptures. The chapter examines how the Indian Soldiers' Fund came to operate as an important charity to obtain and distribute Qur'ans to the soldiers and consolidated donations of religious scriptures from influential persons in Britain and Europe. Even if archival sources do not elucidate any detailed information about the soldiers' uses and meanings of the miniature books, the Qur'an was attributed iconic functions to represent Muslim identities and relationships between the colonial rulers and their subjects.

In a chapter that starts with a questioning of intentions and purposes attributed to uses of miniature Qur'ans, Jonas Svensson provides theoretical reflections and explanations of the desirability of contemporary small versions of the Qur'ans that are mass-produced and popular as marketable commodities. In an attempt to look beyond culture-specific contexts of using the Qur'an, the chapter focuses on the conceptual framework of "affordances" and how potentialities and constrains arise when humans encounter objects and their physical properties. Using James W. Watts' theory of the three dimensions of scriptures to present an overview of common Muslim uses of the Qur'an, it argues that miniature Qur'ans deviate their affordances in relation to the prototypical larger Qur'ans, as representations of the larger versions, but miniaturization leads to a shift in affordances from those linked with the semantic dimension. The diminutive codices are attributed social affordances of being capable to be displayed, worn, conveyed, and given away, and the attractiveness of the books can be found in the aesthetics of size that mobilize emotions in humans.

Addressing Hindu scriptures, Jon Skarpeid examines miniature editions of the Bhagavad Gita produced by four publishers in India and Peru. Special attention is given to the paratextual properties of the books, such as title pages, prefaces, and illustrations, and how these may affect the intended reception. While providing a descriptive overview of various Bhagavad Gitas and their publishers, the chapter examines how the expected uses of the books are included in paratexts and instructions from the publishers. Besides an emphasis on the portability of the small books and their ability to transmit divine power by a mere presence, some of the miniature Bhagavad Gitas have additional mantras and ritual texts included in order to prescribe an ideal approach of the text as an act of religious worship. As the chapter suggests, some of the contemporary publishers maintain conservative views on gender and caste by incorporating illustrations that portray social hierarchies and ritual texts that by tradition are performed only by men. Other publishers have chosen to exclude verses from the Bhagavad Gita that might be considered controversial for users of the small books. These various strategies indicate how publishers communicate ideologies by including paratextual properties to small and larger books.

In the final chapter Yohan Yoo and Woncheol Yun examine miniature *sutras* in practices of Mahayana Buddhism that aim to transform and impute life into statues of Buddha. Based on the religious notions of Buddhist scriptures as embodiments of dharma and Buddha, the authors argue that various *sutras* are regarded as sacred beings and possess an iconicity that is believed to evoke power independently of the semantic content of the texts. After an historical overview of temple practices of installing Buddha statues by placing relics and *sutras* in them, the chapter describes how contemporary lay Buddhists in Korea activate the presence of Buddha by inserting different printed miniature *sutras* into the statues. The religious items have become commodified to the extent that no rituals are required for the installation of Buddha and it is even possible to buy statues with *sutras* already enclosed. Tiny *sutras* printed in codex format are also believed to have protective functions when kept close to the body like amulets. In these religious practices the miniature *sutras* function as representations of the larger texts which are considered to signify dharma.

This volume can be viewed as a first attempt to gather research studies that deal with miniaturization of books in religious traditions and may encourage further empirical and theoretical research on the material aspects of religious books. The volume addresses and makes a contribution to scholarship especially in religious studies, cultural studies, and book history, and will appeal to a broader readership with interest in religious scriptures, publishing, and miniature books.

References

Adomeit, Ruth E. 1980. *Three Centuries of Thumb Bibles: A Checklist*. New York: Garland.

Bondy, Louis W. 1981. *Miniature Books: Their History from the Beginnings to the Present Day*. London: Sheppard.

Bromer, Anne C. and Julian I. Edison. 2007. *Miniature Books: 4,000 Years of Tiny Treasures*. New York: Abrams.

Genette, Gerard. 1997. *Paratexts: Thresholds of Interpretation*. Cambridge: Cambridge University Press. https://doi.org/10.1017/CBO9780511549373

Henderson, James D. 1933. "A Lilliputian Library." *The American Book Collector* IV: 145–150.

Jaffe, Alexandra, Jannis Androutsopoulos, Mark Sebba, and Sally Johnson, eds. 2012. *Orthography as Social Action: Script, Spelling, Identity and Power*. Boston: De Gruyter. https://doi.org/10.1515/9781614511038

Meyer, Birgit, David Morgan, Crispin Paine, and S. Brent Plate, 2010. "The Origin and Mission of Material Religion." *Religion* 40: 207–211. https://doi.org/10.1016/j.religion.2010.01.010

Morgan, David, ed., 2010. *Religion and Material Culture: The Matter of Belief*. Abingdon: Routledge.

Myrvold, Kristina. 2007. *Inside the Guru's Gate: Ritual Uses of Texts among Sikhs in Varanasi*. Lund Studies in African and Asian Religions. Lund: Media-Tryck.

———. 2017. "'Orientalizing' Bibles in Punjab: Christian Missionaries and Book Printing in Nineteenth Century India.'" In *India: Research on Cultural Encounters and Representations at Linnaeus University*, edited by Kristina Myrvold and Soniya Billore, 100–130. Göteborg: Makadam.

Myrvold, Kristina, ed. 2010. *The Death of Sacred Texts: Ritual Disposal and Renovation of Texts in World Religions*. Abingdon: Routledge.

O'Donnell Georgene. 1943. *Miniaturia: The World of Small Things*. Chicago: Lightner.

Shaw, Graham. 1994. "Lithography v. letter-press in India" (Part II). *South Asia Library Notes & Queries* 30: 1-10.

Spielmann, Percy Edwin. 1961. *Catalogue of the Library of Miniature Books*. London: Edward Arnold.

Stam, Deirdre C. 2010. "Talking about 'Iconic Books' in the Terminology of Book History." *Postscripts* 6: 23–38.

Stark, Ulrike. 2009. *An Empire of Books: The Naval Kishore Press and the Diffusion of the Printed Word in Colonial India.* New Delhi: Orient Blackswan.

Veidlinger, Daniel. 2006. "When a Word is Worth a Thousand Pictures: Mahayana Influence on the Theravada Attitudes towards Writing." *Numen* 53: 405–447. https://doi.org/10.1163/156852706778942012

Watts, James W. 2006. "The Three Dimensions of Scriptures." *Postscripts* 2: 135–159.

Welsh, Doris V. 1989. *A Bibliography of Miniature Books (1470–1965).* New York: Kathryn I. Rickard.

———. 1987. *The History of Miniature Books.* New York: Fort Orange.

Yelle, Robert A. 2013. *The Language of Disenchantment: Protestant Literalism and Colonial Discourse in British India.* Oxford: Oxford University Press.

Ritualizing the Size of Books

James W. Watts

James W. Watts is Professor of Religion at Syracuse University. He is author of *How and Why Books Matter* (2019) and editor of *Iconic Books and Texts* (2013) and *Sensing Sacred Texts* (2018).

The Iconic Books Project began its research in 2001 by collecting a database of information and images of iconic books (see The Iconic Books Project n.d.). An iconic book or text is one that is revered as an object of value and power. Its iconic status may be marked by its distinctive form or its typical use for collection, display, or ritual manipulation. Our initial collection of images already included many miniature books: miniature *sutras*, miniature Bibles, miniature prayer books, miniature Qur'ans. They came from around the world and from distant antiquity. Books and other written texts usually draw our attention to their verbal contents, but smaller-than-average books and non-standard sizes of fonts, pages and bindings draw our attention to the book's material form. They make us focus on visual and tactile aspects of books that we usually ignore. I suggest therefore that size provides one means for ritualizing the iconic dimension of books.

Last year, I moved to a different office in my university department. This event forced me to pay attention to the different sizes of books in my own collection. The shelves in my new office can be adjusted to fit the height of the books. So placing books on them required me to confront the relative merits of arranging them strictly by author and topic or whether to shelve the oversized volumes separately. Arranging them by size disrupts the semantic order, but arranging them topically or alphabetically wastes physical space. The material shape of my books resists my desire to treat them only on the basis of their contents. Oversize books call attention to their material form.

Miniature books are not usually designed for standard book shelves so much as for boxes, bags, and pockets, even for belts and chains. Like oversize books, the small format of miniatures both exerts an attraction and generates resistance. Their small size attracts us by evoking our fascination. But our fingers fumble with their tiny pages and their small lettering and fonts can resist easy reading, especially for those of us with presbyopia who have increasing difficulty reading small type.

So the different sizes of books are one of the most common ways in which the materiality of books calls itself to our attention. In this regard, books are both like and unlike other material objects. For example, giant statues and miniature figurines present similar problems for practical manipulation and viewing. The different sizes of works of art, however, are variations in the visual mode of representation that is already part of their primary purpose. They represent what they cannot reproduce. Claude Lévi-Strauss went so far as to argue that representational art is always a form of miniaturization, in sensory range and scope if not always in size.[1] Unlike art, however, many miniature books are, in fact, reproductions of "the real thing," just on a small scale. A fundamental difference between a book and a work of art is that any sufficiently detailed reproduction of a book becomes another version of the book itself.

Like art works, we engage books visually and physically. I term this mode of interacting with books their iconic dimension (Watts 2006). We engage the iconic dimension whenever we recognize an object as a written text because of the appearance of its signs or because of its physical form as a scroll, codex, paper envelope, or digital tablet, for example. But we also interact with books through two other modes that usually overshadow their iconic dimension. The writing on the pages of books can be turned into language through mental and oral performance (its performative dimension). And then the meaning of those words can be interpreted (its semantic dimension). Books differ from works of art and from most other material objects because of the dominance of their performative and semantic dimensions.[2] It is these dimensions that usually receive our attention. The semantic dimension of books particularly preoccupies the attention of scholars.

---

1. Claude Lévi-Strauss argued that all works of art are miniatures, because they are reductions of real experience in scale or sensation. "Being smaller, the object as a whole seems less formidable. By being quantitatively diminished, it seems to us qualitatively simplified. More exactly, this quantitative transposition extends and diversifies our power over a homologue of the thing, and by means of it the latter can be grasped, assessed and apprehended at a glance. [...] The intrinsic value of a small-scale model is that it compensates for the renunciation of sensible dimensions by the acquisition of intelligible dimensions" (Lévi-Strauss 1966, 23, 24).

2. Art works do not usually contain writing that can be performed by turning it into language. They can be interpreted semantically and that interpretation can be ritualized, such as through religious icons. Written texts encourage such a focus

The fact that miniature books contain written text allows them to function like larger books as a basis for semantic interpretation. But their small size resists our usual tendency to reduce books to their semantic contents alone. Micrography and miniature books remind us continually of our senses of sight and touch. Unlike standard books, miniatures never let us forget that reading requires both seeing and touching.

Miniature books function like small statuettes and miniature pictures to attract our gaze and make us marvel at their skilful workmanship. So miniatures attract our senses of sight and touch quite apart from any attempt to read them. Their small size stimulates our fascination with the process of their construction. "How did they do that?" we ask ourselves as we try to read the words and examine the stitching of the binding. More than standard books, miniatures call our attention to the material processes of writing or printing and of manufacturing the book.

Sustained attention to the material form of books and, sometimes, to the processes of their production, is the common way of ritualizing the iconic dimension of books. My use of the word "ritualizing" is informed by ritual theorists who emphasize that ritual is about process as much as form. Scholarly research has therefore focused in recent decades on ways of "ritualizing" rather than on the definitions and forms referred to by the noun, "ritual" (Turner 1969; Grimes 1995, 91; Bell 1997, 72-83; Rappaport 1999, 36–37, 124–126).

Ritualizing anything or any activity inevitably calls attention to the material form of that thing or the physical processes involved in performing that activity. Ritualizing a book draws attention to the material nature of that book: the look of its script or typeface, the feel of its paper or parchment, the look and feel of its binding. Publishers sometimes invest in elaborate decorations and illustrations to draw attention to books' material forms. They hope in this way that their books will gain economic value as iconic or even relic texts. Institutions that display rare and valuable books also draw attention to their visible appearance and material composition. That is partly because codex books are hard to display: you can only show them closed with the binding visible or, if open, only two facing pages at a time. In the display cases of museums and libraries, books cannot function as they were made to function: we cannot hold them in our hands, turning the pages and scanning the text. Books are made to be manipulated, but iconic display often interferes with using them that way. So displays draw attention to their material form and visible features instead.

---

on interpretation even more than art, which shares with writing a tendency to provoke semantic interpretation.

For example, I recently had the opportunity to visit Dublin and see the Book of Kells on display at Trinity College. The Book of Kells is an illuminated Gospel from the eighth century. It is famous for its detailed and whimsical illuminations and full-page illustrations. Ireland claims it as a national treasure, and half-a-million tourists line up every year to see it. But visitors cannot see very much of the book. The Book of Kells has been rebound in four volumes. Two are displayed open at any given time, allowing visitors to view four pages of its 340 folios, which measure only 33 by 25.5 centimeters (13 by 10 inches) each. Most modern readers cannot read Latin, so they cannot read the few pages they are allowed to see.

In order to enlarge the display of this medium-size book, the gallery at Trinity College devotes three rooms to telling the story of the Book of Kells. Wall-sized reproductions of its art surround displays of the raw materials used to create its colorful inks. Parchment strips hanging on racks invite visitors to touch them and find out how the books' pages feel. Visitors are impressed by the number of cows butchered and flayed to create its pages (185 cows).

Though not usually quite so elaborate, other museums also emphasize the physical qualities of the old and rare texts that they display. Ritualized display draws attention to the material book, because for most people reading that book is neither possible nor particularly desirable.

These museum displays and activities ritualize the book as something special. They contrast in almost every way with "normal," pragmatic uses of books. We read the words in most books paying virtually no attention to their physical form and materials. Standardization of the form and sizes of modern fonts, such as Times New Roman 12 point, and of book bindings—quartos, octavos—has the functional effect of making the material book disappear while our minds immediately grasp its words (Plate 2010). Most books have become virtually "invisible" to readers who focus all their attention on the meaning of the text.

Miniature books, on the other hand, call attention to their material form routinely by virtue of their small size. They are harder to manipulate than normal-sized books: opening them and turning their pages requires care and attention. They are harder to read, too, often requiring the use of magnifying lenses. Thus miniaturization serves to ritualize books by drawing ongoing attention to how they look and to their material shape.[3]

---

3. Jonathan Z. Smith argued that ritualization is itself a form of miniaturization: "ritual activities are an exaggeration of everyday activities, but an exaggeration that reduces rather than enlarges, that clarifies by miniaturizing in order to achieve sharp focus. Collecting their terms, ritual is the realm of the 'little,' the 'petty,' the 'trivial.' It is the realm of 'infinite distinctions' and 'micro-adjustments.' Ritual is primarily a matter not of nouns and verbs, but of qualifiers—of adjectives

Ritualizing books by miniaturizing them usually symbolizes different values than other ways of ritualizing books. In contrast to ritualizing iconic texts by enlarging their size or by binding them in expensive materials or by decorating them, miniatures symbolize pragmatic ideals, especially portability and low expense. They are also frequently mass produced. These pragmatic values suit miniature books to a rhetoric of popularization: books for the masses, books for the common people, books for soldiers, books for women, books for children—all in contrast to larger books implicitly intended for scholars, for religious communities, for libraries, that is, for the elite. Miniatures therefore always participate in a dichotomization of size in which small indicates less important, less dominant, less public. However, within the constraints of that social structure, they can also convey status: for example, the child proud of "her books" that rival in number her parents' collection, or the Renaissance upper-class women carrying expensively-illuminated Books of Hours, or the miniature scriptures carried by members of minority religions or by low-rank soldiers. Thus book miniatures index by their size distinctions of public/private, of rank, of majority/minority religion, but within those social categories, they convey legitimacy and prestige (see Bromer and Edison 2007, 128, 133–140).

This common rhetoric about miniature books stands in notable contrast with how they are often used. The use of miniature books as amulets and their frequent production for that purpose shows that small size also has ritual uses, though not so much for public display as for private manipulation.

The production and use of miniature texts as amulets provides our oldest and most pervasive evidence of miniature text production worldwide. Examples date from ancient Egypt, ancient Israel, early Judaism and Christianity, as well as most other textualized religious traditions. Many people carried a miniature book on their person, either hidden away as a private talisman or displayed publicly to index their identity to others. Criticism for using textual amulets is also quite old and wide-spread, and comes predictably from orthodox interpreters of standard (and larger) texts. The criticism frequently associates miniature books as amulets both with religious outsiders and with insiders of lesser status (Parmenter 2006, 177–179). For example, the fourth-century Christian preacher, John Chrysostom, criticized Jewish "scribes and Pharisees" for wearing *tefillin* (phylacteries containing texts from the Torah) and then added sarcastically that "many women now wear the Gospels hung

---

and adverbs. Ritual precises ambiguities. [...] Ritual is 'no big deal.' The object of action that receives ritual attention is, more often than not, commonplace" (Smith 1987, 194–195). So, while I am arguing that the miniaturization of books, and maybe other things, is a means of ritualization, Smith pointed out that ritualization is inevitably a form of miniaturization too.

on their necks" (Canepa 2011, 80). This association has led historians of Late Antiquity to debate whether miniature scrolls and codices were produced specifically for women or not (Haines-Eitzen 2012, 61–62; Luijendijk 2014, 51–56).

So on the one hand, rhetoric about miniature books can celebrate them for popularizing literacy by making books inexpensive and portable. Public gifts and displays of miniature scriptures convey status and respect. On the other hand, rhetoric about miniatures can stereotype their users as at best second-class and possibly religiously or politically deviant in their private, maybe secret, practices. Miniature books therefore can contribute to the ritualization of the private sphere, of the feminine, of childhood—and also of the magical. By their miniaturization, amulets may define magic explicitly, if not semantically, as private ritual practice in contrast to public rituals and to public religious institutions. And notions of privacy frequently raise suspicions of secrecy—that is of unorthodox religious and political practice.

This rhetoric points to the social consequences of ritualizing miniature books. Ritualizing the iconic dimension of any book or written text tends to enhance legitimacy: the book's own legitimacy and the legitimacy of the person or institution that possesses the book and anyone who comes into contact with it. Miniature books and texts facilitate private ritualization—at home or while traveling, or constantly on one's own body. The books' small size allows such rituals to escape ecclesiastical or governmental control more easily than most.

Thus miniature books enabled the ritualization of privacy long before the public-private distinction became a prominent feature of Western culture (for example Landes 2003). Of course, that is true of how amulets function generally. They enable private ritualization out of sight of others. Specifically textual amulets, however, allow individuals to ritualize orthodox scriptures for themselves. By manipulating the miniature scripture or part of scripture, they claim its legitimacy. By doing so, they accept and confirm their place within the social order legitimized by that text, even and especially when their place is a subordinate one. They too have access to the privileged text, if in a reduced size and format as befits their station in life.

Control over the physical text, however, also enables its ritualization in opposition to the established social order in one way or another. That is, the legitimacy generated by ritualizing miniature scriptures and other texts may inspire resistance to one's subordinate status, and these acts may take place out of sight and beyond the control of the authorities.

This potential can be actualized even in today's modern world, and frequently is. An example of such a conflict made news in 2007. In this case, the textual amulet was a miniature not because its text was small but because it was a small fragment of a very large text. The Aleppo Codex is a ninth-century manuscript of the whole Hebrew Bible. Historians regard it as one of the best testimonies to the text of the Hebrew Bible. So it also serves to legitimize the accuracy of Jewish and Christian scriptures. A fire in the Aleppo synagogue in 1947 damaged the Codex which lost almost all the pages of its Pentateuch. Israeli politicians and spies worked secretly to bring the rest of the manuscript from Aleppo to Jerusalem, where it is now displayed in the "Shrine of the Book" as a national treasure. But some members of the Aleppo Jewish community kept fragments of the Codex for themselves as amulets and resisted all attempts by governments and museums to acquire them. The Israeli newspaper, *Haaretz*, reported in November 2007 about one man who did so:

> Sam Sabbagh salvaged the fragment from a burning synagogue in Aleppo, Syria in 1947. [...] Sabbagh believed the small piece of parchment was his good luck charm for six decades. He was convinced that thanks to the parchment, which he kept with him always in a transparent plastic container, he had been saved from riots in his hometown of Aleppo during Israel's War of Independence, and he had managed to immigrate from Syria to the United States in 1968 and start a new life in Brooklyn and make a living. (Pfeffer 2007)

Only after Sabbagh's death in 2005 was the fragment donated to an Israeli museum to be reunited with the Aleppo Codex. So communities ranging from local congregations to nations gain legitimacy from owning and displaying relic texts like the Aleppo Codex and the Book of Kells, while individuals try to keep them for themselves because they offer them prestige, legitimacy, and/or a sense of private protection.

Miniature books and other kinds of miniature texts lend themselves to a range of private uses. These uses raise the value of possessing them. Miniatures are therefore eminently collectible by private individuals. Indeed, much of the published scholarship on miniatures depends heavily on private collections and the catalogs of auction houses (for example: Bondy 1981; Bromer and Edison 2007). That is because displaying miniature books exacerbates because of their small size all the difficulties associated with displaying books in museums and libraries. On the other hand, for private collectors their small size provides practical advantages while the privacy of the collection overcomes some of the difficulties involved in public display of iconic books. Miniatures require smaller containers for display and storage than other books. In many periods of history, miniature books were generally cheaper than other books, though some were exceptionally luxurious. Because they own the books themselves, private collectors are free to manipulate them whenever and however they wish, and can grant that right to their guests. Miniatures therefore have clear advantages for privately ritualizing the possession and manipulation of iconic books.

To sum up: Like other ways of ritualizing iconic texts, miniatures attract our attention to their material form through fascination with technique. This fascination with production represents one way of ritualizing a book: miniaturization ritualizes its physical dimensions. However, like other kinds of ritualization, ritualizing miniatures has social consequences. Because miniatures are often more practical for individuals, miniatures can index private life and religion more than public institutions. While big books index social empowerment, miniatures index relative levels of social disempowerment along lines of age, wealth, gender, rank, and minority status. But within those social structures, their status as books, even books of scripture, provides relative legitimacy. They legitimize their owners' identity—sometimes even their elite positions—within their relatively disempowered position in the social structure.

However, their private use also permits their secret use to legitimize counter-cultural status and personal empowerment, sometimes even resistance by carrying "magical" book amulets or secret books banned by the public authorities. Miniatures can therefore become subversive, because by ritualizing privacy they also carve out a sphere of textual secrecy. So the defenders of orthodoxy and social order often imagine that miniatures are a threat to the public sphere.

All this makes me wonder if digital texts represent our age's form of miniature book. Digitization has certainly made it possible to fit a great deal of text in very small spaces. It has even mystified the process with rhetoric of putting it all "in the cloud." Digitization extends the rhetoric of portability and convenience associated traditionally with miniature books. Tech companies have monetized our fascination with the forms and techniques of miniaturization, now even promising quantum computing at the sub-atomic scale.

But digitization has also brought concerns about privacy and secrecy into public debate. It has sparked clashes between powerful social forces, setting the security agencies of nation states over against the economic power of the computer tech industry. These conflicts have dispersed "the cloud" by drawing attention to the infrastructure of massive computer servers around the world that support the internet, as well as to the miniaturized laptops and phones with which we access it.

Security concerns focus on e-mails and text messages more than published books. Nevertheless, like religious scriptures, digital texts exist in the tension between immaterial "virtual" texts, expensive institutional infrastructure, and miniatures manipulated by billions of people every day. Their conflicting interests get crystalized in discussions of security, privacy, and secrecy, just as discussions about textual amulets focused attention on the same issues hundreds and thousands of years ago. And the new technology also serves clearly talismanic purposes, from the ubiquitous status symbol of the iPhone to high-tech amulets targeted at more differentiated markets, such as microscopically inscribed scriptures on jewelry.

By raising such issues, miniature texts today as always draw our attention to the physical forms of written texts. In this way, miniatures continually undermine the efforts of theologians, philosophers, literati, and futurists to keep attention on the immaterial semantic meaning of texts alone.

References

Bell, Catherine. 1997. *Ritual: Perspectives and Dimensions.* Oxford: Oxford University Press.

Bondy, Louis W. 1981. *Miniature Books: Their History from the Beginnings to the Present Day.* London: Sheppard.

Bromer, Anne C. and Julian I. Edison. 2007. *Miniature Books: 4,000 Years of Tiny Treasures.* New York: Abrams.

Canepa, Matthew P. 2011. "The Art and Ritual of Manichaean Magic: Text, Object and Image from the Mediterranean to Central Asia." In *Objects in Motion*, edited by Hallie G. Meredith, 73–88. Oxford: Archaeopress.

Grimes, Ronald. 1995. *Beginnings in Ritual Studies.* Rev. ed. Columbia, SC: University of South Carolina Press.

Haines-Eitzen, Kim. 2012. *The Gendered Palimpsest: Women, Writing, and Representation in Early Christianity.* New York: Oxford University Press.

The Iconic Books Project. n.d. http://jameswwatts.net/iconicbooks/

Landes, Joan B. 2003. "Further thoughts on the public/private distinction." *Journal of Women's History* 15 (2): 28–39. https://doi.org/10.1353/jowh.2003.0051

Lévi-Strauss, Claude. 1966 [1962]. *The Savage Mind.* Chicago: University of Chicago Press.

Luijendijk, AnneMarie. 2014. *Forbidden Oracles? The Gospel of the Lots of Mary.* Tübingen: Mohr Siebeck.

Parmenter, Dorina Miller. 2006. "The Iconic Book: The Image of the Bible in Early Christian Rituals." *Postscripts* 2: 160–189.

Pfeffer, Anshel. 2007. "Fragment of Ancient Parchment From Bible Given to Jerusalem Scholars." *Haaretz*, November 7. http://www.haaretz.com/news/fragment-of-ancient-parchment-from-bible-given-to-jerusalem-scholars-1.232641

Plate, S. Brent. 2010. "Looking at Words: The Iconicity of the Page." *Postscripts* 6: 67–82.

Rappaport, Roy. 1999. *Ritual and Religion in the Making of Humanity*. Cambridge: Cambridge University Press. https://doi.org/10.1017/CBO9780511814686

Smith, Jonathan Z. 1987. "The Domestication of Sacrifice." In *Violent Origins*, edited by Robert G. Hamerton-Kelly, 191–235. Stanford: CA: Stanford University Press.

Turner, Victor. 1969. *The Ritual Process: Structure and Anti-Structure*. Ithaca, NY: Cornell University Press.

Watts, James W. 2006. "The Three Dimensions of Scriptures." *Postscripts* 2: 135–159.

2

On the Functions of
Miniaturizing Books in Jewish Religion

Marianne Schleicher

Marianne Schleicher is Associate Professor of Jewish Studies at the
Study of Religion at Aarhus University, Denmark. Her research interests lie in the intersection of Judaism, scripture, gender, and the history of religion.

Most literature on miniature books has been written by and for collectors
who have been fascinated with their small size and aesthetic quality. Informa-
tive articles of this kind can be found for example in *Miniature Book News*
and *Antique & Collecting Magazine* or in presentations accessible on the web-
site of the Miniature Book Society (MBS Presentations n.d.). Ever since the
advent of Johannes Gutenberg's printing press in circa 1440 and the emergence of printed miniature books in a Western setting, typesetters, printers,
and binders as well as artists, including Joan Miró and Pablo Picasso, have
taken the opportunity to challenge their craftsmanship by creating work in
the extremely small format and thereby hone their skills. As such, Western
miniature books attract attention to the accomplishments of the producers,
just as they point to the ability of the collectors to appreciate high quality
work. Occasionally, preliminary reflections on the reasons for the existence of
miniature books have supplemented the focus on size and aesthetics, and in
these cases the collectors' literature typically explains the production and use
of miniature books with reference to their portability and therefore people's
easy access to their textual content (Bondy 1981, 1–3; Bromer 1988, 88).
As I shall argue, based on Jewish empirical material, books are never just
containers of text; they are also always artifacts with some kind of symbolic
function. When Louis W. Bondy and Anne C. Bromer thus point to their
portability as something that enables easy access to the textual content, I shall
add that the portability of a book also enables easy access to its artifactual
properties.

The collectors' focus on aesthetics and size affected early academic scholarship on miniature books. Doris Varner Welsh, who wrote the authoritative work *The History of Miniature Books* (published posthumously in 1987), had a professional knowledge of books in that she worked as a cataloguer and editor of historical and ethnographic material at the Newberry Library in Chicago. She took up an interest in miniature books, collected several, and even hand set and printed some (Rickard 1988). Welsh's *History of Miniature Books* stands out with its systematic, historical-critical approach, but nevertheless it also begins with information on size criteria, so important to collectors. According to Welsh, a miniature book cannot be more than 4 inches/ circa 10 centimeters in any direction of the binding, while some definitions, especially in North America, assert that the books should not extend 3 inches or circa 7.5 centimeters (Welsh 1987, 10). The size criteria point to what Welsh considers the origin of Western miniature books and the technological possibilities that followed from Gutenberg's printing press (Welsh 1987, i). In a study of miniaturized religious books like this one, it soon becomes evident that these criteria relate to and privilege the codex format that has been used primarily for religious texts in relatively recent religions, such as Christianity and Islam. While it is not my purpose to argue for new size criteria, I consider the codex bias problematic because the size criteria for the codex may cloud insights on miniaturized books produced by other printing technologies, such as lithography popular outside of Europe, or in other formats, such as clay tablets, scrolls, and *pothi* (see below). An inclusion of other printing technologies and formats could contribute to establishing a comparative perspective on the function of miniaturizing religious books in the broader history of religion. Before I narrow my focus on the functions of miniaturized religious books in Jewish religion and ask how size comes to matter in this particular religious context, I want to include insights on miniaturization from other formats and on how each particular format implies specific functions. I shall therefore briefly give some examples from the history of books.

Early portable writings in the history of books

Mesopotamian clay tablets from circa 2500 BCE, impressed with a partial syllabic script known as cuneiform, are considered to be the earliest example of books. The smallest known of these tablets would actually qualify as a miniature according to modern Western standards in that it measures 2 by 2 centimeters. Such tablets were predominantly used as accounting records and receipts as agriculture developed in the Middle East to include the trade of produce. Subsequently, cultural narratives such as Enuma Elish and legal codes like the Law of Hammurabi were also impressed on the clay tablets (Robson 2009, 68–71; Anderson and Levoy

2002; Kallendorf 2013, 40). In the course of the next two thousand years in the Eastern Mediterranean area, the clay tablets were supplemented with new formats such as metal plates and wooden waxed tablets, as well as papyrus and parchment scrolls. Scrolls had an obvious advantage compared to tablets in that they enabled the storing of uninterrupted narratives and arguments, and were easier to both carry and handle (Roemer 2009, 84; Kallendorf 2013, 41). During the first century CE, stacks of wooden waxed tablets developed into the codex, which almost immediately became the dominant format in the Mediterranean area. A Jewish sect, to be later known as the Christians, was quick to replace scrolls with codices as their preferred medium of storing important narratives and arguments, and did so from the second century CE (Pearson 2013, 246). The many advantages of the codex may explain its popularity: Standard sizes tend to be smaller than the sizes of scrolls and the codex thus increases the ease with which books can be carried and handled. The codex is cheaper to produce than the scroll because it enables the possibility of writing on both sides of the sheet. Most importantly, the codex revolutionized the ease with which one could orient oneself within the book by flicking through its pages, thus allowing for a swift return to/comparison of statements, including critical reflection on long-running arguments and possible inconsistencies. As such, the codex facilitates discussions and problematizations of normative beliefs and practices to a higher degree than scrolls do, thus prefiguring the emergence of many new religions. The oldest known papyrus codex is a fragment of the Gospel of John, chapter 18. It dates from the second century or possibly the first part of the third century CE, and is known as the Rylands Papyrus P52. This papyrus codex qualifies as a miniature fragment according to modern Western standards in that it measures only 9 by 6 centimeters (Nongbri 2005, 46).

The Middle Eastern and Eastern Mediterranean areas were not unique in their production of books. Silk scrolls were produced in China from the seventh century BCE. In addition, the *jiance* format (thin bamboo and wood processed strips held together by parallel bands) and the *pothi* format (palm leaf strips held together by string at one end and attached to a wooden cover) supplemented the silk scroll in the Asian region as a book format as plant-based writing surfaces were easier and cheaper to produce. It is also because of Chinese writing practices that paper was invented. In a Chinese document from 105 CE, the production of paper is mentioned for the first time as a rival to silk as a writing surface (Edgren 2013, 575). Paper soon replaced both plant-based materials and silk in Asia because it was less costly than silk and slightly easier to carry and produce. Paper as a new writing surface also enabled the development of the concertina format in the seventh century CE where paper sheets pasted together at opposite ends were folded into a rectangular object (Pearson 2013, 247–249). Paper was also the preferred writing surface when the Japanese Empress Shotoku in 770 CE ordered the printing of a Buddhist prayer charm in Chinese characters by means of a metal-plate printing method to be distributed in one million copies to ten different temples. It is, in fact, the first known example of printing on paper; it was printed in the scroll format, measuring 5.7 by 47 centimeters (2 ¼ by 18 ½ inches) thus qualifying in height, but not in width, as a miniature book according to modern Western standards (Edison 1967, 1–2; Hunter 1943, 64–76; Znidersic 2004, 144–146). Mesoamerica is also worth mentioning. Paper production developed independently in Mesoamerica in the classical Mayan period of the first millennium CE. For the Mayan people, paper also facilitated cheap and lightweight writing surfaces for their glyphs and advanced number and calendar systems (Vera 2013, 656–657). Meanwhile, the Mediterranean world did not know of paper until the ninth century CE.

Finally, I want to add two points from the history of print. The early engravings and impressions into metal, clay, or wax required some amount of pressure on the stylus. However, once these hard writing surfaces were replaced by plant-based surfaces in both Asia and the Mediterranean area from the third millennium BCE, handwriting with fluid ink could be used and made writing speedier. Also, technological developments beginning with woodblock printing in China in circa 200 CE and continuing throughout Asia, Europe, and America have enabled fast duplication, photo-reduction, and first and foremost mass distribution.

The purpose of mentioning the above examples from the history of the book is to deduct the insight that early writings in small format served as portable memory storage of trade and cultural narratives and arguments. If one follows the development of formats, there is a clear tendency to miniaturize formats not only to enable economization of production, both with regard to effort and financial costs, but also to reduce weight in order to improve portability and permit ease of orientation. If we include methods of impressing alphabetic writing on to surfaces, the development also indicates directionality towards increased speed, easy duplication, and mass distribution. I shall set the overview of the history of the book as an important context for understanding the miniaturization of books.

Theoretical reflections on
the miniaturization of religious texts

In the following section, I shall conjoin related theories on miniaturization to establish an explanatory potential with regard to the miniaturization of religious books and their functions. I shall begin by summarizing my own distinction between hermeneutical and artifactual uses of sacred texts because miniaturized books, and especially religious ones, are always both texts and artifacts. Sometimes users devote attention to the proposed religious worldview communicated through the text and consider whether they should appropriate, transform, or refuse it. Simultaneously, or at other times, the very handling of the sacred text as a physical object transforms it into a manipulable symbol that serves as a hub that establishes connections in all directions, primarily through sensory integration with great consequences for the associations and identifications of the users.[1] To counter a tendency in many academic disciplines to explain the functions of sacred texts with reference to their semantic properties alone, I want to stress the explanatory potential that lies in a reflection on the artifactual properties of miniaturized religious books. To strengthen this focus, I shall turn to insights from a few scholars who have formulated some theories about the miniaturization of other kinds of artifacts and apply them to religious books.

The first theory maintains that miniaturization activates an imaginative creative function in whatever item that has been miniaturized. The theory has been promoted most convincingly by Claude Lévi-Strauss, who, in the book *The Savage Mind* from 1962, reflects on the function of miniaturizing in works of art. Lévi-Strauss insists that art contains an intrinsic aesthetic quality of rendering small-scale models of the world. In the process of miniaturizing, the "graphic or plastic transposition always involves giving up certain dimensions of the object" (Lévi-Strauss 1966, 23). Certain sensible dimensions of the object are renounced, but the remaining sensible dimensions suffice as departing points for creating meaning among the beholders or users in front of an artistic small-scale model of the world. To explain the illusion of wholeness in art, Lévi-Strauss points to how "knowledge of the whole precedes knowledge of the parts" (Lévi-Strauss 1966, 24). The illusory wholeness depends largely on the active participation of the observer to fill in the blanks after the renouncement of sensible dimensions. Filling in the blanks and thus upholding the illusion of wholeness in the work of art, for example a miniature, is a matter of replacing sensible dimensions with intelligible ones—a creative process that is no longer in the hands of the creator, who has removed him-/herself from the object, but a creative process left to the observer or user.[2]

---

1. For a recent and more detailed introduction to this distinction, as well as the role of sensory integration in artifactual use, see Schleicher 2017.

2. Susan Stewart reaches a similar conclusion in her aesthetic and semiotic study on the reduction or exaggeration of scale, but combines it with thoughts on desire and control, reminiscent of the conclusions in Dehouve and Gores to

Jonathan Z. Smith has also touched upon the active role of people handling miniaturized artifacts. In his article "Trading Places" from 1995, Smith argues that a shift occurred in ritual settings in late antiquity from archaic temple cult to private homes (Smith 1995, 21). As a part of this shift, miniaturized and portable artifacts, such as little shrines, statues, amulets, and phylacteries, supplemented a ritualization of narrative and discourse that enabled the domestic ritual setting to trade places with the archaic temple (Smith 1995, 24–25). Smith identifies displacement, miniaturization, and portability of religious artifacts as driving forces in late antiquity toward relative individual religious agency, including access to religious narrative and discourse that facilitated the end of the priestly monopoly on religious rituals.[3]

In line with Smith's ideas, Danièle Dehouve argues that become dislodged from a first context and portable in a way that allows for individual handling. Dehouve, however, contributes to the theoretical reflections on the modification of the dimensions of the ritual object with three propositions. First, miniaturization might be a way to "provide structure to the world" (Dehouve 2016, 509).[4] Second, miniaturization causes the positioning of the object "within reach of the human senses" (Dehouve 2016, 512). Third, miniaturization implies a process of iteration and thereby multiplication of a motif in different scales, which facilitates dynamism and creation (Dehouve 2016, 524). Dehouve's propositions deserve elaboration. I shall begin with her last point that multiplication in different scales reveals an aspect of iterability that emphasizes that no copy or imitation is the same. The positioning of a copy or an imitation in a different time and space will inevitably create a

---

be summarized below (see for example Stewart 1993, 37–69). Stewart directly applies Lévi-Strauss' understanding (on page 48).

3. Smith's understanding of miniaturization as a driving force for religious developments in late antiquity is applied and supported by Ian S. Moyer and Jacco Dieleman, who argue that elements from Egyptian temple religion were transposed into miniature cult statues, favoring the itinerant and domestic praxis of holy men in late Greco-Roman Egypt (Moyer and Dieleman 2003, 49, 67–69).

4. Dehouve's preliminary typology of miniaturization is rich in empirical details from Mesoamerican ritual contexts. However, I do not understand why she turns to Blumenberg to reflect on structuration, when she could have contextualized her own use of Lévi-Strauss (Dehouve 2016, 505) by referring to Lévi-Strauss' understanding of miniaturization in the arts as combining the ambitions of both the bricoleur and the engineer. While the bricoleur, according to Lévi-Strauss, creates structure by means of events, the engineer creates events by means of structure, and the artistic creation lies midway in his or her attempt at ordering the world. Bricolage, art, and science are all means of introducing some kind of order into the universe (Lévi-Strauss 1962, 9–10, 22, 30).

new context of interpretation that will influence the significance of whatever is copied or imitated, just as the process of iteration always implies the possibility of an intended or accidental variation on the model, thus allowing for new creations.

To exemplify the aspect of iterability in processes of miniaturization, I shall point to Ian Reader's analysis of the miniaturization of small-scale pilgrimage routes in Japan, downscaled from a parent pilgrimage route, such as the eighty-eight sites route on the island of Shikoku. Shortage of time, strength, and economy prevented many Buddhists from traveling to Shikoku to pilgrimage together with the once historic, but soon imaginative figure of Kobo Daishi on the island of his birth along a 1,500 km route. As an alternative, miniature versions of the 88 sites route on Shikoku were established from 1691 onwards all over Japan. This multiplication of miniature routes implied new distinct ritual practices with dual references to the Shikoku route and the immediate context of the miniaturized route, thus "bringing people from different regions into contact with temples and places with deep connections to Japanese history" (Reader 1988, 53). Furthermore, it enabled the appropriation of a powerful ritual and a protest against the primacy of the region hosting the parent pilgrimage, thus facilitating dynamic change in regional identity and power relations (Reader 1988, 55–56). In this way, Dehouve and Reader argue that the creative potential in processes of miniaturization originates from the aspect of iterability.

Dehouve's initial propositions state that miniaturization "provide[s] structure to the world" and causes the positioning of the object "within reach of the human senses" (Dehouve 2016, 509, 512). These are presented as two distinct aspects of miniaturization. However, I shall argue that they are related observations. My argument builds on Steven J. Gores in his study of miniature portraits in eighteenth-century England, where he notices that sensing things renders the impression of relating to, possessing, and handling them. Gores compares the possessive aspect of the miniature portrait to that of maps where the process of miniaturization transforms something which is "inherently too large and complex for the comprehension or control of the individual eye into something that is easily mastered" (Gores 1997, 592 n12). Maps create the illusion that the world can be overlooked and controlled by subdividing it into areas, reflecting whatever interests the topographer has, be it in national borders or geological, demographic, or botanical characteristics. Similarly, a miniature book offers its reader/holder the impression that the entire content of a book can be held within the palm of a hand, come in handy, and be handled. Usages of miniature portraits in eighteenth-century England testify to how middle-class people could now afford to commission miniature portraits and thus gain access to "representing an absent other"

(Gores 1997, 574) and to signal their loyalty to him or her. The miniature portrait was mostly worn underneath the clothes close to the body to demonstrate emotional attachment to someone in a subtle way and, at the same time, allowed the bodily contact to indicate intimacy as a characteristic of the attachment. In addition, miniaturizing the absent person into a portable artifact is, according to Gores, a matter of turning the portrayed one into something that can be handled and possessed by the individual, of "domestication of the desired 'other,'" presenting "its possessors with a sense of security arising out of assurance of their affection being returned by the beloved" (Gores 1997, 576). The entitlement to such assurance might originate from the fact that smallness in combination with the materiality of the miniature allowed for affordable ornamentation as an "investment of emotions in ties between the lovers" (Gores 1997, 577). In this manipulation of the miniature portrait, Gores suggests that the frequent inclusion of monograms and locks of hair from the beloved turned the miniature portrait from a metaphoric representation of the beloved into a metonymy. It renders the miniature portrait as a kind of talisman, drawing down the presence of the absent other into the manipulable object (Gores 1997, 577) or, in the words of Lévi-Strauss, it upholds an illusory wholeness combined with the illusion of control.

I shall argue that such investments are important in the context of miniaturized books in Jewish religion in that books that are believed to contain divine words or include references to God seem to have been ornamented more often than secular ones, which indicates a wish to invest in or even manipulate desired, intimate relations with the divine. I shall also draw upon Gores' observation that the increased possibility of sensing is relevant to all miniaturized objects because smallness permits objects to be close to the body in ways that activate sensory responses, which explains the link between manipulability of the artifact and its activation of the senses (see Schleicher 2017).

Analysis of miniaturized books in Jewish religion

The theoretical reflections above indicate that miniaturization of artifacts activates an imaginative creative function that allows the individual to compensate for the renounced sensible dimensions by creating meaning relevant to his or her upholding of a relevant, albeit illusory, wholeness, just as the individual may vary the authoritative use of the model. They also suggest that bodily contact enables manipulability and illusions of close relations to and mastery of what it is a metonomy of. In the remaining part of this chapter, I turn to examples of miniaturized Jewish books to evaluate how their size has enabled easy access to their textual and artifactual properties. I explore the different functions of scrolls and codices and to what extent the miniaturized versions serve the early function of books to store memories of trade, cultural narratives, and arguments. Furthermore, I evaluate if miniaturized books in Jewish religion can reflect some developments in the general history of books, with miniaturization, speedy rendering of alphabetic writing on to various surfaces, easy duplication, and distribution enabling the economization of production with regard to both effort and financial costs, but also with regard to weight as an important factor for their portability and ability to establish ease of orientation. These evaluations will finally lead me to answer the questions on the general functions of miniaturized books and how the size of these small books comes to matter.

Community rules

The oldest surviving "miniature" books were produced in the scroll format and are versions of the *Community Rule* (1/4QS) found among the Dead Sea Scrolls. The *Community Rule* describes daily practices and rituals as well as initiation processes of the sect, legitimized by salvific ethics and a theology adhered to by Jewish sect members who wrote the Dead Sea Scrolls in the second and first centuries BCE. Manuscripts 4QS-i and 4QS-f, as they are called, measure 4.4 and 7.6 centimeters in height respectively and are written not on papyrus, but represent the world's oldest extant parchment scrolls as well as the first extant Jewish miniature books. Two leading experts on the Dead Sea Scrolls, Philip S. Alexander and Geza Vermes, conjecture that these manuscripts are "probably examples of miniature scrolls, designed to be carried around on the person" (Alexander and Vermes 1998, 5). In other words, the sect members miniaturized the rules for their community to allow for portability, probably because the textual content was considered so important for salvation that its easy access was needed no matter where a sect member was located.

Prayer books

The oldest surviving prayer book stems from circa 840 and is written in the codex format. It is 10 by 7.5 centimeters (4 by 3 inches) and thus qualifies as a miniature according to modern Western standards (see Woollaston 2013). From the ninth century onward, the Jewish prayer book was added to the private library of most Jewish families. It primarily contained prayers of which some were renderings of the biblical Psalms.

Tobias Foa published the first printed prayer book in 1555 that measured only 7 by 4.5 centimeters. On the first page, Foa added his publisher's remarks, stating that the prayer book was intended for use in homes as well as for those on the road. Jews in Europe were often engaged in trade, where they benefitted from networks of relatives dispersed along Jewish migration routes as far away as China. When between Jewish homes, these travelers were in need of external memory storage to help remember the fast and feast days during the Jewish year. Accordingly, Foa's prayer book was equipped with a liturgical calendar at the end of the book, which set precedence for so many prayer books to follow. Some editions came to include the weekly portions from the Torah and the Prophets, and the biblical passages for the high holidays. In the absence of a nearby religious community with scrolls fit for liturgical use, the composite prayer book became the Jewish *vade mecum* and, therefore, in the course of history, the most miniaturized Jewish book (Feffer 1969, 38). The prayer book enabled lay Jews to perform most rituals, individualized as these performances might be, and granted them access to a profane codex version of some of God's words. Simultaneously, because the prayer book would be the only book possessed by traveling Jews, prayer books also came to include secular information, such as dates for sailing vessels, coaches, road maps, and currency exchange rates for relevant countries (Rivkin 1939, 208; Feffer 1969, 39). The popularity of the Jewish prayer book confirms Smith's recognition of the development of the history of religion toward individualized rituals through miniaturization, but it also confirms the basic function of writing, that is, the external storage of information.

Smith's theory on the developments toward individualization of religious agency is confirmed by the distribution of prayer books to Jews of all genders and ages. In Amsterdam, the publisher Meir Crescas decided to ensure the correct pronunciation of the prayers among the young, and so in 1739 he published an easy to read, handy, miniature prayer book with vowels, measuring 6 by 4.1 centimeters (2 3/8 by 1 5/8 inches) (Feffer 1969, 39; see also Kedem Auction House n.d.a). Another prayer book titled *Meah Berachot* (100 blessings) measuring 4 by 3.6 centimeters stems from the eighteenth century and includes three blessings relevant to women's traditional chores of bread making, ritual bathing and kindling the Sabbath lights in addition to traditional prayers, prayers for the safety of travelers, when hearing thunder, and when wearing new garments for the first time (Facsimile Editions 2017). This prayer book stands out in that all prayers are handwritten by a *sofer*, that is, a professional scribe who usually writes on parchment. The book contains an illuminated title page and twenty-nine miniature panels illustrating the activities to which the blessings relate. A beautiful leather case furthermore protects the content. In line with Gores, the investments in this prayer book with regard to both the material costs, the time-consuming production, including the insertion of prayers for women, indicate that bonds to a woman, possibly a bride, were to be proven or even enhanced by having this book made for her. On the small Tunisian island of Djerba, another prayer book was printed in 1946 with a children's version of the grace after meals, thus also facilitating children's expression of devotion (eBay 2017a).

Along with the rise of emigrants to America, sales of miniature prayer books rose. In Fürth, Germany, the first of four eight-centimeter high editions were printed. The title page specifies this prayer book is for travelers about to cross the ocean to America.[5] In other miniature prayer books from this period, named poets from the middle of the nineteenth century onward composed new prayers for those embarking on sea vessels and trains, both pointing to the vulnerable stage of transition in the life of the owners and a possible function as an amulet to ward off dangers on the way. Miniaturization of prayer books in the context of emigration thus connotes both hermeneutical and artifactual usage.

Army service among Jews during peace or wartime also occasioned editions of miniature prayer books. Rabbis in Bohemia gave miniature prayer books to Jewish soldiers when they enlisted in the army from the end of the nineteenth century to the First World War (Rivkin 1939, 211n). Jews who enlisted in the armies of the Allied forces during the Second World War were also equipped with Jewish prayer books conveying the presence and protective power of God. Today, armies still produce prayer books for Jews. In 2006, the US Army produced an "ecumenical" Jewish prayer book for all Jewish congregations. In Israel, the Israeli Defense Forces provide their soldiers with Hebrew Bibles, a complete set of objects for prayer including miniature prayer books (eBay 2017b). In comparison, the British Armed Forces have embraced the digital format and only offer prayer books to soldiers of different religions as online PDF files (Her Majesty's Armed Forces 2006), thus compromising the artifactual uses, including the functions as amulets.

Psalms

The Book of Psalms belongs to the Writings in the Hebrew Bible, with only a small degree of sacredness in comparison with the Torah. Still, the Psalms has been the most loved part of the Hebrew Bible throughout the ages and has always been the most likely candidate to serve as an amulet for protection or a talisman for good luck (see Schleicher 2009, 56–58). Handwritten copies in Hebrew of the Psalms were given to newly-wed couples from antiquity onward, among other things to secure their share in the world-to-come and to ward off demons and disasters (bGit 35a). The earliest surviving miniaturized version of the Psalms stems from 1565 and was printed by Robert Etienne

---

5. Until the awareness of the 1842 Fürth prayer book, historians believed that immigration to America from Germany did not begin until after the revolutionary uprising among liberals and working-class Germans against the aristocracy in 1848–1849. However, the costly affair of setting up such a print and the title page itself have corrected scholarly opinion and directed attention to the wave of immigration prior to these revolutions (Rivkin 1939, 210–211).

in Paris. Even today, Jews of a mystical inclination consider recitation of all the 150 Psalms to be an efficient means to ward off evil. It therefore comes as no surprise that copies of the Psalms have become miniaturized to such an extent that both their appearance and functions are more amulet-like or talismanic than book-like. This interpretation is supported by a new invention in Judaica jewelry, that is, USB keys that come, for example, in silver coating and with a single precious stone, attached as a pendant to a necklace (World of Judaica 2017). Here, the artifactual properties of the book dominate, but the digital format also permits the portability of the text and its hermeneutical use, if combined with an electronic device.

Haggadah shel Pesach

Pesach, also known as Passover, is one of the most important Jewish holidays. The book that commemorates the Exodus from Egypt is not the Hebrew Bible, but the *Haggadah shel Pesach* (the Passover narrative). The first *Haggadah shel Pesach* was probably written in the thirteenth century and constitutes a ritual manual for the first evening during Passover to be celebrated in Jewish homes. This lay and domestic celebration implies active participation from everyone present, who should read the narrative, think, ask questions, eat symbolic food, and open the main door of the house hoping for the Messiah. If the Haggadah is not in the hands of those present at the Passover table, it will lie in their bosom or next to their plate to be within reach whenever the recitation of the Haggadah resumes because everyone is obligated to follow the recitation. In other words, ease of access to and orientation in the textual object explains the frequent miniaturization of the *Haggadah shel Pesach*. Jonathan Z. Smith in fact mentions the domestic Passover ritual as an empirical example that supports his theory that miniaturization, together with narrativization, enabled domestic rituals and thus the religious agency of individuals (Smith 1995, 22).

The *Haggadah shel Pesach* quotes from the Torah, draws upon specifications from the Mishnah, and often includes illuminations. One of the earliest and most beautiful examples is the Golden Haggadah from Barcelona from 1320 with fifty-six miniature illuminations (The British Library n.d.). While the Golden Haggadah is not a miniature, the illuminations are. These illuminations testify, in line with Lévi-Strauss, to the artist's imaginative attempts to fill in various narrative and conceptual lacunae that occurred as a result of miniaturizing the whole Book of Exodus into the Haggadah text.

An extant miniature Haggadah from 1721 measures 9.2 by 6.1 centimeters. The *sofer* Meshullam Zimmel ben Moshe of Polna produced it in Vienna on parchment. It was intended as a gift from Meir Poesing to his wife Juetl according to the dedications inside the book (see for example The Israel

Museum, Jerusalem 2017). In accordance with Steven J. Gores' argument, this bears witness to how investments in small objects may represent investments in emotional bonds.

Easy access to the textual content is not the only reason for miniaturization. Avraham Haba is one of several artists who have challenged the codex format of miniature haggadot by subverting expectations of formats and writing surfaces. Eggs belong to the festive meal on the first evening of Passover. They must be eaten hardboiled to symbolize tasting the Egyptian hardship. However, in 1967 Haba wrote the entire Haggadah on a six-centimeter high egg by means of micrography and thus combined two central artifacts for the Passover ritual: that is, the Haggadah and the egg (Kedem Auction House n.d.b). Beyond the imaginative function of such miniaturization, it testifies to Haba's artistic skills as well as invests in and demonstrates his personal bonds to Jewish culture and tradition.

Purim Megillot

At the carnivalesque festival during winter known as Purim, Jews listen to the reading of the Book of Esther in the synagogue from a scroll. Each Jew, man or woman, follows the reading by looking at his or her own private miniaturized scroll because of the commandment to understand every single word of the story. Having one's own Esther scroll thus permits individual agency, not only in domestic settings, but also in liturgical ones.

Esther scrolls were and are still typically handwritten by a *sofer,* that is, a scribe. It was common for a bride's parents to give a beautifully written Esther scroll as a gift to the bridegroom at Jewish weddings. In line with Gores, people invested in personal ties also to men by means of ornamented miniaturized books.

In the Middle East and India, miniaturized Esther scrolls were not decorated, but their cylinders or encasements were often made of precious materials. In the Ashkenazi region, that is, among German-speaking Jews, scribes could include illuminations. Esther scrolls from the Sephardic area, that is, where Jews would be Spanish speaking, would follow the Muslim practice of only decorating miniature Esther scrolls with floral or geometrical motives (Feffer 1969, 35–36). Similar to Ian Reader's observations on how miniatures offer the possibility to vary the models to mark local dissociation from the authoritative model, Esther scrolls that abided by local ornamental traditions demarcated the cultural region to which the commissioning Jews belonged.

Hebrew Bibles and Torot

John Clein from Leyden published the oldest miniature Hebrew Bible in the codex format in 1529. It measured 9.9 by 6.8 centimeters (Welsh 1987, 63).

As technology advanced, miniature Hebrew Bibles were sometimes printed in such a small type that the text became unreadable. Such miniature Bibles are referred to as *abiblia* and are often distributed with a magnifying glass attached to them (see for example: PBS 2008; Welsh 1987, 7). Generally, complete Hebrew Bibles had no liturgical function, but rather belonged as an important text for studies and an identity marker in Jewish homes and institutions of religious training, all from basic Hebrew classes to rabbinical academies. Miniaturization of this text can therefore point to a need to access its textual content in case one had to travel, hide one's religious affiliation, and/or migrate.

The Torah in the codex format is called a *humash* or *hamishah humshey torah*. Cantors use a *humash* to learn the vowels attached to the consonants in the Torah scroll, which cannot contain any vowels if it should be fit for liturgical use. The printing of miniaturized *humashim* is known from 1540 (Morse-Harding 2015). It has facilitated the preparations of cantors and lay Jews who were called to read from the Torah during synagogue service. In this respect, a *humash* very much exemplifies how books basically function as external memory storage. In addition, the miniaturization of the Torah in the codex format could also enable close contact to God's own words if one had to travel, conceal one's religion, and/or migrate, even though the sacredness disappears to some extent because of the liturgically invalid formats, materials, and processes of production.

The most concentrated manifestation of sacredness lies in the scroll format applied to the first part of the Hebrew Bible; that is, the Torah, God's teachings to Moses. In late archaic times, the priests and the Levites orchestrated readings of the Torah to the people (Neh 8:8), but in the last centuries before the Common Era, the Torah escaped the sole control of these specialists and became distributed in different, sometimes variant handwritten versions among lay people, along with the increase of literacy.

From the second century BCE, practices of reciting specific Torah passages, known as the *shema*, each morning and evening, are documented. These passages were miniaturized into micrographic renderings on parchment, placed in small cylinders attached to the doorposts of Jewish homes, known as *mezuzot*, and in the *tefillin* boxes placed by men on their forehead and on their upper left arm, closest to the heart, signifying mental focus and sincerity during recitation. Such *tefillin* and *mezuzot* were found in the excavations at Qumran, testifying to the devotional use of these miniaturized fragments among the members of the Dead Sea Community. In Jewish-Greek writings from around the beginning of the Common Era, Josephus *(Antiquities* IV, 8:13) and Matthew (23:5) refer to the *tefillin* boxes by the Greek word *phylacteries*, meaning amulets. The Greek word itself and the metonymic transposition of God's presence through his words into the *tefillin* and *mezuzot* confirm both Danièle Dehouve and Steven J. Gores' arguments about the metonymical and manipulable functions of miniaturization.[6]

In 70 CE the Romans burned down the Jerusalem Temple. The portability and accessibility of God's presence through the Torah have added to our understanding of how temple-less Judaism as a religion came to survive the national catastrophe and exile that followed. Around 600 CE, the Babylonian Talmud prescribed that every man should write a Torah scroll for himself, and if he could not, he should have one made (bSan 21b; bMeg 27a). This commandment ensured the distribution of Torah scrolls and favored domestic or small communal settings and individual religious agency in the absence of a cultic center. Only parchment scrolls from the skin of a kosher animal (bMeg 19a, bShab 79b), written in the original language, the Assyrian script, and in ink (mYad 4:5) were fit for liturgical use.[7] In other words, the early rabbis insisted on the scroll format, which might be related to the parting of the ways between rabbinical Jews and Jesus-following Jews. The latter group, as they gradually consolidated themselves as Christians, favored the codex. The scroll format of the Torah does not facilitate easy orientation, but it points to the history of Jews as recipients of the *Sefer haTorah*, that is, the scroll of the Torah. Moses wrote a scroll on God's command and ordered the Levites to place it next to the two tablets as a means of narrative guidance to the Israelites on how to live (Deut. 31: 24–27). *Sefer* (scroll or book) in Hebrew is derived from the root *s-p-r* (to narrate), which reminds us of how the scroll format offered a better medium for narration than tablets. In the rivalry with Jesus-following Jews, the rabbis chose not to authorize the codex format for the ritual use of their most sacred text. Instead, the rabbis prescribed investments in the artifactual properties of the scroll to signal their loyalty to the covenant between Moses and God as a means to enhancing their primacy and access to a metonymical representation of God despite the exilic and competitive situation.

Through the ages, many lay and mystical Jews have considered any liturgically valid Torah scroll as a mediator between the practicing Jew and God, able to grant various sorts of blessings such as fertility, protection, and good health. A famous example of an amuletic and talismanic, not miniaturized, but very small scroll is the *Zghair Derna*, the "little" one from the Jewish

---

6. This supports Heather Coffey's analysis of miniaturized Qur'ans where she writes that "[a]ll small manuscripts have the *potential* to be amuletic, and that this potential is intrinsically linked to devotion, which renders the numinous accessible through close use" (Coffey 2009, 103, Coffey's italics).

7. For more on the artifactual properties of the Torah scroll, see for example Schleicher (2010, 13–17) and Sabar (2009, 139–142, 152, 159).

community of Derna in modern-day Libya. Its smallness has attracted legends about how it adroitly moves and intervenes to offer blessings and prevent evil. Here, it is striking how its adroitness "incarnates" the mobility of any miniaturized Torah scroll.[8]

Small scrolls, but not exactly miniatures according to modern Western standards, have been made through the ages. A miniaturized scroll from the Balkans made in 1750 is fastened to a suitcase, which indicates its smallness as important to it portability and maybe the owner's profession as an itinerant preacher, typical of the period and region (eBay 2017c).

Only a few miniaturized scrolls would qualify both for Jewish liturgical use and as miniatures according to modern Western standards. The liturgically valid miniature scrolls are typically quite recent and reflect the elite ambitions of Jewish professional scribes similar to the ambitions of book printers who have used the miniature format to showcase their skills. The world's smallest handwritten miniature Torah scroll, which abides by all requirements to be liturgically fit, measures only 5 centimeters in height and has a magnifying glass as a screen built into the lid of its silver case (The Yeshiva World 2014). The function of this scroll is hardly liturgical but rather testifies to artifactual properties such as the skills and religious affiliation of the *sofer*.

A scroll whose smallness was crucial for its liturgical application, however, was used on October 24, 2014, where it facilitated women's access to religious agency at the Western Temple Wall in Jerusalem. After having been refused access to the women's area with a full-sized scroll, women from the feminist organization "Women of the Wall" smuggled a miniature Torah scroll into the women's area. Thanks to the miniaturization of the scroll, they were able not only to perform the first women's Torah reading at the Western Temple Wall, but a twelve-year-old girl named Sasha Lutt was also among the readers as part of her *bat mitzvah*, which establishes her reading as the first *bat mitzvah* ceremony at the Western Temple Wall (Ferber 2014). While the miniature scroll is liturgically fit, it is not normative in Israeli Judaism for women to read from it. It was the smallness and the concealability of the scroll that enabled this religio-political statement concerning women's access to religious agency in a communal setting. In accordance with Lévi-Strauss, Dehouve, and Reader, miniaturization facilitated a variation on the model including performances of protest and alternatives, and the "filling out of blanks" in the life of these religious women.

I want to end my account of miniaturized books in Jewish religion with a true story about a non-miniature, but nevertheless small, Torah that adds to

---

8. For more on the legends about the Zghair Derna, see Sabar (2009), Ben-Amos (2011) and Goldberg (2013).

our understanding of the miniaturization of religious texts. The scroll was written on deerskin, which is very rare in that the skin of one deer only provides one sheet and it takes around 80 sheets to make a scroll. The deerskin scroll was made in around 1800 in Eastern Europe. It belonged to Rabbi Yaakov Meir who had inherited it from his grandfather who had it made to accompany him on the road, as he was a traveling merchant. Instead of wooden cylinders, the Meir scroll had copper ones with the consequence that early on in the life of this scroll the copper had already transferred rust onto the sheets, rendering the scroll liturgically unfit. During Nazi occupation, Rabbi Meir was sent to Auschwitz. Not knowing what awaited him, he hid the deerskin scroll in a secret pocket, made from another sleeve, inside the sleeve of the coat that he was wearing. Its non-kosher status was not important to him. Upon arrival in Auschwitz, he was told to remove his clothes. The Jew who was tasked with collecting the clothes of the newcomers secretly removed the scroll from Rabbi Meir's coat and brought it to Rabbi Meir's barracks three days later. All the Jews in the camp shared this scroll, which points to a more communal use of miniaturized Torah scrolls in comparison to the individualized use of other religious miniature books in a codex format. During spring 1945, Rabbi Meir was sent on the death march across Germany as the Nazis wanted to prevent the liberation of the death and concentration camps by the Allied forces. During this march, a Nazi soldier shot Rabbi Meir, who was once again carrying his scroll up his sleeve. Large bloodstains spread to the portions of Tazria and Metzora (Lev. 12–15), indicating recent use as these four chapters were read during the two weeks before and after his death. Perceived as fate, many years later in the 1970s, Rabbi Meir's grandson, Yaakov Maor, happened upon the deerskin scroll in Vienna. Here, he identified it thanks to family narratives about the scroll, its copper cylinders, the rust, Rabbi Meir's blood on the Leviticus chapters, and its disappearance in 1945. Yaakov Maor's claim to the scroll was accepted and he took it with him to Israel where he lived and where he was able to return it to his mother, the daughter of Rabbi Meir. Mother and son arranged for Rabbi Meir's blood to be scraped off the scroll, and they subsequently buried the blood in Jerusalem. The family also had a new Torah cover made that was embroidered with a quote from Numbers 10:35 on how the ark had traveled to the Promised Land, and combined with the names of towns through which their family had traversed with the scroll before entering Israel. In spite of its liturgically defect status, they still invested in its preservation as it represents several bonds to dead and living family members, regions of their past and present, as well as atrocities inflicted on them and all Jews, which some of them had survived. This ornamental investment is a matter of external memory storage. Had the deerskin scroll not been small, it would not have been a source of both individual and communal meaning making and devotion during the encampment. It would not have served as a hub for family histories, world history, traversed territories, pain, and joy (Rizel 2016).

Conclusion

In my analysis of the miniaturization of books in Jewish religion, I have found that all examples of miniaturized books to some extent serve the basic function of books as an external memory storage that provides access to canonized wordings of cultural narratives and information to be performed as a means to maintain and signal the user's Jewishness.

The miniaturized examples of community rules, Hebrew Bible codices, as well as Torah codices and scrolls indicate that reduction in size has allowed for easy access to divinely inspired texts and their metonymical representation of God as artifacts primarily among lay individuals. As a variant of easy access, the portability of these books also explains the embracing of miniaturization, especially in times of exile and persecution among both lay Jews and itinerant specialists.

The theoretical reflections of Jonathan Z. Smith inspired me to look at miniaturization as a process that facilitated individualized religiosity. His thesis found support in the uses of prayer books and small haggadot at the Passover meal among Jews of all genders and ages; in men's and women's readings from private Esther scrolls during the synagogal Purim service; in Bible and Torah codices that have enabled private study and reading preparations; and finally in women's Torah readings in a ritual context where such readings used to be a male privilege.

While all of the handwritten examples demonstrate the skills of the *sofer*, the meticulous production of books, as in the case of the world's smallest scroll, has also afforded the *sofer* an opportunity to demarcate his, and lately also her,[9] religious affiliation. This may be an overlooked artifactual aspect of miniature publications among Christian printers too, but supported by the fact that many of the early printers, including Gutenberg, prioritized the printing of Bibles.

Steven J. Gores considered miniaturization a process that enabled an artifact to gain amuletic and talismanic properties because of the metonymical character of miniature paintings. I applied this theory to miniaturized books in Jewish religion and found that the prayer books, the Psalms, and parts or full versions of the Torah support Gores' thesis in that they have all been used

---

9. The first female scribe, Jen Taylor Friedman, was educated in 2007. See for example her completion of what seems to be the first scroll written by a woman in a Reconstructionist congregation (Friedman n.d.)

to ward off evil and attract divine blessings, most likely because God's words are believed to constitute their sacred and thus numinous content.

The iterability of a greater model that follows from miniaturization explains its imaginative function of filling in the gaps and the dynamic potential to alter the model. This idea, presented by Claude Lévi-Strauss, Danièle Dehouve, and Ian Reader, found support in the miniature paintings of many haggadot that filled in the omissions of the Exodus narrative, in the regional differences in the ornamentation of miniaturized Esther scrolls, and in the protest among "Women of the Wall" against authoritative models of patriarchal liturgy by means of a miniaturized Torah scroll.

The final insight of the analysis, inspired by Gores, is how ornamentation has been used to invest in emotional bonds and personal ties. Gift-giving by means of miniaturized books, as well as the renovation of the Meir scroll, testify to how investments in miniaturized books have been made to establish, maintain, and cherish bonds with individuals, collectives, even to geographies and historical events.

I therefore conclude that miniaturized books in Jewish religion have served and still serve many different functions. The early function of books that stored memories of cultural narratives and arguments pertains to the textual content and invites hermeneutical uses. However, the empirical material also demonstrates how the continuation of Jewish practices and beliefs in the course of history, despite exile and persecution, depended not only on the textual content of Jewish religious books being stored, but also on the books being small enough for individuals to handle and hide. Handiness and concealability are thus important functions of miniaturization, as mentioned in much of the collectors' literature. However, what the collectors do not explain is the implications that follow from handiness and concealability. The perspective on artifactual uses of miniaturized books in Jewish religion opens up a deeper function of miniature books, explained largely by sense activation.

By interpreting the empirical material from the insights presented by Lévi-Strauss, Dehouve, and Gores, the analysis indicates that closeness to the body and the activation of the senses lead to the illusion, not only of wholeness and the processes of filling in the blanks, including associations to individual and collective representations, but also to the illusion of manipulability, close relations to, and mastery of the miniaturized artifact. In this way, manipulability through sense activation is another important function of miniaturization, which also explains how miniaturized books have facilitated individual religious agency among both specialists and lay people in the course of Jewish religion.

References

Alexander, Philip S. and Geza Vermes. 1998. *Qumran Cave 4, XIX: Serekh ha-Yahad and Two Related Texts*. Oxford: Clarendon Press.

Anderson, Sean Eron and Marc Levoy. 2002. "Cuneiform Tablets." *IEEE Computer Graphics and Applications* 22(6): 82–88. https://doi.org/10.1109/MCG.2002.1046632

Ben-Amos, Dan (ed.). 2011. *Folktales of the Jews—Volume 3: Tales from Arab Lands*. Philadelphia: The Jewish Publication Society.

Bondy, Louis W. 1981. *Miniature Books: Their History from the Beginnings to the Present Day*. London: Sheppard.

British Library. n.d. "Golden Haggadah." Online Gallery. http://www.bl.uk/onlinegallery/sacredtexts/golden.html

Bromer, Anne C. 1988. "Art for Miniature Art's Sake." *Journal of Decorative and Propaganda Arts* 7: 88–95.

Coffey, Heather. 2009. "Between Amulet and Devotion: Islamic Miniature Books in the Lilly Library." In *The Islamic Manuscript Tradition*, edited by Christiane Gruber, 78–115. Bloomington: Indiana University Press. https://doi.org/10.2307/j.ctt2005ssv.8

Dehouve, Danièle. 2016. "A Play on Dimensions: Miniaturization and Fractals in Mesoamerican Ritual." *Journal of Anthropological Research* (Winter): 504–529.

eBay, 2017a. "1946 Djerba Tunisia MINIATURE SHABBAT PRAYER BOOK Antique/Judaica/Jewish/Hebrew." http://www.ebay.ca/itm/1946-Djerba-Tunisia-MINIATURE-SHABBAT-PRAYER-BOOK-Antique-Judaica-Jewish-Hebrew-/390779900010?hash=item5afc4c106a:g:IIkAAOxydlFS-LSD

eBay, 2017b. "LOT IDF Judaica Tefillin Bag Antique Tfilin Teffilin JEWISH Phylacteries Rare." http://www.ebay.ca/itm/LOT-IDF-Judaica-Tefillin-Bag-Antique-Tfilin-Teffilin-JEWISH-Phylacteries-Rare-/202015933502?hash=item2f0916843e:g:zz0AAOSwrqlZiDO6

eBay, 2017c. "Miniature Travelling Torah Scroll Parchment Wimpel Wooden Case Tik Balkan Ca1750." http://www.ebay.com/itm/Miniature-Travelling-Torah-Scroll-Parchment-Wimpel-Wooden-Case-Tik-Balkan-Ca1750-/371248960666

Edgren, James Sören. 2013. "The History of the Book in China." In *The Book: A Global History*, edited by Michael F. Suarez, S. J. and H. R. Woudhuysen, 573–592. Oxford: Oxford University Press.

Edison, Julian I. 1967. "World's Oldest Printing on Paper." *Miniature Book News* 8: 1–2.

Facsimile Editions, 2017. "Me'ah Berachot." http://www.facsimile-editions.com/en/mb/

Feffer, Solomon. 1969. "Hebrew Miniature Books." *Jewish Book Annual* 27: 35–41.

Ferber, Alona, 2014. "Defying Regulations, Women of the Wall Sneak Tiny Torah Scroll into the Kotel." *Hareetz.* October 24. http://www.haaretz.com/israel-news/1.622560

Friedman, Jen Taylor. N.d. "Milestones." www.hasoferet.com

Goldberg, Harvey E. 2013. "The Ethnographic Challenge of Masorti Religiosity Among Israeli Jews." *Ethnologie Française* 43(4): 583–590. https://doi.org/10.3917/ethn.134.0583

Gores, Steven J. 1997. "The Miniature as Reduction and Talisman in Fielding's *Amelia.*" *Studies in English Literature 1500–1900* 37(3): 573–593. https://doi.org/10.2307/451050

Her Majesty's Armed Forces. 2006. "Armed Forces Operational Service and Prayer Book." London: Ministry of Defense. http://health.nzdf.mil.nz/assets/Uploads/JSP587-BritishArmedForces-Prayer-Book.pdf

Hunter, Dard. 1943. *Papermaking: The History and Technique of an Ancient Craft.* New York: Dover.

The Israel Museum Jerusalem. 2017. "Miniature Passover Haggadah." http://museum.imj.org.il/imagine/collections/item.asp?itemNum=354497

Kallendorf, Craig. 2013. "The Ancient Book." In *The Book: A Global History*, edited by Michael F. Suarez, S.J. and H.R. Woudhuysen, 39–53. Oxford: Oxford University Press.

Kedem Auction House. n.d.a. "Miniature Siddur—Amsterdam, 1739—Variant." Books and Manuscripts. https://www.kedem-auctions.com/content/miniature-siddur-amsterdam-1739-variant

———. n.d.b. "Avraham Haba—Passover Haggadah—Micrography on an Egg." https://www.kedem-auctions.com/content/avraham-haba-passover-haggadah-micrography-egg

Lévi-Strauss, Claude. 1966. *The Savage Mind.* Chicago: The University of Chicago Press.

MBS Presentations. n.d. *Miniature Book Society.* https://www.mbs.org

Morse-Harding, Chloe. 2015. "Miniature Books." *Brandeis Special Collections Spotlight.* http://brandeisspecialcollections.blogspot.dk/2015/07/miniature-books.html

Moyer, Ian S. and Jacco Dieleman. 2003. "Miniaturization and the Opening of the Mouth in a Greek Magical Text (*PGM* XII.270-350)." *Journal of Ancient Near Eastern Religions* 3: 47–72. https://doi.org/10.1163/1569212031960320

Nongbri, Brent. 2005. "The Use and Abuse of P52: Papyrological Pitfalls in the Dating of the Fourth Gospel." *Harvard Theological Review* 98(1): 23–48. https://doi.org/10.1017/S0017816005000842

PBS. 2008. "Miniature Hebrew Bible, ca. 1850." http://www.pbs.org/wgbh/roadshow/season/13/dallas-tx/appraisals/miniature-hebrew-bible-ca-1850--200802A39

Pearson, David. 2013. "Bookbinding." In *The Book: A Global History*, edited by Michael F. Suarez, S.J. and H.R. Woudhuysen, 245–257. Oxford: Oxford University Press.

Reader, Ian. 1988. "Miniaturization and Proliferation: A Study of Small-Scale Pilgrimages in Japan." *Studies in Central and East Asian Religions* 1: 55–66.

Rickard, Kathryn I. 1988. *A Lady and Her Books: The Biography of Doris Varner Welsh*. Montreal: du Parnasse.

Rivkin, Isaac. 1939. "A Pocket Edition Prayer Book for German Jewish Emigrants to America, 1842." *American Jewish Historical Society* 35: 207–212.

Rizel, Shlomo. 2016. "From Auschwitz to Israel, the Saga of a Long-Lost Mini-Torah: How a Journalist Made a Priceless Personal Discovery." *Chabad.org News*. January 11. http://www.chabad.org/news/article_cdo/aid/3193812/jewish/From-Auschwitz-to-Israel-the-Saga-of-a-Long-Lost-Mini-Torah.htm

Robson, Eleanor. 2009. "The Clay Tablet Book in Sumer, Assyria, and Babylonia." In *A Companion to the History of the Book*, edited by Simon Eliot and Jonathan Rose, 67–83. Oxford: Wiley-Blackwell.

Roemer, Cornelia. 2009. "The Papyrus Roll in Egypt, Greece, and Rome." In *A Companion to the History of the Book*, edited by Simon Eliot and Jonathan Rose, 84–94. Oxford: Wiley-Blackwell.

Sabar, Shalom. 2009. "Torah and Magic: The Torah Scroll and Its Appurtenances as Magical Objects in Traditional Jewish Culture." *European Journal of Jewish Studies* 3(1): 135–170. https://doi.org/10.1163/102599909X12471170467448

Schleicher, Marianne. 2017. "Engaging All the Senses: On Multi-sensory Stimulation in the Process of Making and Inaugurating a Torah Scroll." *Postscripts* 8(1/2): 39–65. https://doi.org/10.1558/post.32694

———. 2010. "Accounts of a Dying Scroll: On Jewish Handling of Sacred Texts in Need of Restoration or Disposal." In *The Death of Sacred Texts: Ritual Disposal and Renovation of Texts in World Religions*, edited by Kristina Myrvold, 11–29. London: Ashgate.

———. 2009. "Artifactual and Hermeneutical Use of Scripture in Jewish Tradition." In *Jewish and Christian Scripture as Artifact and Canon*, edited by Craig A. Evans and H. Daniel Zacharias, 48–65. London: T&T Clark.

Smith, Jonathan Z. 1995. "Trading Places." In *Ancient Magic and Ritual Power*, edited by Marvin Meyer and Paul Mirecki, 13–27. Leiden: Brill. https://doi.org/10.1163/9789004283817_003

Stewart, Susan. 1993. *On Longing: Narratives of the Miniature, the Gigantic, the Souvenir, the Collection*. Durham: Duke University Press.

Vera, Eugenia Roldán. 2013. "The History of the Book in Latin America (including Incas and Aztecs)." In *The Book: A Global History*, edited by Michael F. Suarez, S. J. and H. R. Woudhuysen, 656–670. Oxford: Oxford University Press.

Welsh, Doris V. 1987. *The History of Miniature Books*. Albany: Fort Orange Press.

Wiseman, Donald J. 1955. "Assyrian Writing-Boards." *Iraq* 17(1): 3–13. https://doi.org/10.2307/4241713

Woollaston, Victoria. 2013. "The World's Oldest Jewish Prayer Book? Hebrew Text Predates Earliest Known Copy of the Torah by Four Centuries." *Mail Online*. October 2. http://www.dailymail.co.uk/sciencetech/article-2441588/The-worlds-oldest-Jewish-prayer-book-Hebrew-text-predates-earliest-known-copy-Torah-CENTURIES.html

World of Judaica. 2017. "Sterling Silver 2 Gigabyte Disk on Key with Digital Book of Tehillim." http://www.worldofjudaica.com/jewish-jewelry/necklaces-pendants/p_925_sterling_silver_8_gigabyte_disk_on_key_with_digital_book_of_tehillim

Yeshiva World. 2014. "World's Smallest Torah Scroll Up for Auction." https://www.theyeshivaworld.com/news/headlines-breaking-stories/218946/worlds-smallest-torah-scroll-up-for-auction.html

Znidersic, Martin. 2004. "Small is Beautiful (But is It Useful?): Miniature Books through the Ages." *Logos* 15(3): 144–146.

3

Words in a Nutshell:
Miniaturizing Texts in Early Modern England

Lucy Razzall

Dr Lucy Razzall is a Teaching Fellow in Shakespeare and Renaissance Literature at University College London. Her research focuses on literature and material culture in early modern England.

Object number WB. 236 in the British Museum is a carved wooden sphere small enough to nestle in the palm of the hand, and somewhat resembling a walnut. It is scarcely seven centimeters in diameter at its widest point, but when opened along a hinge it reveals the entire story of Christian salvation depicted in tiny detailed relief in its interior. Made from boxwood in a Netherlandish workshop at some point in the early 1500s, it is one of the finest surviving examples of intricately carved wooden beads that enjoyed particular popularity in this region during the first decades of the sixteenth century. The exterior of the bead is decorated with Gothic tracery and flowers, and it opens into two halves, each of which can be opened again, by two tiny doors on the upper half, and a hinged flap on the lower. All of these interior surfaces show key scriptural events in relief, from Moses and the serpent to the Marriage of the Virgin, the Annunciation, the Nativity, events from the life of Christ and the Passion, with Christ bearing the cross and the Crucifixion carved in the most intricately detail relief in the shadowy recesses at the very heart of the object. Fragments of scriptural verses are inscribed in Latin around the external and internal circumferences of the sphere and its internal panels.

Beads such as this one were objects for private devotion in late medieval Europe, and they may have been part of a rosary, or suspended alone from a belt (Scholten 2017; Wetter and Scholten 2017). In their miniaturization of important events from the Christian story, particularly Christ's suffering, they intensify the user's devotional recollection of them. Although there are surviving examples of sixteenth-century prayer beads carved from ivory, bone, and metal, boxwood appears to have been the most popular material, and the distinct resemblance, both inside and out, of wooden examples to nutshells lies behind the term "prayer nut," the modern name frequently given to these objects.

Prayer nuts invite devotional interaction in several sensory ways. Used like a rosary, or as part of a rosary, they are intended to be touched. Their carved surfaces are invitingly tactile, and natural substances such as wood or ivory would respond to touch, warming gently in the hand. The innermost parts of the British Museum example, especially the Crucifixion, make the most of the object's three-dimensional visual potential, drawing the eye into the tiny details of the thronged scene, in which human figures bearing weapons, animals, and architectural details are crowded into a miniature vaulted space. They are also often textual objects; in the British Museum example, each circular scene is bordered with familiar phrases from the gospels and Lamentations.

Unlike a rosary, a prayer nut requires both hands at once, so that it can be opened to reveal its contents. In material as well as spiritual terms then, it is also a book-like object, a stimulus for private devotion that encloses the story of salvation at the fingertips. We might compare it to another (slightly later) devotional object from the Low Countries, a seventeenth-century "book" now in the Metropolitan Museum of Art (Accession Number 17.190.303) which opens to reveal carved ivory plaques like pages that can be unfolded in concertina fashion, bearing scenes from the Passion. When closed, this object is a similar size to a prayer bead, at 7.6 cm by 4.1 cm, and it may likewise have been worn on a chain around the neck or suspended from the waist. Both objects can be opened and closed in the intimate space of the palm of the hand, and play on the compelling effects not only of miniaturization, but also of enclosure and containment.

Prayer nuts celebrate the material and technical virtuosity of the carver, who miraculously condenses important biblical events into a tiny space. As in a real nut, a mysterious exterior conceals rich sustenance within. More so than in other miniature objects, there is a particular extremeness of scale in prayer nuts, as in the ivory book of the Passion: what is compressed and contained in a space as small as a nutshell is a story of universal salvific significance. This image, of a narrative of epic proportions enclosed in the smallest of containers, has an ancient pagan parallel that was widely known in early modern Europe. In the seventh book of his *Natural History*, Pliny the Elder evokes several impressively miniature objects in a passage about "quicknesse of Eie sight":

> *Cicero* hath recorded, that the whole Poeme of *Homer* called Ilias, was written in a piece of parchment, which was able to be couched within a nut shel. [...] *Callicrates* vsed to make Pismires and other such like little creatures, out

of yvorie so artificially, that other men could not discerne the parts of their body one from another. There was one *Myrmecides,* excellent in that kinde of workmanship: who of the same matter wrought a chariot with foure wheeles and as many steeds, in so little roome, that a silly flie might couer all with her wings. Also he made a ship with all the tackling to it, no bigger than a little bee might hide it with her wings. (Holland 1634, 167)

There are multiple distancings, reductions, and enclosures happening at once here. Pliny also notes that another great writer, Cicero, has written about the existence of a copy of Homer's *Iliad* so tiny it was "couched within a nut shel." In one sentence, the greatest work of ancient Greek literature is reduced to a "piece of parchment" of the most miniscule of proportions, comparable with carved ivory creatures, chariots, and ships so small they might be hidden by an insect. While Pliny's *Natural History* is itself a work of compression, attempting to summarise the known world in the space of a single book, the *Iliad* is also a masterpiece of reduction. Homer famously begins "in the middle of things," compressing the ten years of the Trojan War into a period of barely forty-two days, and the eighteenth book of the poem features a well-known image of ekphrastic condensation, the shield of Achilles, which contains the entire cosmos. Thus Pliny's account of miniature objects brings together multiple forms of literary and material compression in just a few lines.

Other versions of this rumour about the *Iliad* "within a nut shel" succeeded Pliny in Greek and Roman literature (Squire 2011, 1-2), each rescaling Homer's epic to an improbably miniature size. Like the sixteenth-century Netherlandish prayer beads, such images of the *Iliad* in a nutshell play around with visual and verbal representation, forcing upon the viewer (or reader, or listener) a particularly acute awareness of scale in visual and intellectual terms. Michael Squire has pointed out that "by objectifying the *Iliad*, turning it into a wonder of writing, the '*Iliad* in a nutshell' inverts the epic tradition of representing vision in words": the poem is transformed into an artifact as well as a text, and then encapsulated inside another intriguing artifact, so that both demand not only reading but seeing as well (Squire 2011, 10-11). Both nutshell and parchment also demand the tactile intimacy of unclasping and unfolding for the revelation of their contents to be complete.

After Philemon Holland's influential English translation (cited above) of much of Pliny's *Natural History* was first published in in the early seventeenth century, the fantastical *Iliad*-in-a-nutshell became a commonplace motif of virtuosic compression in early modern England. Engaging with the popularity of this image, this chapter will explore its implications in early modern literary culture. In her examination of "Renaissance culture's fascination with the inscrutable," which "is borne out by its frequent invocations of the paradox of *multum in parvo*, or much in little, which posits that the smallest spaces are more replete, and thus symbolically larger, than more expansive ones," Jessica Wolfe adopts a rather cynical attitude towards what she describes as the "cramped, detail-packed spaces of elaborate devices (mechanical or rhetorical)" in this period (Wolfe 2004, 163, 182). Minutiae such as the *Iliad*-in-a-nutshell were, she suggests, "frequently denigrated as trivial or excessively artful," because they reflected "the preciosity or idleness of their owners" (Wolfe 2004, 182). This chapter will tread a less suspicious approach, taking the nutshell at face value as a convenient way of expressing literary concerns about the challenges of size and scale—particularly regarding the desirable feat of being both small and compendious at the same time in printed texts. Although the frequently-appearing *Iliad*-in-a-nutshell might seem merely a convenient rhetorical flourish in early modern writing, this chapter proposes that closer attention to this image might help us to consider broader questions about the intertwining of physical and literary scale in some early modern printed books, as both texts and material objects.

Literary, literal, and metaphorical size

In what follows, I argue that the miniature book is is not just a frivolous curiosity in early modern England, but a manifestation, at the extreme end of the scale, of anxiety about how a book's physical size is related to its literary magnitude. A literally weighty book might be mentally burdensome as well, while a miniature book, although it might involve impressively virtuosic acts of writing, also suggests that any potentially unwieldy text can be rendered smaller, literally and metaphorically. Although a miniature book might present its own practical challenges – is it actually possible to read the *Iliad* in so tiny a format? – the idea of the miniature can also imply simplification, and something more readily handled. Pliny's image is of one of the most expansive works of literature squeezed into the tiniest of spaces, and in early modern England, the book most often miniaturised was another text that was both literally and metaphorically weighty, the Bible (Stewart 1984, 38). Attempts to rescale the Bible did not necessarily always involve miniaturization in the most literal sense, however, but were concerned with bringing it down to size in other ways in order to render it more manageable—something that might sit more easily in both the hands and in the mind.

The mystery scribe of the legendary *Iliad*-in-a-nutshell had a counterpart much closer to home in early modern England. The Elizabethan chronicler John Stow was one of several historians to refer to "a strange peece of worke, & almost incredible" which "was brought to passe by an Englishman, born within the Citie of London & a Clearke of the Chancerie, named Peter Bales." A calligrapher, by "his industrie and practise of hys pen," Bales,

> contriued & writ within the compasse of a peny, in Latine, the Lords prayer, the Creede, the ten Commandements, a prayer to God, a prayer for the Queene, his Poste, his name, ye day of the moneth, the yere of our Lord, & the raigne of the Queene: […] he presented the same to the Queens Maiestie in the heade of a Kyng of Golde, couered wyth a Christall, and presented therewith an excellent Spectacle by him deuised for the easier reading thereof, wherewith hir Maiestie read all that was written therein, wyth greate admiration, & commended the same to the Lordes of the Councell, and the Embassadours, & did weare the same many times vpon hir finger. (Stow 1580, 1187)

As well as this miniature royal gift, Bales produced a copy of the Bible "'in an English walnut no bigger than a hen's egg. The nut holdeth the book: there are as many leaves in his little book as the great Bible, and he hath written as much in one of his little leaves as a great leaf of the Bible'" (Disraeli 1881, 275). Like the proverbial miniature *Iliad*, Bales' penny and the Bible in a nutshell do not survive today, but as on a seventeenth-century gold ring containing the words of the Lord's prayer which does, while the text might have been "all but invisible to the naked eye," the assurance of its presence must have lent "both curiosity and prophylactic properties" (Mack 2007, 207). Bales provided "an excellent Spectacle" for "easier reading" of the words condensed onto the penny, and presumably the miniature Bible was legible only with a similar aid. In such objects, the diminutive physical format becomes exponential to the metaphorical weight of the textual content: these most sacred of words are so small that they cannot easily be read, but their miniaturization emphasises their infinite value. As Susan Stewart puts it, in objects like Bales' Bible in a nutshell, "the labor involved multiplies, and so does the significance of the total object" (Stewart 1984, 38).

The significance of scale in early modern print culture (rather than manuscripts), which I am mainly concerned with here, presents more complex questions about the relationship between size and the labor of both making and reading. The early seventeenth century saw the first examples in English of miniature printed books. In 1601, the poet and antiquary John Weever published *An Agnus Dei*, a devotional text telling the life of Christ in verse, which measured approximately 1¼ inches x 1³⁄₁₆ inches, and was for subsequent centuries the smallest book printed in the English language (Bromer and Edison 2007, 68). The year 1614 saw the publication of a verse summary of scripture in two miniature volumes, by the prolific writer John Taylor: *Verbum Sempiternum* (the Old Testament) and *Salvator Mundi* (the New Testament), which became instantly popular, and were reprinted thirteen times by 1721 (Bromer and Edison 2007, 70). Although the format of these books is certainly miniature, using paper folded to almost the smallest possible size, the text is not printed in a correspondingly miniature typeface, so there are only a few words on each page, and they can be read relatively easily. While their physical format offers a literary challenge to the author, who must condense text into a limited number of words, their size also has implications for the other agents involved in producing them, challenging "the typesetter, printer, illustrator, and binder to hone their skills" (Bromer and Edison 2007, 12). In print culture, potential acts of miniaturization are restricted by the material limitations of the particular medium—the size of a sheet of paper, and pieces of type, and the particular ways in which they must be deployed in the printing process.

Acts of virtuosic compression in print culture are less about the manual skill involved in producing a carved prayer bead, or a Bible in a nutshell, and more about the effective use of the possibilities offered by print. In the letter to the reader at the beginning of his mid-seventeenth-century educational text *Reading and spelling English made easy: Wherein All the Words of our English Bible are set down in an Alphabetical order and divided into their distinct Syllabls*, Thomas Lye directs his work to parents, who "generally throughout this *whole Kingdom*, are at constant, *vast expences*, for the ingenious education of their dear *Children*." There are "many excellent Means already prescribed" for teaching children how to read and write, but his project offers a new model of instruction, he claims, dissecting scripture into the most miniature of units, the syllable and the letter. "Probably," he says, "thou hast heard of an *Iliad* in a Nutshell, or seen the Ten Commandments cut on a small Penny. But didst ever yet behold the *whole Bible*, every word therein, distinctly set before thine eye in a few pages?" Trumpeting the originality of his own project in these opening lines, Lye juxtaposes the proverbial "*Iliad* in a Nutshell" with another image of miniaturised text, a penny bearing the Ten Commandments, which the reader might actually have "seen," to foreground a third example that for his rhetorical purposes, is much rarer: "the *whole Bible*" in "a few pages" (1673, A2r,v). In his book, every word in the Bible is listed alphabetically, and then broken down into its constituent syllables of just a few letters each. The entire biblical text becomes a rich source for learning how to read and write the English tongue, and Lye claims that students of this method will at the same time benefit spiritually from the familiarity with the scriptures that it encourages.

Lye's explanatory letter is followed by an advertisement for some of his other educational texts, as well as other works for young readers available from the same publisher, including Thomas White's *A Little Book for Little Children; wherein is set down several Directions for Little Children, and several, remarkable Stories both Ancient and Modern, of Little Children* (Lye 1673, A4v). Both the title of this work and Lye's letter to the reader reveal a preoccupation with the literal and metaphorical implications of size. White's book is described as a "Little" one, for children who are correspondingly "Little," and it contains stories of other "Little Children." Here, the repetition of "Little" connects the scale of the book with that of its readers, suggesting that it is appropriately matched to "Little Children" in both practical and intellectual terms, a common didactic technique in early modern theological texts for children (see Razzall 2017). Meanwhile, Lye warns "Let no man object the *Difficulty* of this Book, and that it is so *massy* a weight, as will not *only press,* but *crush* such tender shoulders," drawing a similar parallel between intellectual and physical weightiness. Dispelling such conjecture, he reminds his readers "do but consider, that every word in this Table is drawn out into *little easy syllabls* (which is not done in any *Primers, Psalters,* or other Books used by Children) and then judg which are most *easy* to be learned, *This,* or Those." Though the scale of his ambitious book might make it appear too weighty for "tender shoulders," it in fact performs an act of miniaturization not seen in other educational works, dissecting scripture into its constituent vocabulary, and then individual words into "*little easy syllabls.*" Octavo-sized, it is significantly smaller than a Bible, though at over seventy leaves, it occupies more than just "a few pages."

As these texts suggest, books can convey a sense of solemnity through their literal weightiness that might threaten to overwhelm in both material and intellectual terms: the Great Bible of 1539, the first officially commissioned translation in English, was so named because of its size, and other early modern Bibles were usually physically imposing volumes. At the same time, however, small books in the religious context of post-Reformation England could also be intensely powerful objects, and potentially concerning to authorities because of their physical size, which meant that controversial material could be could be easily smuggled or hidden. In often confessionally-charged ways, "life-transforming experiences that came from the page were far more likely to be found in small than in great books," suggests Margaret Aston (2004, 174; see also Kearney 2009), challenging the assumption that physical scale always equates directly to spiritual value. Small books offer practical convenience that may be matched by literary content that is condensed, neater, and thus easier to handle in intellectual terms, too.

This upending of the correlation between physical and metaphorical weightiness resonates widely in early modern writing, especially at moments where writers are self-conscious about the relationship between the physical appearance and literary value or purpose of their work. Stephen Gosson's famous euphuistic attack on the theatre, *The School of Abuse* of 1579, is prefaced with a defensive dedicatory letter, in which he writes:

> The title of my booke, doth promise much, the volume you see is very little: and sithence I cannot beare out my folly by authority, like an Emperoure, I will craue pardon for my Phrenzye, by submission, as your woorshippes too commaunde. The Schoole which I builde, is narrowe, and at the first blushe appeareth but a doggehole; yet small Cloudes cary water; slender threedes sowe sure stitches; little heares haue their shadowe; blunt stones, whetter kniues; from harde rockes, flow soft springes; the whole worlde is drawen in a mappe, Homers *Iliades* in a nutte shell, a kings picture in a pennye; Little Chestes maye holde great treasure; a few Cyphers contayne the substance of a riche Merchant; The shortest Pamphlette maye shrowde matter. (1579, *3v-*4r)

Gosson moves through a series of comparable images to assert that his "very little" volume contains much of value, despite its diminutive size. The proverbial *Iliad*-in-a-nutshell is enmeshed in a collection of other curiosities, both natural and manmade—including clouds, threads, stones, chests, and pamphlets. The very materiality of this text comes to the fore, turning the reader's attention to the physical properties of the object they hold in their hands, in order to clarify its literary worth. In a similar vein, in his 1638 *Meditations on the holy sacrament of the Lords last Supper*, the prolific writer and preacher Edward Reynolds reflects on the stark contrast between the humility of the material substances involved in sacraments—water, bread—and their powerful effects. "Whence is it that there should lie so much power in the narrow roome of so small and common elements?" he asks, continuing:

> Is not even in works of Art, the skill of the workman more eminent in the narrowest and unfittest Subjects? Are not the Iliads of *Homer* more admirable in a Nutshell than in a volume? doe not Limmers set the highest value on their smallest draughts? and is there not matter of admiration, and astonishment in the meanest and most vulgar objects? (Reynolds 1638, 16)

Like Gosson, Reynolds pushes the correlation between smallness and value to the extreme, alluding to the skill of painters and limners whose "meanest and most vulgar objects" might be the most impressive. Set amidst such artifacts, the *Iliad*-in-a-nutshell becomes a curiosity comparable with the other miniature things that populated early modern collectors' cabinets—portraits, models, and clocks, for example, in a reincarnation of Pliny's virtual collection of carved ivories. Such objects often aspire to be encyclopedic in some way, but in turn become encyclopedized themselves (Wolfe 2004, 161–202). Pliny's textually copious nutshell, dislodged from its ancient origins and relocated to a distinctively early modern setting cluttered with other material objects such as those invoked by Gosson and Reynolds, is part of a bigger picture that scrutinises the relationship between the material medium and intellectual value of literary works.

Conclusion

In the 1623 Folio text of *Hamlet*, Shakespeare's hero remarks to his friends Rosencrantz and Guildenstern that "Denmark's a Prison" to him. They disagree, suggesting "your Ambition makes it one; 'tis too narrow for your minde," but Hamlet proclaims "O God, I could be bounded in a nutshell and count my selfe a King of infinite space; were it not that I haue bad dreames" (Shakespeare 1623, 262). Hamlet uses the nutshell as a paradigm of the miniature, the opposite of "infinite space," but in his image the two become the same thing, in a neat paradox. The image is an even more fantastical version of the legendary *Iliad*-in-a-nutshell—in this nutshell, Hamlet encloses not just one literary work, but his entire imagination. Denmark feels confining and restricting to Hamlet, but at the same time, he can conceive of finding "infinite space" for his mind in a nutshell. His image invokes a similar thrill to that of the *Iliad*-in-a-nutshell, of containing the impossibly large in the tiniest of spaces. Hamlet's nutshell provides him with a space to think in, an object that is at once constraining and liberating. As the other textual moments examined in this chapter have revealed, Pliny's mysterious miniature book, which like Hamlet's nutshell remained only virtual in early modern writing, offered another concrete site for thinking about size and scale in the relationship between container and contained, in printed books as material objects.

References

Primary sources

Gosson, Stephen. 1579. *The School of Abuse, Conteining a pleasant invective against Poets, Pipers, Plaiers, Iesters, and such like Caterpillars of a Commonwelth*. London: Thomas Woodcocke.

Holland, Philemon. 1634. *The historie of the world: commonly called, The naturall historie of C. Plinus Secundus*. London: Adam Islip.

Lye, Thomas. 1673. *Reading and Spelling English made Easie*. London: A. Maxwell for Thomas Parkhurst.

Reynolds, Edward. 1638. *Meditations on the holy sacrament of the Lords last Supper*. London: Felix Kyngston.

Shakespeare, William. 1623. *Mr. VVilliam Shakespeares comedies, histories, & tragedies*. London: Isaac Jaggard and Edward Blount.

Stow, John. 1580. *The chronicles of England from Brute vnto this present yeare of Christ*. London: Ralphe Newberie.

Taylor, John. 1614. *Verbum Sempiternum. Together with Salvator Mundi*. London: John Beale for John Hamman.

Weever, John. 1606. *An Agnus Dei*. London: Val. Sims for Nicholas Lyng.

Secondary sources

Aston, Margaret. 2004. "Lap Books and Lectern Books: The Revelatory Book in the Reformation." In *The Church and the Book*, edited by R.N. Swanson, 163–189. Woodbridge: Boydell. https://doi.org/10.1017/S0424208400015801

Bachelard, Gaston. 1994. *The Poetics of Space: The Classic Look At How We Experience Intimate Places*. Translated by Maria Jolas. Boston, MA: Beacon.

Bromer, Anne C., and Julian I. Edison. 2007. *Miniature Books: 4,000 Years of Tiny Treasures*. New York: Abrams.

Disraeli, Isaac. 1881. *Curiosities of Literature. A New Edition, edited, with memoir and notes, by his son, the Earl of Beaconsfield*. 3 volumes. London. Frederick Warne & Co.

Kearney, James. 2009. *The Incarnate Text: Imagining the Book in Reformation England*. Philadelphia: University of Pennsylvania Press.

Mack, John. 2007. *The Art of Small Things*. London: British Museum Press.

Razzall, Lucy. 2017. "Small chests and jointed boxes: Material texts and the play of resemblance in early modern print." *Book 2.0* 7: 21–32. https://doi.org/10.1386/btwo.7.1.21_1

Scholten, Fritz. 2017. *Small Wonders: Late Gothic Boxwood Microcarvings from the Low Countries*. Rotterdam: Rijks Museum.

Stewart, Susan. 1984. *On Longing: Narratives of the Miniature, the Gigantic, the Souvenir, the Collection*. Baltimore: John Hopkins University Press.

Squire, Michael. 2011. *The Iliad in a Nutshell: Visualizing Epic on the Tabulae Iliacae*. Oxford: Oxford University Press.

Welsh, Doris V. 1989. *A Bibliography of Miniature Books (1470–1965)*. New York: Kathryn I. Rickard.

Wetter, Evelin and Fritz Scholten, eds. 2017. *Prayer Nuts, Private Devotion and Early Modern Art Collecting*. Special Issue of *Riggisberger Berichte 22*. Riggisberg: Abegg-Stiftung.

Wolfe, Jessica. 2004. *Humanism, Machinery, and Renaissance Literature*. Cambridge: Cambridge University Press.

4

Small Things of Greatest Consequence:
Miniature Bibles in America

Dorina Miller Parmenter

Dorina Miller Parmenter is Associate Professor of Religious Studies at Spalding University in Louisville, Kentucky. Her research interests include material uses of the Christian Bible.

A miniature Bible is in many ways the exemplary iconic book, with power, status, and/or identity concentrated in the object's recognizable material properties (see Watts in this volume; Parmenter 2006). For example, when a person wears a Bible charm on a necklace or bracelet, or carries a leather-bound, gold-tooled Bible that contains 800,000 words in 500 pages yet is small enough to fit in a pocket, the activity is not about reading the text, but about the feelings triggered by the material practice of touching and seeing the miniature book (Parmenter 2012).

Because the iconic power of a Bible derives from the manipulation of the book as an identifiable material object, the efficaciousness of a Bible's ritualization is only indirectly dependent on the biblical text, and it does not need to directly contain the "real"[1] or complete text to "do its work" (Fea 2016; Parmenter 2006, 2012; Watts 2006). Thus books that bear the familiar visual image and perhaps even the formal or informal title of "Bible" might contain biblical selections, such as the four Gospels (as was the case with many medieval treasure bindings), or the New Testament (such as common pocked-sized Gideon volumes, with Psalms and Proverbs), or verses and prayers relevant to a particular demographic (like soldiers' Bibles). The textual content of these volumes does not affect their ritual display, use, or signification as "Bible," or authoritative and powerful Christian scripture. This demonstrates that when the iconicity of a Bible predominates in particular uses of the book, it allows for variability of the text contained between the recognizable covers.[2] Therefore,

---

1. Of course, there is not and never has been a "real" or original biblical text (Beal 2011).

2. The iconic dimension also explains how the image is effective (to signify status, legitimacy, community, etc.) when there is no visible text at all, as with two-

the miniaturization of a Bible to create a smaller-sized object also permits the condensation of the text—not only in font size, but also in semantic content.

This chapter shall address a genre of miniature printed Bibles called "thumb Bibles" that began in the seventeenth century in England, but flourished in nineteenth-century Protestant America with numerous new editions that broke with their English prototypes. Because these miniature "Bibles" were produced by printers and binders who also made other books using the same methods and materials, and little is known about how they were used by those who owned them, what is available for analysis are their texts and illustrations. Unlike many other miniature books, including the popular miniature scriptures of various religions that were published in Britain beginning in the late nineteenth century, these miniature tomes are quite readable without magnifying tools. In a thumb Bible the biblical text is versed or summarized, supposedly for the understanding of children, and consequently, with the contents miniaturized, the font can remain of a legible size. But even though the semantic dimension is significant to the genre, the whole package of the thumb Bible—container and text—functions as an iconic representation of a "real" Bible, thus providing legitimacy to its owner in the present and to the owner's use of other Bibles in the future.

English prototypes for North American thumb Bibles

The designation "thumb Bible" appears to derive from the popularity of the English folklore character Tom Thumb, a boy who is no bigger than his father's thumb. The first use of the term attached to the genre uses the French title for the boy in a Parisian miniature book printed in 1800 called *Bible du Petit Poucet* (Adomeit 1980, xiii, 365). Tom Thumb first appears on an English title page of this genre on a *Verbum Sempiternum* printed in London in 1849 (Adomeit 1980, 263–264). This date coincides with the popularity of the Barnum Circus performer and American dwarf Charles Stratton, who toured Europe and the United States in the 1840s with the stage name of General Tom Thumb (Adomeit 1980, xiii). The term "thumb Bible" has stuck to this genre and is now used retrospectively to describe a miniature printed book that is "an abstract, an epitome, a summary, a synopsis, a paraphrase, or an abridgement" of the Bible (Adomeit 1980, xiii).

The first editions of thumb Bibles were produced in London in the early seventeenth century. The earliest (and the smallest printed book in England to date, 1.3 by 1.1 inches or 33 by 27 millimeters) was by the well-known poet John Weever (1576–1632) and printed in 1601. The book titled *An Agnus Dei* (Lamb of God) contained 128 pages of rhymed couplets to illustrate the

dimensional images of a Bible, or for closed objects like Bible charms for jewelry, which shall be addressed at the end of the chapter.

life of Christ (Adomeit 1980, 193–194; Metzger 2004). More influential was a similar volume by the English "Water Poet," John Taylor (1580–1653). The first edition of Taylor's *Verbum Sempiternum* and *Salvator Mundi* appeared in 1614 (Adomeit 1980, 198), followed by thirteen more English editions until 1721. The book was revived by many different American printers starting in 1765, and then taken up again in England starting in 1849 (Bromer and Edison 2007, 70). These Taylor Bibles contain a rhymed summary of each book of the Bible. For example, the first couplet for Genesis (out of eight total) is "JEHOVAH here of Nothing all things makes / And Man, the chief of all, this God forsakes" (Taylor 1614). In addition to a dedication and epistle acknowledging royal patronage (also seen in Weever Bibles), Taylor (1614) includes an address to the reader:

> With care and pains out of the Sacred book,
> This little abstract for thee have took:
> And with great reverence have I cull'd from thence,
> All things that are of Greatest consequence.

In 1698 or 1699 the London and Boston printer Benjamin Harris, known for producing the *New England Primer*, created a macrominiature[3] Bible very much like John Taylor's called *The Holy Bible in Verse* (Welch 1972, 159; Welsh 1987, 65; Nichols 1926, 73). While the Weever and Taylor Bibles do not contain any specific references to children as the intended audience for thumb Bibles, the Harris *Holy Bible in Verse* identifies itself as "Very pleasant and profitable, and greatly tending to encourage Children and Others to Read, and also to understand what they Read in that sacred Book" (Nichols 1926, 75; Edison 1968, 3). It contains ten woodcuts identical to the *New England Primer*, making it the first illustrated tiny Bible of this genre, and also demonstrating the intention of the small volumes for children's Protestant religious education (Nichols 1926, 74). Collector Doris Welsh indicates that there were twelve editions of Harris rhymed Bibles printed during the early eighteenth century in London, Scotland, and Boston (Welsh 1987, 65; see also Nichols 1926, 74; Welch 1972, 159-161), but that they were not as "concise, expressive and to the point" and thus not as popular as the Taylor thumb Bibles (Welsh 1987, 65).

---

3. Because *The Holy Bible in Verse* slightly exceeds 3 inches or 76 millimeters, most collectors do not classify it as a miniature book (falling between 1 and 3 inches or 25 and 76 millimeters), but a macrominiature (of 3 to 4 inches or 76 to 101 millimeters) (see Byrne 2016, 3; Bromer and Edison 2007, 114). Therefore, for most collectors it does not classify as a thumb Bible, either. But other than differing by a few millimeters in size, *The Holy Bible in Verse* fits all the other criteria for miniature thumb Bibles, and is included in this study because of its apparent influence on the genre.

In eighteenth-century London, new illustrated miniature books with sum-
maries of the Bible in prose were created that surpassed the rhymed ver-
sions in popularity. The first was *Biblia, or a Practical Summary of y* Old &*
New Testaments with sixteen engraved plates, published by R. Wilkin in 1727
(Adomeit 1980, 214–215; Welsh 1987, 66). It was reprinted 1771 by W.
Harris and by Elizabeth Newbery in 1774, both bearing the title *The Bible in*
Miniature, or a Concise History of the Old and New Testaments (the Newbery
Bible has "Miniuture" in the title, see Adomeit 1980, 228-230; Welsh 1987,
66). Ruth Bottigheimer claims that these summaries were "initially intended
for adults [… but] manifestly read by children" (Bottigheimer 2004, 301).
Unlike the whimsical thumb Bibles in verse, the language of these prose
Bibles is much more solemn, as one can see in the style of the preface of *The*
Bible in Miniuture (sic):

> It is a melancholy reflection, that in a country, where all have a Bible in their
> hands, so many should be ignorant of the first principles of the oracles of
> God. How infinitive wisdom from the beginning hath in divers manners,
> communicated his will to man; and how all former dispensations of the di-
> vine care and love to him receive their completion in JESUS CHRIST.

> To give the reader a taste of this, the supreme exercise of the soul here on
> earth, is the pure design of this Treatise; which, if read attentively, will, with
> God's assistance, answer the proposed end. (*The Bible in Miniuture* 1780,
> 1–4)

The preface is followed by a short theological treatise on the characteristics of
God, and a summary of Genesis that begins: "The great Almighty Lord God
hath revealed himself by his glorious works in the creation of the heavens and
the earth" (*The Bible in Miniuture* 1780, 12–13).

Collector Ruth Adomeit claims that the Elizabeth Newbery prose thumb
Bible of 1780 (*The Bible in Miniuture*) is "probably the best-known […] and
the one most often found today" (Adomeit 1980, 229). Unlike most other
editions of thumb Bibles, which are extant in only a few copies each, Adomeit
found that she could not keep track of all of the different copies that were
available. The prose Bible summaries of Wilkin, W. Harris, and Newbery
were printed under various titles in at least twenty-eight editions in England
in the nineteenth century (Welsh 1987, 66), and were the prototypes of at
least eighty-seven different editions of thumb Bibles printed in America.

American modifications to English thumb Bibles

North American editions of miniature Bibles at first showed little variation
from their English prototypes, but gradually became more explicitly Protestant
in how they encouraged the users of miniature Bibles to not only learn about
Christian theology and salvation, but also to venerate the "original" Bible
used by adults, which is the object that is essential to Protestant identity.

While the covers of thumb Bibles mimicked the appearance of larger Bibles (for example, by having the title "Bible" prominently gold-stamped on the leather cover and spine), often the illustrations and the introductory text referenced the differences between the children's and adults' Bibles, inviting children to aspire to read the entirety of the sacred Word. Since the small versions synecdochally represent the "real" Bible, one can deduce that one of the purposes of these thumb Bibles was that children could learn how to revere the Bible and identify as Bible-oriented people through their own special book.

The first American editions of the small, rhymed, Bible summary printed in the colonies were the macrominiatures of the printer Benjamin Harris, *The Holy Bible in Verse*, produced between 1717 and 1773 (Welsh 1987, 65; Nichols 1926, 79–82; Welch 1972, 159–160). It is not surprising that with Harris' success with the Protestant *New England Primer*, one of the most popular books in the American colonies with hundreds of editions and millions of copies printed (Lacey 2007, 40), that the designs used for the woodcuts would be repeated in *The Holy Bible in Verse*.[4] For example, in the syllabary of the *Primer* the "B" emblem is an image of a book with BIBLE written across the open pages, accompanied by the text "Thy Life to Mend / This *Book* Attend" (Lacey 2007, 41). This image was used as the illustration for the title page for each of the four editions of *The Holy Bible in Verse* printed in America (Welch 1972, 159–161), and similarly used in the title page designs of other American miniature Bibles. The reference of the tiny book to "original" Bibles also occurs in Benjamin Harris' epistle to the "Christian Reader" in the opening pages of *The Holy Bible in Verse*: "*Children*, read [this book] with Gravity, and you'll find it an excellent Antidote against a weak Memory. That you may turn *Berean*[5] and run oftener to its sacred Original, is the Prayer of thine" (Harris 1717, n.p.).

A 1765 Boston edition of John Taylor's *Verbum Sempiternum* and *Salvator Mundi* is the first extant thumb Bible (to meet the traditional size criteria) printed in the American colonies (Adomeit 1980, 3–4), perhaps with a few earlier editions in the 1750s (Bromer and Edison 2007, 70). The 1765 edition is a copy of the text from early eighteenth-century English editions, including a dedication to Prince William, Duke of Gloucester, who had died

---

4. While ten of *The New England Primer*'s woodcuts are repeated in *The Holy Bible in Verse*, the copies that are available indicate that new, single-image cuts were made for the miniature Bible, whereas the *Primer* used one block with six stacked images to illustrate the verses associated with six letters per page (see Nichols 1926, 74; Lacey 2007, 40–47).

5. A possible reference to Acts 17:10–15, where many Bereans convert after hearing Paul preach the Gospel.

in 1700. At least fifteen different editions of Taylor Bibles were produced in America until the end of the nineteenth century. Many of them, like the 1765 edition, have "Bible" and "The New Testament" on separate title pages from the Latin title pages of "*Verbum Sempiternum*" and "*Salvator Mundi*," and many have the word "Bible" gold-tooled on the spine. One copy of the 1765 edition, now at the Lilly Library in Bloomington, has a contemporary printed bookplate identifying "Elisha Badcock, His Bible; 1765," and has remnants of metal hinges that once held the small volume closed (see Figure 4.1).

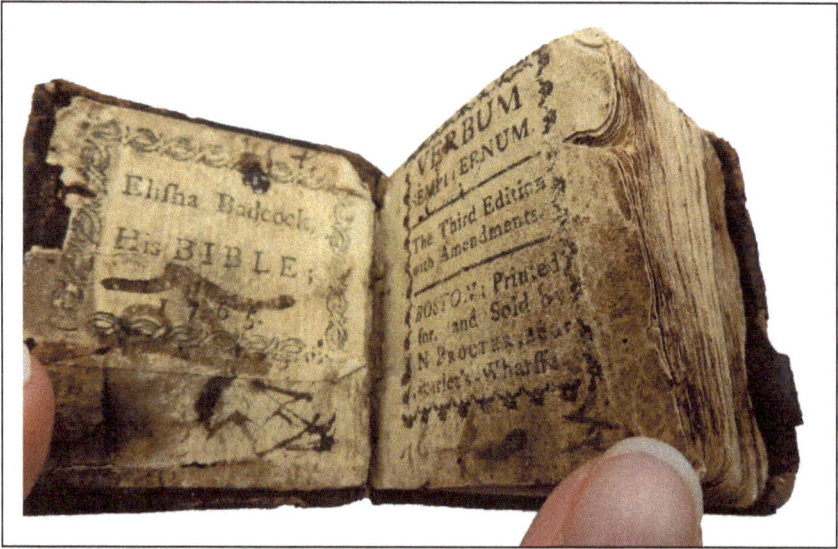

Figure 4.1: *Verbum Sempiternum and Salvator Mundi* by John Taylor. Third Edition with Amendments, printed for and sold by N. Proctor near Scarlet's-Wharffe, Boston, 1765. Courtesy, The Lilly Library, Indiana University, Bloomington, Indiana [A1]. Photo by the author.

Several late eighteenth- and early nineteenth-century American editions that follow the text of a Taylor Bible make some unique and significant changes to the prototype. It became common to drop the Latin *Verbum Sempiternum* and *Salvator Mundi* titles, as does one post-Revolutionary (circa 1800) edition (Adomeit 1980, 153–154); the only titles are "Bible" at the beginning of the book, and "The New Testament" after the text with Old Testament Apocrypha. The only illustration in this edition is a rough woodcut of a person holding an open book with the word "Bible" across the pages. While it is common to see thumb Bible illustrations repeated in multiple editions, there are no other thumb Bibles with an image similar to this one; however it is similar to imagery in other illustrated devotional literature such as *The*

History of the Holy Jesus from 1746 where the figure is clearly a woman (see Lacey 2007, 152). The title page of this volume, *The Bible: The ninth Edition*, is remarkably lacking in information: the place of publication is "New England" and it is "Printed for the Purchaser."[6] Dropping the common dedication to the Duke of Gloucester, it is dedicated "to the Rev. Clergy of the United States of America," who are addressed as "most hopeful Sires" in their address, which has been shortened and simplified by "The Editors" from the traditional John Taylor introduction. The epistle and the directives to the reader are signed "J. Taylor," but also have been shortened from the seventeenth-century prototype. Similarly, a few other editions of the Taylor-type from 1796–1815 are dedicated to "His Excellency G. Washington, President of the United States of America," who is addressed as "most hopeful George" (see Adomeit 1980, 155–156; Welch 1972, 426–427). Starting in 1805 some dedications were "To Christians of All Denominations in the United States of North America" (Adomeit 1980; 22-23). The "Bible" emblem from the *New England Primer* was used again for the title illustration of a miniature Bible titled *Salvator Mundi* and printed by Thomas Fleet of Boston in 1801-1802, who also recycled some woodcuts from his editions of *The Prodigal Daughter* to provide other images for the volume (Welch 1972, 427; see Lacey 2007, 57–62).

Many early American prose thumb Bibles followed the Newbery editions of *The Bible in Miniature, or a Concise History of the Old and New Testaments.* An early American illustrated version of 1795–1797 has a unique title page illustration even though the remaining engravings follow their English prototypes. In a picture not much bigger than one inch tall (circa 2.5 centimeters), an attentive boy stands next to a man who is touching the edge of an open book on a podium with "Holy Bible" written across the pages (Adomeit 1980, 161-162). This volume itself looks very much like a miniature gold-tooled Bible of the era, including having "Holy Bible" stamped on the spine, so the small book in a child's hands is both a replica of and an aspiration for the "real" Bible that he or she will have someday.

It was previously mentioned how the first English prose thumb Bibles used more solemn and dense language for unidentified but perhaps adult readers, but in nineteenth-century American editions of the same type, the language is edited to reflect children as the targeted audience. The preface for an 1811 *Bible History* (a version of *The Bible in Miniature, or Concise History*) retains the same "melancholy reflection" on the state of Bible reading, but changes the last paragraph to create a different tone:

> It is hoped, the perusal of this little treatise will so attract the young mind, as to excite a curiosity and love for the scriptures at large. They are indeed

---

6. Considering the rough execution of this volume, this lack of information might be a way for an unestablished printer to avoid early US copyright issues.

valuable writings; and are profitable for doctrine, reproof, and instruction. Teaching us, that denying ungodliness and worldly lusts, we should live soberly, righteously, and godly in this present world. (Wood 1811, 5–7)

New American editions of thumb Bibles

New American types of prose thumb Bibles emerged in the first half of the nineteenth century that were influenced by English prototypes but did not recycle the older text or illustrations. They were more obviously and consistently produced for children and reflected common nineteenth-century views of children's capacities as well as religious education in the home, guided by mothers (see Morgan 2005). One of these is *Miniature Bible or Abstract of Sacred History* by Thomas G. Fessenden, printed in Battleborough, Vermont, in 1816 (see Figure 4.2). Beneath the title is printed "For the use of Children" and the text of Proverbs 21:6: "Train up a child in the way he should go: and when he is old he will not depart from it." The wood engraving for

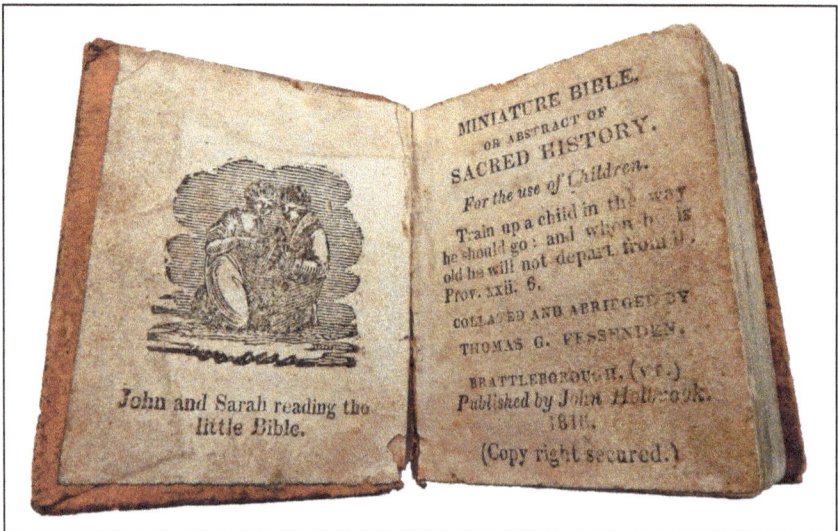

Figure 4.2: *Miniature Bible or Abstract of Sacred History* by Thomas G. Fessenden. Published by John Holbrook, Battleborough, Vermont, 1816. Courtesy, The Lilly Library, Indiana University, Bloomington, Indiana [A39]. Photo by the author.

the frontispiece shows a boy and a girl kneeling on the ground, huddled over a small book, captioned "John and Sarah reading the little Bible" (see Adomeit 1980, 56).[7] The preface states that "The object of this publication is to allure the attention of infant minds to the sacred and important truths

---

7. For a similar image see the frontispiece to *A Short History of the Bible and Testament* by Alfred Mills (Hartford, CT: Cooke and Hale, 1817) with "Eliza, William, and Julia reading the Little Bibles" (Adomeit 1980, 57).

of the Bible" (Fessenden 1816, 5). It concludes with the hope that it "will be found well adapted to the capacity of children; and while it amuses the fancy, will improve the understanding, ameliorate the heart, and serve as an introduction to a more intimate acquaintance with the volumes of divine inspiration" (Fessenden 1816, 6-7). The summary text of each book of the Bible is straightforward and simple. For example, Genesis begins: "By this book we are informed that in the beginning God created the heavens and the earth, the firmament, and the waters, and every plant and every moving creature that hath life" (Fessenden 1816, 11).

The Child's Bible with Plates by a Lady of Cincinnati,[8] first published in 1834 by Truman, Smith, and Company of Cincinnati, was a very common prose thumb Bible, printed in many locations in the northeast United States in the nineteenth century (Adomeit 1980, 94–101). The frontispiece engraving has three children surrounding an open, regular-sized book, with the caption "There are the Bears tearing the children. Oh what wicked children they were!" (see Figure 4.3). This refers to a later image in the volume, illustrating

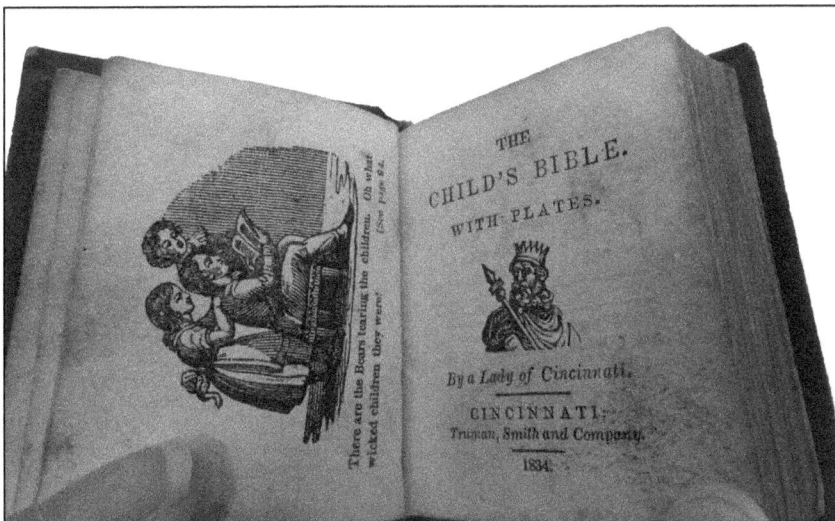

Figure 4.3: *The Child's Bible with Plates* by a Lady of Cincinnati. Truman, Smith and Company, Cincinnati, 1824. Courtesy, The Lilly Library, Indiana University, Bloomington, Indiana [A75]. Photo by the author.

---

8. There has been some speculation that this "Lady" was Harriet Beecher Stowe (Smith 1984, 5; repeated by Dalton 2016, 58), presumably due to her family's association with Truman, Smith, and Company, her authorship of other books of children's Christian literature, and her residence in Cincinnati in 1834, but neither the Harriet Beecher Stowe Center in Cincinnati nor several Harriet Beecher Stowe scholars whom I contacted confirmed this.

Elisha's curse on forty-two small boys who taunt him, who are subsequently mauled by bears (2 Kings 2:23–24), an image common to illustrated American thumb Bibles like this one that "tells us how dreadfully sinners must be punished" (A Lady of Cincinnati 1834, 9). Children are directly addressed in the preface as well as in the summary of Bible narratives. With the story and illustration of "Abraham offering Isaac" readers are asked,

> Do you not think he was obedient to let his father take cords and bind him, and he make no resistance? He was an obedient, good boy, and grew up a good man. The Lord blessed him greatly. He had very few troubles, and much prosperity through his whole life. (A Lady of Cincinnati 1834, 37)

While some seventeenth- and eighteenth-century thumb Bibles were illustrated, nineteenth-century books in the genre explicitly used pictures as the hook to interest children and eventually inspire them to further Bible use. In *The Child's Bible with Plates*, children are told that

> [w]e have made this small book, dear children, on purpose for you. As we knew you liked pictures, we have given you a number. After you read this through, you will wish to know more about the Bible. Your mamma will get you one, or let you take hers, and you will learn much more than we had room to tell you. (A Lady of Cincinnati 1834, 10)

Similarly, *The Little Picture Bible for Young Children* of 1841, with an open book for the title page illustration, begins the Introduction with the following:

> In this tiny book, my dear young readers will find, not only the *Bible in miniature*, but many pictures of some of the most interesting events related in the Bible [...] I hope those who read it will have their interest excited, and wish to learn more, and that they will gladly turn to their Bibles that they may do so [...] This little volume is designed to lead them to read and love the Bible, which, more than any other book in the wide world, will make them wise and happy. (*The Little Picture Bible for Young Children* 1841, 5–6)

Unlike miniature books of prayers or devotions which may have been produced in small sizes for ease of access (for example, being worn on the body or carried in a purse or pocket; see Welsh, 1987, 13) or because the size facilitated secrecy (see Watts in this volume), it seems that the reason for the miniature size of these American thumb Bibles was its appeal to children. The only clues for how these books were used are in the books themselves. We have already seen that they were directly addressed to children in their contents and their illustrations. Some volumes indicate on the title page that they are "intended as a present for youth" (*The Bible in Miniature* 1815 in Adomeit 1980, 275–275), and therefore were perhaps given as gifts by parents or teachers for religious milestones or as Sunday school rewards (de Hamel 2001, 259; Eclectibles 2017). From the high numbers of thumb Bibles already in collections and still available for purchase today, they clearly were neither rare nor unique, but widely produced and marketed (Welsh 1987, 66-67). From the evident wear on many of the extant books one can deduce that they were used in some way, and not kept on a shelf. The small Bibles provided children with an object that gave them practice with a Bible's iconic and semantic use, generating positive personal and social affect (see Parmenter 2012), and anticipating their use of a "real" Bible in similar ways.

The end of thumb Bibles:
Miniature Bibles as souvenirs, amulets, and talismans

The production of children's thumb Bibles came to a close at the end of the nineteenth century as printers acquired thinner paper and the ability to mass produce photographically-reduced images, which led to the creation and sale of full-text miniature Bibles. With the development of these miniature Bibles, the connection between smallness and children becomes less prominent. Anyone could possess a tiny version of a "real" Bible, and therefore it appears that the function of the small books changed. They no longer indicated an intention for future Bible use and reading, but instead the small objects were sold as souvenirs, amulets, and talismans.

The first publication of a full-text miniature Bible was by David Bryce and Son of Glasgow and Henry Frowde of London in 1896 (see Myrvold in this volume; see Figure 4.4). The first run was 25,000 copies, but by the middle of the twentieth century hundreds of thousands of Bryce Bibles were published in a variety of different formats (Bromer and Edison 2007, 76). 876 pages measuring 1.75 by 1.5 inches (forty-four by thirty-eight millimeters) or smaller, these volumes were not readable without extraordinary myopia, so all copies came with a miniature magnifying glass, either in a pocket inside the book cover, in a book sleeve, or in a metal case which could function as a locket.

There is no indication that Bryce Bibles or their even smaller microminiature[9] New Testaments (0.75 by 0.5 inch or nineteen by thirteen millimeters) were meant for children. The text was a reduced facsimile of Oxford University's King James Authorized Version with 28 illustrations, "appointed to be read in churches"—these were "real" Bibles, just smaller. While David Bryce wrote that his small Bibles were useful for reading (Bromer and Edison 2007, 76), packaging promised curiosity rather than readability. One could purchase the "Smallest Bible in the World: Complete and Illustrated" with a variety of paper, cloth, or leather bindings, or in souvenir editions for kings' coronations in 1902 and 1911 (de Hamel 2001, 266) or for events like the Glasgow International Exhibit of 1901. One version of a Bryce Bible came

---

9. Microminiature books are those measuring less than one inch (Bromer and Edison 2007, 11).

chained to a miniature lectern, in a box with a printed lid explaining the history of chaining precious Bibles in churches in England (see Bromer and Edison 2007, 77); other lectern Bibles were packaged for the 1911 tercentenary commemoration of the Authorized Version.

Figure 4.4: The Holy Bible. Published by David Bryce and Son in Glasgow and Henry Frowde in London, 1896. Property of Kristina Myrvold. Photo: Kristina Myrvold.

Bryce's lectern Bibles provide an interesting juxtaposition between nostalgia for Bibles as treasured rarities of the past, so valued that they needed to be chained in place, and objects so common or taken-for-granted in the present that they require a spectacle in miniature to be noticed. All of the Bryce miniatures and microminiatures present mass-produced Bibles in a curious and compelling format to garner special attention. The magnifying glass promises the comforting possibility of reading the text,[10] but based upon how the Bryce Bibles were marketed as curiosities and souvenirs, it appears that the primary function of the small objects is not for semantic use, but for physical contact, visual display, and/or remembrance, all of which are significant elements in the iconic dimension of scriptures. Like all Bibles, they are objects associated with sacred power, social and personal identity, and affection, but these qualities are concentrated with the awe of technological curiosity and the nostalgia of the souvenir. And unlike thumb Bibles that miniaturize the biblical text for the purpose of opening up the larger world of the Bible in

---

10. Even though David Bryce wrote that "many" people read from his tiny Bibles, including a minister who used it as his pulpit Bible (Bromer and Edison 2007, 76), I suggest, following Susan Stewart (1993) that the *possibility*, not the practicality, of the semantic aspect of the full Bible is important for how the books function as iconic and/or nostalgic objects.

future use, these curious reductions rely on memories and are therefore recollecting prior biblical uses or prior events that are commemorated (see Stewart 1993).

Printers and promoters in the United States took the lead from Bryce to create and display miniature Bibles. "The World's Smallest Bible," an 1895 Bryce New Testament microminiature on display at the 1933 Chicago World's Fair, was touted as a technological wonder produced in the "Century of Progress," "not created with the idea of being practical for anyone to read under ordinary conditions" but "made to show the almost superhuman skill and patience of the engravers" (*The World's Smallest Bible* 1933, 1). The descriptive booklet and the postcard that accompanied the display of this marvel indicate that this tiny tome was "actually printed" from hand-engraved plates (*The World's Smallest Bible* 1933, 3) and "[p]archment bound—sewed with silk thread," which "[r]equired nearly 4 years to complete" (Postcard of The World's Smallest Bible 1934). Since there is no other verification that Bryce and Son made special editions of this type, one might speculate that the promoters of the "Century of Progress" were aggrandizing the mystifying production technique of photo-reduction that made the Bryce miniatures and microminiatures possible.[11] After observing "this amazing 'Book of Books'" (*The World's Smallest Bible* 1933, 1) at the Chicago World's Fair, and hearing the claims that it is unsurpassed in craftsmanship and value, one could purchase a World's Fair souvenir miniature Bible (a photoreduction of the four Gospels, 42 by 30 millimeters) of one's own, not made by Bryce, but by the International Company of Cincinnati, Ohio. Some Bryce and Son biblical miniatures and microminiatures were sold in the United States under the imprint of Frederick A. Stokes Company of New York (Phillips 2014).

In the 1920s and 1930s, mass-produced, photographically-reduced "Midget Bibles" were sold in bulk to be used as Church gifts or re-sold for fundraisers. Advertisements in the novelty catalogs in which the Midget Bibles were sold claimed: "Measuring but 1 x 1 ⅝ inches, it can readily be carried in a smallest pocket, in a lady's purse, etc., and the Bible is thought by many to bring Good Luck to its owner" ("Midget Bible" 1928, 375). Similarly, in the 1940s, "midget" Holy Bibles (1.5 by one inch, or thirty-eight by twenty-six millimeters), made with thin paper, glued bindings, and paper covers were hung with a ribbon on a variety of greeting cards made by Sorin Bible and Card of Cincinnati, Ohio. They also made a claim to be distributing "The World's Smallest Bible" on these cards, which were patented to prohibit others from making similar products. One card includes a Christmas prayer for

---

11. However, microminiatures were hand-set and printed by other publishing houses around the same time; see Bromer and Edison 2007, 115.

God's blessings to "Keep you and those to you most dear/Safely through another year" with the accompanying "Little Bible to Keep You Safe From Harm." Another card from Sorin with a miniature Bible attached, intended to be given to American soldiers fighting in the Second World War for whom the Bible "'Twill keep you safe from harm," included a reproduction of a letter from Franklin D. Roosevelt that advocated for "the Bible for all who serve in the armed forces of the United States" (Greeting Card from Mrs. Seiler to Jack Vaughan 1943).

With less readability and less durability, these and other miniature mass-produced Bibles are no longer for use as books to be read, but instead can be interpreted as amulets that ward off misfortune and talismans to better one's fortune. As iconic objects they also are mini-spectacles, sending a message about the owner's identity in relation to the Christian tradition or potential for or realization of Christian piety. The text inside, which likely was never consulted, apparently makes little difference. The Bibles on the cards from Sorin Bible and Card from the 1940s contain "over 220 pages": microscopic analysis reveals that this means all of Matthew, Mark, and Luke, but only chapters 1-6 of John.[12] Contemporary versions of these Bibles are produced in China and sold as keychains in Christian bookstores and novelty catalogs and websites so one can carry the word of God with you always or to give a gift of the "Good Book" ("Bible Keychains" 2017). But when examined with a microscope one can see that they contain an odd assortment of biblical books (Genesis, Exodus, Leviticus, 1 and 2 Timothy, Titus, Philemon, Hebrews, James, and 2 and 3 John), and numerous errors in the text.

This trend away from any possibility of biblical reading in increasingly smaller biblical displays involving curious textual technologies culminates in the microprinted Micro Book and various Nano Bibles available today. The Holy Bible Micro Book, made by the Toppan Printing Company of Tokyo and measuring 4 by 4 millimeters, was displayed and sold at the New York World's Fair of 1965 (Bromer and Edison 2007, 117). Too small to have any immediate iconic value, the display and use of such a small item is dependent upon its housing in a clear plastic case whose packaging encourages it to be seen and touched as a pendant, key holder, or personal accessory. Similarly, the Jerusalem Nano Bible is a silicon wafer of five millimeters square, reduced and engraved using "Israeli nanotechnology" with either Hebrew or Greek on a single surface, and readable only with an electron microscope with one thousand times magnification. This chip, sold as a "small bible, big faith […]

---

12. Similarly, novelty "Midget Bibles" in the 1920s advertise "TWO HUNDRED AND FIFTY PAGES of the NEW TESTAMENT" without mentioning what content that might be ("Midget Bible" 1928, 375). A copy of this book was not available for examination with a microscope.

where spirit and technology meet" is marketed to jewelers or sold embedded in pendants, pins, and watches, so it can be displayed and worn on the body (*Jerusalem Nano Bible* 2016). A similar product is a Crystal Bible, available with the entire text of the King James Version Bible, the Vulgate, or the Septuagint reproduced onto a "tiny glass crystal" through "nanotechnologies." When set into jewelry and worn on the body,

> [y]ou and your loved ones can now wear the Holy Bible anytime! [...] The Word of God promises health for your body, prosperity for your finances, absolute peace in your heart and mind, long life, and most importantly eternal life filled with no more tears, no more sorrow and absolute bliss in the company of the Creator of the universe! (*Crystal Bible* 2016)

As souvenirs to enhance nostalgia for the past, amulets to protect users from harm, and talismans to bring good fortune, these miniature (and smaller) Bibles produced since the late nineteenth century and displayed as curious objects in close proximity to the body concentrate and harness the power attributed to the Bible. But unlike the thumb Bible genre of miniature books popular in the United States in the nineteenth century, the textual or semantic dimension of the Bible has completely dropped out in favor of what literary theorist Susan Stewart calls "minute writing experiments with the limits of bodily skill in writing" (Stewart 1993, 38), which one could also extend to the mechanical technologies that result in microscopic texts. She writes that "the remarkableness of minute writing depends upon the contrast between the physical and abstract features of the mark. Nearly invisible, the mark continues to signify; it is a signification which is increased rather than diminished by its minuteness" (Stewart 1993, 38). Detached from any specific words, the amplified signification is imprecise, and allows for the power generated by tiny books like miniature Bibles to be perceived in many different ways. This is one of the primary characteristics of the iconic function of texts, where signification is generated by the book's visuality and materiality, rather than by its semantic properties.

Conclusion

The iconic and semantic dimensions of scripture operate in relation to one another, so that how the Bible as a physical object is shown, seen, and touched relates to how the biblical text is read and interpreted, and vice versa (see Watts 2006). This exploration of different types of miniature Bibles has demonstrated that the degree to which biblical texts and illustrations are available results in different kinds of iconic uses. A thumb Bible, readable but short and selective, aimed to give the owner a longing for more, which could be found in future Bible use. American thumb Bibles, specifically for children, attempted to cultivate Christian, Bible-reading adults. A thumb Bible thus was an icon in the sense that it was a material image and likeness of a "real" and ideal Bible. A Bible too small to read, whether complete or with selections, does not signify biblical textuality, but augments the power connected with the iconic object, which has been building from past associations. One might imagine that children who learned that "real" Bibles are sacred and transformative may not have implemented fully the ideal of becoming Bible readers, but instead reflected back upon their lessons learned to become users of Bibles as powerful objects.

References

Primary sources

A Lady of Cincinnati. 1834. *A Child's Bible with Plates*. Cincinnati: Truman, Smith and Company.

Fessenden, Thomas G. 1816. *Miniature Bible or Abstract of Sacred History*. Battleborough, VT: John Holbrook.

Greeting Card from Mrs. Seiler to Jack Vaughan. 1943. *The Portal to Texas History*. https://texashistory.unt.edu/ark:/67531/metapth379846/m1/3/

Harris, Benjamin. 1717. *The Holy Bible in Verse*. Boston: John Allen.

"Midget Bible." 1928. Advertisement in novelty catalog, 375. Racine, WI: Johnson, Smith and Company.

Taylor, John. 1614. *Verbum Sempiternum Together with Salvator Mundi*. London: Jo. Beale for John Hamman.

The Bible in Miniuture, or a Concise History of the Old & New Testaments. 1780. London: E. Newbery.

The Little Picture Bible for Young Children. 1841. New Haven: S. Babcock.

The World's Smallest Bible. 1933. Cincinnati: International Company.

Postcard of the World's Smallest Bible. 1934. Chicago: World's Fair.

Wood, S. 1811. *Bible History*. New York.

Secondary sources

Adomeit, Ruth E. 1980. *Three Centuries of Thumb Bibles: A Checklist*. New York: Garland.

Beal, Timothy. 2011. *The Rise and Fall of the Bible: The Unexpected History of an Accidental Book*. New York: Houghton Mifflin Harcourt.

"Bible Keychains." 2017. *Oriental Trading*. http://www.orientaltrading.com/bible-keychains-a2-19_136.fltr

Bottigheimer, Ruth B. 2004. "Catechistical, Devotional, and Biblical Writing." In *International Companion Encyclopedia of Children's Literature*, Volume 1, Second Edition, edited by Peter Hunt, 299–305. New York: Routledge.

Bromer, Anne C. and Julian I. Edison. 2007. *Miniature Books: 4,000 Years of Tiny Treasures*. New York: Abrams.

Byrne, Stephen. 2016. "Miniature Books Bound to Impress." A Presentation given to the British Printing Society, Annual Convention, March. http://www. mbs.org/presentations/Presentation_by_Stephen_Byrne_to_the_British%20 Printing_Society.pdf

Crystal Bible. 2016. http://www.crystal-bible.com/

Dalton, Russell W. 2016. *Children's Bibles in America: A Reception History of the Story of Noah's Ark in U.S. Children's Bibles*. London: Bloomsbury.

de Hamel, Christopher. 2001. *The Book: A History of the Bible*. London: Phaidon.

Eclectibles. 2017. *A Lady of Cincinnati The Child's Bible*. http://www.eclectibles. com/product-p/27011007.htm

Edison, Julian I. 1968. "American Thumb Bibles." *Miniature Book News* 12: 2–6.

Fea, John. 2016. *The Bible Cause: A History of the American Bible Society*. New York: Oxford. https://doi.org/10.1093/acprof:oso/9780190253066.001.0001

Jerusalem Nano Bible. 2016. https://www.jerusalemnanobible.com/

Lacey, Barbara E. 2007. *From Sacred to Secular: Visual Images in Early American Publications*. Newark: University of Delaware Press.

Metzger, Bruce M. 2004. "Curious Bibles." In *The Oxford Companion to the Bible*, edited by Michael D. Coogan and Bruce M. Metzger. *Oxford Biblical Studies Online*. http://www.oxfordbiblicalstudies.com/article/opr/t120/e0163

Morgan, David. 2005. *The Sacred Gaze: Religious Visual Culture in Theory and Practice*. Berkley: University of California Press.

Nichols, Chares L. 1926. "The Holy Bible in Verse." *American Antiquarian Society* April: 71–82.

Parmenter, Dorina Miller. 2006. "The Iconic Book: The Image of the Bible in Early Christian Rituals." *Postscripts* 2: 160–189.

———. 2012. "How the Bible Feels: The Christian Bible as Effective and Affective Object." *Postscripts* 8: 27–37.

Phillips, Elizabeth M. 2014. *The Early Miniature Books Collection* (GB 7B). Special Collections and University Archives, Rutgers University Libraries. http:// www2.scc.rutgers.edu/ead/baab/EarlyMiniBooksf.html

Smith, Charlotte M. 1984. "The Joys of Miniature Books." *Books at Iowa* 41: 33–42. http://digital.lib.uiowa.edu/bai/smith2.htm

Stewart, Susan. 1993. *On Longing: Narratives of the Miniature, the Gigantic, the Souvenir, the Collection*. Durham, NC: Duke University Press.

Watts, James W. 2006. "The Three Dimensions of Scriptures." *Postscripts* 2: 135–159.

Welch, d'Alté A. 1972. *A Bibliography of American Children's Books Printed Prior to 1821*. Worcester, MA: American Antiquarian Society.

Welsh, Doris V. 1987. *The History of Miniature Books*. Albany, New York: Fort Orange Press.

5

Diminutive Divination and the Implications of Scale:
A Miniature Qur'anic *Falnama* of the Safavid Period

Heather Coffey

Heather Coffey is an Assistant Professor of Art History at OCAD University. In addition to her penchant for small things, her research examines the art and architecture of the Mediterranean basin as an arena of Christian and Islamic cross- and intercultural fertilization from *circa* 1200–1600.

The scale of surviving Qur'ans within the Islamic manuscript tradition remains an infrequent focus of scholarly investigation, despite being a fundamental component of the history of the Qur'anic codex and its material manifestation. The consequence of size upon the parameters and practicalities of its devotional use, its technical execution, and the signification of overt or underlying ideologies is especially potent when contending with extremes of scale expressed through miniaturized or gigantic proportions.

In a previous publication, I countered the longstanding bias against the inclusion of miniaturized Qur'ans and other religious texts prevalent in the study of Islamic book arts, where a preference for monumentality had led to their omission from sustained scholarly treatment (2009a, 78–115; Coffey 2009b). When briefly mentioned in exhibition catalogues, miniature Islamic books have invariably been classified as *sancak* (banner) Qur'ans, an Ottoman Turkish tradition wherein miniature manuscripts were placed in metal boxes or receptacles of fabric attached to military standards and deployed on the battlefield. While this martial interpretation holds true for some artifacts, this classification has become both restrictive and reflexive, stymying deeper theorizations of the intersection of scale, signification, and function of miniaturized manuscripts. Recognizing the amuletic function of miniscule text, I argued that Qur'anic codices of diminutive dimensions participated in an intentionally crafted "textual intimacy" between owner and object.

One Qur'anic manuscript treated briefly in my article (2009a)—Adomeit Miniature Islamic Manuscript C12 (hereafter "Adomeit C12")—is deserving of longer consideration. This is a Safavid Qur'an preserved in the Adomeit

Collection in the Lilly Library at Indiana University that measures 6.3 by 5.7 centimeters per folio and bears an inscribed date of May 26, 1551. Adomeit C12 distinguishes itself from other surviving miniature Qur'ans in its inclusion of a terminal *falnama* ("Book of Divination," alt. "Book of Omens," attributed to the sixth Shi'i Imam Ja'far al-Sadiq, d. 765). A *falnama* is a form of bibliomancy—the art of divination by means of a codex—which most commonly occurred in one of two prominent formats in Safavid Persia.[1] The first format, preserved in Adomeit C12, is a ruled grid inserted at the end of a Qur'anic manuscript wherein the letters of the Arabic alphabet are arranged schematically and paired with short auguries. A *falnama* may alternatively refer to a large-scale illustrated codex, fully independent of the Qur'an, wherein a plethora of painted illustrations are paired with longer presages that similarly convey the beneficial or detrimental nature of proposed courses of action. After first attending to the appearance of miniaturization in the Qur'anic record, this investigation will demonstrate how C12's *falnama* immerses this small specimen along the dialogical spectrum of bibliomantic practices characteristic of the Safavid period. Arguing that miniaturization is inherently relational, Adomeit C12 will demonstrate that its replication of divinatory materials found in codices of larger dimensions not only attests to the ubiquity of divination in the Safavid period, but also to the ongoing naturalization of miniaturization within the Qur'anic record.

How old is miniaturization?
Extremes of scale in the earliest centuries

Miniaturization as a term encompasses a process in progress, an act already completed, or an ongoing state of being—that is, one can say an object *is being* or *has been miniaturized* or is a *miniature version* of something else. One can also speak of an object rendered *in miniature,* which refers to either the spontaneous diminution of scale upon its production and/or its participation in an established genre that delights in, and is characterized by, minuteness. I would further argue that miniaturization is inherently relational, prompting an automatic and reflexive mental visualization of the larger object, or cat-

---

1. The Safavid dynasty ruled Persia from 1501–1722 as a theocracy, establishing Twelver Shi'ism (*Ithna 'Ashariyya* in Arabic) as the state religion. They traced their lineage to Sheikh Safi al-Din (1252–1334), who founded the Safaviyya Sufi order at Ardabil in north-western Iran, from whom they derived the name "Safavi." They also traced their descent from 'Ali ibn Abu Talib, the son-in-law of the Prophet Muhammad, "and claimed semi-divine status as reincarnations of the [previous] Shi'i imams" (Blair and Bloom 1994, 166). The Safavids ruled first from the city of Tabriz, and then moved their capital city to Qazvin in 1555, and again to Isfahan in 1591 (see, for example, Savory *et al.* 1995, 769–774).

egory of objects, to which it refers. Even if no immediate material referent exists, the very fact of an object's startlingly minute rendering instigates a swift cognitive and comparative recollection of objects of normative or conventional scale.

When one miniaturizes a book, the resulting symbolic vectors are two-fold. Small-scale books stimulate the cognitive specter of books of larger dimensions, but also instigate comparison to the reader's own corporeal dimensions. This is enacted through the intimate interaction minuteness requires. Opening, perusing or reading the text immediately reinforces its diminution through juxtaposition to the size of the palm that holds it, the fingers that turn its pages, and the eyes that strain to read its contents. In her celebrated meditation on narrative and signification, Susan Stewart declares:

> The body is our mode of perceiving scale, and, as the body of the other, becomes an antithetical mode of stating conventions of symmetry and balance on the one hand, and the grotesque and the disproportionate, on the other. We can see the body as taking the place of origin for exaggeration, and, more significantly, as taking the place of origin for our understanding of metonymy (2001, xii).

If the conventional distance between the eye and the page or folio is approximately fourteen inches (Spector 2009, 77), this is decreased substantially through miniaturization out of the simple inability to read the text without bringing the book closer to the eyes that struggle to decode its fine details. Adjusting their physical posture to better see its pages, the reader absorbed in a diminutive text "becomes the lectern that receives the book: chest, arms, lap, or thighs. This proximity is the territory of embrace, of possession, not to be entered without permission" (Spector 2009, 77). While twenty-first century readers might take such somatic conceptualizations of reading for granted, early Islamic sources suggest that prolonged and proprietary interactions with miniaturized Qur'anic codices may—at least initially—have been considered treacherous to proper ritual adherence and developing standards of behavior, thereby leading to institutional, if not, theological, preference for largescale manuscripts (Saleh 2017).

Indeed, extremes of scale are readily identifiable among early Kufic Qur'ans from the first centuries of Islam. The early Abbasid period witnessed the emergence of a group of monumental Qur'ans of striking dimensions, such as the manuscript called BNF Arabe 324c, which measures 53 by 68 centimeters and the fragments of another preserved in FLB Ms. orient. A 462 (Déroche 2003, 261; 1983, entry 45, 75–77). Also emblematic of this category of Qur'ans is the manuscript of the 'Uthman or Tashkent Qur'an (Déroche 1992, 27–33; 2013, 56–77; George 2010, 87–88; Small 2011, 19–20). Often considered "the largest extant Qur'an written on parchment" (Ekhtiar *et al.*

Figure 5.1: Folio from the Tashkent Qur'an, attributed to Syria, Yemen, or North Africa, late eighth or early ninth century, 55 by 70 cm, ink on parchment, MMA 2004.87, verso, Metropolitan Museum of Art, New York. Credit: Purchase, Lila Acheson Wallace Gift, 2004. https://www.metmuseum.org/art/collection/search/454661.

2011, 25), this gradiose manuscript represents an enormous investment into the transmission and transcription of the sacred text. Of Syrian, Yemeni or North African manufacture, the manuscript has been dated to the late eighth or early ninth century. A considerable portion of its remaining folios is now preserved in the *madrasa* library in the Tellya-Sheikh Mosque in Tashkent, Uzbekistan, giving it its name (Ekhtiar *et al.* 2011, 25–26). A number of its original folios, however, were unbound and dispersed upon its repository in the imperial library in St. Petersburg in 1868 or 1869 after Russian colonial expansion into Central Asia (Ekhtiar *et al.* 2011, 26; Shebunin 1891, 69–70; Jeffrey and Mendelsohn 1942, 175; Déroche 2013, 59). One such folio, now preserved in the Metropolitan Museum of Art, measures a whopping 55 by 70 centimeters and is written in brown ink in twelve lines of early Kufic script (see Figure 5.1). The text can be identified as a portion of *Surat al-Anbiya,* the twenty-first *surah* or chapter of the Qur'an ("The Prophets," 21.103–111; Ekhtiar *et al.* 2011, 25). The even placement of the calligraphy, which may well have required the labor of numerous scribes, creates a harmoniously balanced contrast between horizontal and vertical calligraphic letterforms in an early version of Kufic that is almost entirely uncluttered by diacritical marks and devoid of any vowel signs to ensure the proper recitation of the text. This was no simple transcription: close examination of individual words reveals the subtle pooling of ink at the bottom edge of letterforms, suggesting the folios may have been fixed on a slanted board because of their large size (Déroche 2013, 65). Estimates suggest the Qur'an was originally composed of more than one thousand folios, each of which required the entire hide of a single animal to produce one two-sided sheet of thick parchment. François Déroche calculates a staggering 362 square meters (alt. 3,896 square feet) of trimmed parchment were required to complete the commission, possibly divided into multiple volumes (Déroche 2013, 65).[2] The practical limitations on its portability suggest a stationary object, possibly divided into multiple volumes, and commissioned for public congregational Qur'anic recitation in a grandiose urban mosque. Déroche has posited that it served as an "imperial presentation copy" from the second half of the eighth century, specifically under the aegis of the third Abbasid caliph Al-Mahdi (r. 775–786) (Déroche 2013, 76). Surely the reading and recitation of the sacred text was the secondary function of such a monumental manuscript, as its intentionally elaborate size anticipates public display and is not strictly necessary for this purpose (Déroche 2003, 261). By literally and experientially "magnifying God's words" (Déroche 2013, 77) the manuscript cultivates a somatic sensation of wonderment and envelopment upon approach.

In diametrical opposition to such largesse, several miniature parchment folios also survive from the ninth to early tenth centuries, marking the entrance of miniaturization into the material history of the Qur'anic codex. One such parchment folio, also preserved in the Metropolitan Museum of Art, measures a mere 3.8 by 7.3 centimeters and was produced in the Central Islamic Lands in the ninth century (Ekhtiar et al. 2011, 27) (see Figure 5.2). The parchment folio features fourteen lines of Kufic[3] script on each side that together recount a segment of *Surat al-Furqan*, the twenty-fifth *surah* of the Qur'an ("The Criterion" 25.22–40) (Ekhtiar et al. 2011, 27). While the verse is not characteristically associated with magico-religious purposes, all Qur'anic verses are inherently protective or prophylactic as the Word of God. Any Qur'anic manuscript (*mushaf*) is an earthly manifestation derived from the so-called *al-Kitab* or *Umm al-Kitab* ("[the] mother of the book" in

---

2. To appreciate the degree to which the dimensions of the Tashkent Qur'an deviate from convention, see the chart envisioning comparable amounts of parchment required for four early copies of the Qur'an in Déroche (2013, 65).

3. Despite its horizontal orientation and small format, the Metropolitan Museum folio has been linked to an early form of Kufic calligraphy evocative of Estelle Whelan's "Group 2" (the majority of which are vertically-oriented manuscripts and of larger size (Ekhtiar et al. 2011, 27; Blair 2006, 2011-2016; Whelan 1990: 119–121).

Figure 5.2: Folio from an undated Qur'an. Attributed to the Central Islamic Lands, ninth century, 3.8 x 7.3 cm, ink, opaque watercolor, and gold on parchment, MMA 62.152.2, recto, Metropolitan Museum of Art, New York. Credit: Rogers Fund, 1962. https://www.metmuseum.org/art/collection/search/451677

Arabic), an ultimate celestial scripture referenced on three occasions in the Qur'an in *Surat an-Nisa*, the third *surah* of the Qur'an ("The Women" 3:7) in *Surat al-'Imran*, the thirteenth *surah* of the Qur'an ("The Family of Imran" 13:39); and most prominently in *Surat az-Zukhruf*, the forty-third *surah* of the Qur'an ("The Ornaments of Gold;" also called "Luxury" 43:4); and in approximately forty *hadiths* (Geoffroy and Daftary 2000). The relationship between the written text and its heavenly prototype invests it with perceived sacrosanct power, ensuring that even proximity to a Qur'an is sufficient to bestow blessing, or *baraka* (Nasr 1972, 51). Despite its lone preservation as a single folio, the modest dimensions of the parchment, and the small-scale Kufic calligraphy preserved upon it, the specimen attests to the presence of diminution in the ongoing formation of the early Qur'anic codex. It is unlikely that this folio originally functioned as a small-scale talisman of rolled parchment containing verses extracted from the holy book, despite the ubiquity of talismans and amulets across the Islamic world (Kriss and Kriss-Heinrich 1962; Fodor, 1990; Canaan 2004; Al-Saleh 2010; 2014; Ruska, Carra de Vaux, and Bosworth 2000; Gruber 2016, 33–52; Leoni 2016, 53–68). This is because the text contained on its surface is randomly selected from verses from the middle of the *surah*, while the compositional density of the transcription—which fits over two hundred words onto the recto alone—signals a desire for the compression of Qur'anic text. The compression is motivated less, one suspects, by a desire for the economic use of costly materials but rather to sustain ease of use by an individual owner. That is to say, when miniaturized, this specimen witnessed not simply a decrease in the scale of its dimensions, but naturally also in the length of the total number of folios required for its completion. The folio may have originally been bound as a single-volume manuscript of the entire Qur'anic text or else derives from a subdivision of the Qur'an into miniaturized sequential volumes. Other folios thought to derive from this same manuscript are preserved in the New York Public Library, which feature the end of *Surat an-Nisa*, the fourth *surah* ("Women" 4.172-76), and the opening lines of *Surat al-Ma'ida*, the fifth *surah* ("The Table" or "The Table Spread" 5.1–7; Schmitz 1992, 281 and figure 296).

Figure 5.3: Folio from a miniature Qur'an, location of production unknown, ninth century, 3.8 cm by 6.8 cm, ink and opaque watercolor on parchment, DIA 25.72.A, recto. Credit: Detroit Institute of Arts, USA Founders Society Purchase/Bridgeman Images.

Another early miniature Qur'anic folio can be found in the Detroit Institute of Arts (see Figure 5.3). The horizontal parchment of this manuscript is very similar in size to the previous example, measuring 3.8 cm by 6.8 cm. Its precise place of production in the Islamic world is unknown. The Qur'anic text is also arranged in fourteen lines of carefully transcribed Kufic script written in brown ink with red diacritical marks. Despite water damage along the upper edge and the bottom right corner of the parchment, the text can be identified as a portion of *Surat al-Anam* ("The Cattle" 6:125–129). Given that the text is interrupted mid-verse, it clearly belonged to a series of folios. Furthermore, the Kufic calligraphy is here confined to one side of the parchment only. Unless part of a Kufic Qur'an that was deliberately left unbound and stored in a pouch or Qur'an box, the pacing of the text—if consistent—indicates that over four hundred folios would have been needed to form a complete transcription of the Qur'an. While not an impossible number of folios to bind into a single codex, it is equally possible that the specimen originally belonged to a series of thin and equally portable codices corresponding to one of the many subdivisions of the holy text into recitational units active in this early period.

Provocative new research by Walid Saleh argues that "the early religious tradition was inimical to portable Qur'ans," and that larger copies of the Qur'an were favored by early Islamic theology in its first centuries (Saleh 2017). The *Kitab al-masahif* of Ibn Abi Dawud (circa 929), for example, notes that the Prophet's second successor, 'Umar ibn al-Khattab (r. 634–644) "abhorred Qur'ans in small script and was delighted when he saw large copies" (Déroche 2003, 261; Saleh 2017).[4] Saleh argues that this preference for large and substantial Qur'ans coexisted with a predilection for an abstract and unadorned aesthetic. The "ideal" Qur'anic manuscript in this early period avoided verse endings and counting apparatuses, diacritical marks and vowel signs, with little to no illumination and ornamentation, so as not to impinge on the fidelity of God's recitation carefully transcribed. The bare and uncluttered progression of Kufic letters across the parchment "was enough to evoke the perfect utterance of God's mind" (Saleh 2017, 7). The portability and convenient accessibility of a Qur'an written in small dimensions, capable of being carried on one's person, was considered "subversive," and innately theologically "transgressive," for it imitated memorization of the sacred text and physically compensated for any lapses of mental recollection (Saleh 2017, 3). The advent of small-scale Qur'ans, a development reflected in surviving miniaturized Qur'anic folios such as those now preserved in the Metropolitan Museum of Art, the New York Public Library, and the Detroit Institute of Arts, was nonetheless inevitable as the Islamic manuscript tradition unfolded across subsequent centuries, perhaps driven onwards by a desire for these very same benefits in conjunction with a desire for portability, proximity, personal ownership, and ease of consultation.

Such folios are strikingly earlier in date than the majority of miniature Qur'anic codices on display in international Islamic art collections, which commonly date from the fifteenth to the nineteenth centuries. They document that miniaturization is not an anomalous occurrence within the Islamic manuscript tradition, but an intrinsic participant in its development, and a phenomenon already present throughout its formative centuries. Certainly,

---

4. I would like to extend my warmest gratitude to Walid Saleh for generously sharing his unpublished conference paper during the writing of this article, and for his assistance in translating the content of the folio in the Detroit Institute of Arts, USA Founders Society Purchase/Bridgeman Images, DIA 25.72a.

diminutive single-volume Qur'ans had become an established component of Islamic books arts by the Safavid period and thereafter, wherein the material record suggests that individual ownership of a small-scale Qur'an across the Islamic world was more prevalent, at least among those who could afford to commission a manuscript (Coffey 2009a, note 2, 109, and Appendix 3.2, 104-106; Coffey 2009b). Furthermore, the naturalization of a miniature Qur'ans within religious practice in later centuries is a precondition for the widespread use of the Qur'an for divination, which requires a frank dependence on the Qur'an as a physical object and embraces its codex form.

Adomeit C12: Diminutive divination in the Safavid Period

Adomeit C12 is an octagonal Qur'anic manuscript composed of 280 folios made of highly polished rag paper (see Figure 5.4). The Qur'anic text is transcribed in minute *naskh* script in black ink. Precious materials have been used throughout the manuscript's production, such as the abundant gold and lapis

Figure 5.4: Opening of *Surat al-Fatiha*, miniature Qur'an, Safavid Iran, 26 May 1551, 6.3 by 5.7 cm, opaque watercolor, ink, and gold on paper, Adomeit Miniature Islamic mss. C12, folio 1v. Credit: Courtesy Lilly Library, Indiana University, Bloomington, Indiana.

illumination surrounding *Surat al-Fatiha* ("The Opening"), the first *surah* of the Qur'an, ensuring only one other specimen in the Adomeit collection can rival its luxury. The folios are bound in a stamped leather binding flecked with gold paint, now greatly worn. Each folio measures no larger than 6.3 by 5.7 centimeters in totality and bears a written surface of 3.8 by 3.8 centimeters, containing an average of twelve lines of text. The colophon gracing the bottom of folio 277v confirms its Safavid provenance and mid-sixteenth-century context of divinatory and occult practices so diffuse throughout the majority of Shah Tahmasp's reign (r. 1524–1576). This social acceptance of such practices is epitomized by the inclusion of a terminal *falnama* among the back matter of the manuscript, assuring that its owner used the pocket Qur'an for individually tailored consultation.

Figure 5.5: Qur'an case, possibly Safavid Iran, 8.1 cm in diameter and 3.5 cm (case), 27 by 3 cm (chain), silver, Adomeit Miniature Islamic mss. C12, obverse. Credit: Courtesy Lilly Library, Indiana University, Bloomington, Indiana.

The diminutive manuscript is accompanied by a large round metal case that measures 8.1 centimeters in diameter by 3.5 centimeters. The case sports a looped chain 27 centimeters in length, or 13.5 centimeters when the loop is stretched taught. This pairing reflects how the two items were gifted to the library as part of the collection of Ruth E. Adomeit, not necessarily their shared historical origin (Rauscher 2009, 52–77; Coffey 2009a, 84–85) (see Figure 5.5). Although Adomeit conceived of the two as a unit in the organization of her collection, it is unlikely that the case was originally created in tandem with this Safavid miniature Qur'an in sixteenth-century Persia. The lid of the case features an unknown architectural structure in *repoussé* while the bottom of the case is incised with a six-sided seal of Solomon. However, the diameter of the case is almost two centimeters larger than the codex itself, whose largest dimension is 6.3 cm. This indicates that the manuscript would have been jostled inside the case if it were not kept in a stationary position. The inherent portability bestowed by its miniaturization is compromised by the substantial wear and tear risked to the manuscript were the metal case to serve a mobile function. The discordant geometric shapes between the two items further heighten the potential for damage: the metal case is circular, while the manuscript is octagonal. The length and thickness of the intricately linked chain also raises questions: the looped chain is too short to be securely or comfortably affixed to a person's body or object, especially given the fact that the chain cannot be undone to facilitate fastening.

The extravagant materials and execution of Adomeit C12 rivals, if not surpasses, most other surviving miniature Qur'ans from the Safavid period, and a great many from the preceding Timurid period. Contemporaneous to C12 is one of several single-volume miniature Qur'ans preserved in the Ghassan I. Shaker collection, which dates to approximately 1550 (Safwat 2000, 72–73). This Shirazi manuscript contains 268 folios written on cream-colored and highly polished rag paper. The text block, delineated by blue and gold rulings, measures 4.6 cm by 4.6 cm and averages seventeen lines of script transcribed with a deftly-cut nib in black ink in *ghubar* script—meaning "dust-like" due to the miniscule size of the letters, which sprinkle across the folio as minute markings similar to dust particles (Safwat and Zakariya 1996, 184; Blair 2006, 259–260). Given that non-miniaturized Safavid Qur'ans of Shirazi provenance typically range in size from 32 to 90 centimeters, this is a significant reduction (Tanindi 2016, 109). *Surah* headings and verse markers are written in gold ink using tiny *riqa* script. Folio 1r even bears the remains of the Qajar seal impression of Muzaffar al-Din Shah (r. 1896–1907) dating to 1890–1891, before he ascended to the throne, attesting to the esteemed lineage of the manuscript's ownership (Safwat 2000, 72). Folios 1v and 2b compress the opening lines of *Surat al-Fatiha* into a micro-octagonal written surface. The text is nestled amidst a rich blue field of color articulated by shimmering gold cloud scrolls and delicately curving tendrils dotted with orange, white, yellow, and violet blossoms. This lush painted armature stimulates the continuous centrifugal movement of the eye towards the inner transcription of divine text. It nonetheless lacks the crispness of the circular illuminated medallion.

Figure 5.6: *Surat al-Fatiha* and the opening of *Surat al-Baqara*, miniature Qur'an, Safavid Iran, March 1670, 8.3 cm by 8 cm (single folio), opaque watercolor, ink, and gold on blue-dyed paper, 41/1999, folios 2v-3r. Credit: Courtesy The David Collection, Copenhagen. Photographer: Pernille Klemp.

Even more striking is a Safavid Qur'an now preserved in the David Collection in Copenhagen. Dating to 1670, this octagonal manuscript was commissioned by one Abd al-Samad al-Musawi and completed by the calligrapher Abdallah ibn Muhammad Hussain ibn Ali al-Mazandarani (see Figure 5.6). Its constituent folios are tinted a velvety blueish-purple throughout the entire manuscript. Folios 1v and 2r contain a spectacular *fihrist* (a table of contents) that lists all titles of the *surah*s of the Qur'an arranged in a diamond-shaped checkerboard, identified as such in the top register where *hadha Fihrist Kalam Allah* ("This is the Table of Contents of the Word of God") is inscribed in red ink. Folios 2v and 3r begins the transcription of Qur'anic verses in *naskh* script executed in sumptuous chrysography, further offset by gold cloud bands. So named by rubricated cartouches, *Surat-al Fatiha* ("The Opening" 1:1–7) appears on the right while the initial lines of *Surat al-Baqara*, the second *surah* ("The Cow" 2:1–286), consume the left folio. The consistent use of gold writing on a blue substrate across the entirety of the manuscript, albeit condensed onto a miniaturized octagonal writing surface, is strongly reminiscent of the famous Blue Qur'an. Now unbound and scattered across international collections,[5] the date and place of production of this magnificent multivolume Qur'an has been the source of extensive debate. The manuscript has cumulatively been attributed to the eighth, ninth, or tenth centuries and to Mashad, Baghdad, Qayrawan, and more generally, to North Africa, Spain, Sicily, and elsewhere (Bloom 2015, 196–204). Its horizontal folios measure approximately thirty by forty centimeters and contain fifteen lines of Kufic script lacking diacritical marks and vowel signs, but featuring verse markers executed in silver-inked rosettes, now oxidized. The distinguishing feature of this horizontal manuscript—its chromatic and material juxtaposition of iridescent chrysographic lettering on richly blue-colored sheepskin has been illuminated by new technological investigations. Its blue color derives from "an indigotin-bearing plant material," that is, either indigo or woad pigment, evenly-distributed either by dyeing the sheepskin or by painting the color, mixed with a binder, atop the surface of the parchment with a brush or cloth (Porter 2018, 577–581). Microscopic analyses further reveal that the Blue Qur'an was written in gold leaf applied to letterforms already transcribed onto the sheepskin by an adhesive (Porter 2018, 581–584). Unlike the Blue Qur'an, the calligrapher responsible for the specimen from the David collection likely mixed finely-powdered gold with an adhesive such as gum or glair (egg white) to create an ink replete with suspended gold particles, also known as "shell gold." Of the two techniques, it is the latter method of crysography that required a larger quantity of the precious metal (Porter 2018, 581), regardless of the miniature stature of the calligraphy involved. Nevertheless, despite the indisputable opulence and somewhat archaizing aesthetic of the mini Copenhagen manuscript, it does not contain a divinatory mechanism such as the *falnama* preserved in Adomeit C12.

---

5. For a detailed list of owning institutions and the pertinent shelf marks of surviving folios, see "Appendix A: List of Pages by Date of Appearance" and "Appendix B: List of Pages Known by Verses (Based on George [2009] With Additions)" (Bloom 2015, 216–218).

Fine distinctions: *Fal-i Qur'an* versus *Falnama*

Divination itself encompasses a compilation of practices including the fore-telling of the nature of future events, the search for portentous omens, and the discovery of what is hidden or obscure by supernatural or magical means (Fahd 1966, 758). Many such activities existed across Islamic history as semi-licit magico-religious practices and were relatively overlooked by theologians (Gruber 2006, 210; Lory 2016, 13 and 31). Tolerance of these customs is best explained by the conflation of divination with the transmission of divine truth and the seeking of guidance (*istikhara*) from God, who alone knows the future (Gruber 2006, 210). Adomeit C12's *falnama* exists on a continuum of broader prognosticative and auspicious activities commonly utilized within the wider Islamic world chronologically and geographically. This includes the wearing or carrying of talismans and amulets, the consultation of astronomi-cal and astrological charts, ornithomancy, geomancy, rhapsodomancy, clero-mancy, kledonomancy, scapulimancy, oneiromancy, and so on (Gruber 2006, 209–210; 2016, 33–52; Lory 2016, 13–32; Mavroudi 2009, 221–229). Yet Adomeit C12's small-scale *falnama* specifically belongs to a subcategory of the divinatory arts, namely bibliomancy, or divination or prognostication by means of a codex. The codex in question was not always confined to the Qur'an, although it was arguably the most important, but also extended to volumes of poetic works by Persian Sufi writers such as the *Diwan* ("Collec-tion of Poems") of Hafiz (d. 1390), the *Mathnawi-i manawi* ("The Spiritual Couplets") of Rumi (d. 1273) and *Haft awrang* ("The Seven Thrones") of Jami (d. 1492) (Farhad 2015, 139), and to prophetic traditions collected by al-Bukhari and others (Lory 2016, 21).

The Persian term *falnama* ("Book of Divination" or "Book of Omens") is inherently elastic and encapsulates multiple mechanisms for bibliomancy within the Persian-Turco world. One use of the term, corresponding to that which is found in Adomeit C12, refers to a codicological addendum or extension inserted after the conclusion of the Qur'anic text and specifi-cally used for Qur'anic prognostication. It is arranged in a geometric table or grid-like format that follows the conclusion of the final *surah* of the Qur'an and a terminal prayer (*du'a-yi khatim*) that closes the Qur'anic text (Coffey 2009a, 86; Gruber 2011, 39). In this situation the term *falnama* may be used interchangeably with the term *fal-i Qur'an* ("Divination by the Qur'an"). Technically, *fal-i Qur'an* specifically refers to the *process* of divination by the Qur'an, while the term *falnama* refers to the series of folios placed at the end of a Qur'anic manuscript described above that serve as the *material vehicle* for *fal-i Qur'an*. Nor are these the only terms employed: various alternate titles frequently introduce *falnama*s found in the closing folios of Qur'anic manuscripts, such as *Fal-i Mushaf* ("Divination by the Codex")*, Fal-i Kalam*

Allah ("Divination by God's Words"), *Fal-i kalam-i masjid* ("Divination of the Sacred Text"), *Tafaʾul kalam-i Allah* ("Divining the Word of God") or simply *Min Kalam* ("Of the Word") (Bağci and Farhad 2009, 20).

To confuse matters further, the term *falnama* is regularly used to indicate a second category of bibliomancy altogether. These are freestanding codices or treatises of augury fully independent of the Qur'an, which, upon maturation of the genre, were characteristically illustrated and adhered to a completely different codex format, one lacking a divinatory grid in favor of seriated paintings interlarded with versified and prosified auguries (Farhad and Bağci 2009b; Tokatlian 2007). However, exceptions to these two categories appear fairly regularly within the Islamic manuscript tradition. These two *falnama* formats are best viewed as the two well-established ends of a spectrum or range of bibliomantic variants. To give but one example, the Nasser D. Khalili Collection of Islamic Art is home to a Shirazi Qur'an completed in July-August 1552 and attributed to Shah Tahmasp (Farhad and Bağci 2009a, 88–89). Its *falnama* consists of four folios (201v–203r) that eschew a brightly illuminated and ruled geometric grid of Arabic letters and short Persian phrasings to reveal the seeker's prognostication (Farhad and Bağci 2009a, 89). Instead, extensive versified instructions combine Persian poetry and prose written in *nastaʿliq*[6] calligraphy interspersed with Qur'anic verses transcribed in *muhaqqaq*.[7] Each

---

6. Together with *taliq*, *nastaʿliq* was one of two "hanging" styles of calligraphic scripts especially well-suited to writing in Persian. In fact, the term *nastaʿliq* is a contraction of *naskh-i taʿliq*, indicating a hanging or suspended *naskh*. Developed in fourteenth-century Persia, *nastaʿliq* became the preeminent script for the transcription of literary texts and lyric poetry. Although its invention is repeatedly credited in historical texts to the Timurid calligrapher Mir ʿAli Tabrizi, it is more accurate to credit him with its refinement and canonization. The fluidity of the script results from such features as its distinct diagonal slope downwards from right to left, a sweeping elongation of letters such as *sin* and *kaf*, a lack of adherence to the baseline, and the foreshortening of letters due to "the stacking and overlapping of letters and words" (Blair 2006, 270–286, especially 274–275).

7. *Muhaqqaq* refers to one of the so-called "six pens" (*al-aqlam al-sitta* in Arabic) systematized by the Abbasid vizier and calligrapher Abu ʿAli Muhammad ibn ʿAli, known as Ibn Muqla (d. 940), and further refined by his successors Abu'l-Hasan ʿAli ibn Hilal, also known as Ibn al-Sitri or Ibn al-Bawwab (d. 1022) and Yaqut al-Mustaʾsimi (d. 1298). These six proportional cursive scripts include *naskh, thuluth,* the above-mentioned *muhaqqaq, rayhani, tawqiʾ* and *riqa*. Letters transcribed in *muhaqqaq* script are relatively more vertical than those executed in *naskh* or *thuluth*, and are complemented by evenly-spaced ligatures and a distinctive horizontality. *Muhaqqaq* is further characterized by a narrow zone below the base line wherein the bowls on descending strokes are "shallow, elliptical, and sometimes extend to encircle the following letter" (Blair 2006, 141–195, especially 157, 160, 171–173, 195).

letter of the alphabet is then the subject of a distich, followed by a lengthy prose gloss and Qur'anic verse. The glosses commence with *ay khudavand-i fal, bedan va agah bash* ("O seeker of the *fal*, know and be aware"), beseeching the seeker directly (Farhad and Bağci 2009a, 89).

Although a small number of *falnama*s predate the Safavid era, the production of bibliomantic materials gained increasing urgency under the patronage of Shah Tahmasp. Bibliomancy was so commonly practiced that "[a]dding divination texts to the end of Qur'ans was, if not systematic, then at the very least symptomatic of Qur'anic production in Iran during the tenth/sixteenth century, especially during the reign of Shah Tahmasp" (Gruber 2011, 29). It is difficult to concretize the various forces behind this ascent of divinatory practices and the occult arts. Kathryn Babayan argues for a pervasive "mood of antinomianism," characterized by mounting objection to, and flouting of, the legal, ethical and moral duties upheld by religious communities (Babayan 2009, 245). More pointedly, Shah Tahmasp's own rule corresponded with the impending turn of the millennium according to the Islamic calendar (r. 930-983 AH/1524–1576), inciting a courtly atmosphere of cosmological and apocalyptic fervor (Babayan 2009, 247ff; Gruber 2011, 43).

The *Falnama* of Adomeit C12

The terminal *falnama* of Adomeit C12 comprises the final folios of the manuscript (Coffey 2009a, 86). Upon the completion of the 114th and final *surah* of the Qur'an, *Surat an-Nas* ("Mankind," 114:1–6) on folio 277v, the reader is then required to complete some informal prayers. These are followed by a *du'a-yi khatim* on 278r, a formal prayer to mark or "seal" the conclusion of the Qur'anic text. It is on 278v-279r that the reader finds explicit instructions on the use of the Qur'an for divination positioned above the start of the grid (see Figure 5.7). The divinatory grid extends from the bottom of 279r and across 279v and 280r. The ease with which the Adomeit C12 opens to its back folios—the looseness of the binding—suggests these folios were referred to frequently. The instructions begin in Persian as follows:

> In the name of God, the Most Merciful, the Most Compassionate: Imam Jafar Sadiq says that whoever desires to know the future of his affairs through divination by the Qur'an should first perform ablutions. He should hold the full text of the Qur'an and three times utter the salutation [now in Arabic]: 'Prayers and peace of God be upon Muhammad, and his family.' (Coffey 2009a, 106; Gruber 2011, 39–40)[8]

---

8. For a complete English translation and Persian transcription of the *falnama* of Adomeit C12, folios 278v–280r, please see Appendix 3.2 in Coffey 2009a, 106–108, prepared by Sheida Riahi.

Figure 5.7: Folio from a *falnama* (end of instructions for divination and inception of divination grid), miniature Qur'an, Safavid Iran, 26 May 1551, 6.3 by 5.7 cm, opaque watercolor, ink, and gold on paper, Adomeit Miniature Islamic mss. C12, folio 279r. Credit: Courtesy Lilly Library, Indiana University, Bloomington, Indiana.

After this, the querent is prompted to read *Surat al-Fatiha* once ("The Opening" 1:1–7) and *Surat al-Ikhlas* ("Unity" or "Purity," also called "Monotheism" 112:1–4) three times. The querent should then recite an additional prayer contemplating God with purity and sincerity while opening the Qur'an to a random folio. The prayer (a *du'a,* now in Arabic) reads in translation:

> O Lord, I have trusted in You and have made divination by Your Book, so show me what is concealed in Your hidden mysteries and (what is) in Your hidden world. With Him are the keys to the things that are beyond the reach of a created being's perception: no one knows them but He and He knows all that is on land and sea; and not a leaf falls without His knowing; and neither is there a grain in the darkness of the earth, nor anything living or dead that is not recorded in (His) clear decree. (Coffey 2009a, 106)

Figure 5.8: Continuation of *falnama* (divination grid), miniature Qur'an, Safavid Iran, 26 May 1551, 6.3 by 5.7 cm, opaque watercolor, ink, and gold on paper, Adomeit Miniature Islamic mss. C12, folio 279v. Credit: Courtesy Lilly Library, Indiana University, Bloomington, Indiana.

Returning to Persian, the instructions direct the seeker to hold the Qur'an open on the resulting folio and to "count seven pages further" and then look to the right margin of the folio. The reader then identifies the seventh line down the page and pinpoints the first letter of the seventh line. Herein lies the seeker's prognostication. Referencing the letter against the divination grid at the back of the codex then reveals the consequence or outcome associated with this divinely selected letter. Alternatively, the reader may verify whether the all-important seventh line commences with a verse of mercy (*ayat-i rahmat*). "If so, then he can proceed [with his requested action] but if not," the reader is warned, "he should renounce [carrying it out]" (Coffey 2009a, 106).

The divination grid listing the meanings of all possible letters follows these instructions. The composition of the divination grid is characteristically schematic in its form and resulting aesthetic. Its octagonal edges mimic the contour of the folio. Nested frames in blue and black ink and gold paint delineate the written surface. The letters of the Arabic alphabet—used for both the Arabic and Persian language—are arranged vertically along the right margin and are offset from the page through the use of alternating blue and gold paint. The outcomes associated with each letter are written in pithy Persian phrases that extend horizontally along the breadth of the grid, which is bisected by vertical lines. The outcomes associated with each letter suit an array of concerns through their generic content. The letter *jim* asserts "Hard work in one's affairs will produce unexpected fortune," *ra* soothes "this is a sign of grandeur: you will have a long life and good fortune as well," and the letter *ha* confirms "your enemies will be destroyed and you will be free from bad-mouthing and gossip" (Coffey 2009a, 107).

Painted in isolation against the right margin, each letter invites meditation upon its minute form. The blue and gold paint juxtaposed against the stark black ink of the predictions immediately draws the eye to the letters' shape against the cream-colored paper, prompting mental recognition of their names and the sounds they represent. Despite their isolated or offset presentation in the divination grid, in practice every letterform is inherently unstable when used to form written words—the calligraphed letters of the Arabic alphabet subtly change shape in response to their placement in a word, whether the letter appears in an initial, medial, final or isolated position in response to the script used, its size, and the hand of the calligrapher. The tiny Arabic letters are independent signifiers wherein their grammatical and semantic potential is momentarily suppressed. They nonetheless blossom with an innate revelatory capacity, despite their small size, as Arabic is the language of the Qur'an and of "God's 'reciting,' his verbatim speech; and of *Allah*'s eternal, uncreated word" (Graham and Kermani, 2006, 115) (see Figure 5.8).

Use of Adomeit C12's miniaturized *falnama* demands a tactile and interactive experience of the codex, because the meaning of the resulting letter can only be understood through the physical manipulation of the tiny book. For the purposes of divination or augury, opening the manuscript at random affects a surprise, which, although experienced by the seeker, grants agency not to the individual but to Allah, the ultimate determiner of fate. The individual merely acts as a vessel, channeling the will of God while opening the divine recitation faithfully and exactingly transcribed. Nor is the opening of the Qur'an at random necessarily at odds with decorum governing its proper recitation, which need not be sequential for personal devotion. Several Qur'anic *surah*s are considered apotropaic or curative and are recited independently in times of need. These include *Surat al-Falaq* ("The Daybreak" 113:1–5) and *Surat-an-Nas* ("Mankind" 114:1–6), the final two chapters of the Qur'an, collectively termed *al-mu'awwadhitayn*, the so-called "*surah*s of refuge," typically recited as sequential short prayers (Canaan 2004, 131; Savage-Smith 1997, 59; Sobieroj 2006, 365–366, 371; Coffey 2009a, 89; Gruber 2011, 32). Reliance upon a *falnama* does, however, suggest a degree of literacy, at least if used alone (as the size of the manuscript suggests) to ensure proper adherence to the preparatory prayers, for identification of the resulting letter, and most importantly, to understand the fortuitous or inauspicious outcome revealed in the grid itself. One cannot discount the possibility that a consistent user of the divination chart could memorize its required preparations and listed outcomes through repetition. However, whether comprehension was relatively effortless and swift or halting and laborious, the handling of the diminutive codex was unavoidable, thereby continuously reinforcing the paradoxical status of the Qur'an as at once an immaterial and eternal celestial scripture and also an exalted material object, subject to a relatively codified format of production. The nexus for these two simultaneous modes was, of course, the individual, who carried the Qur'anic text within the heart and mind through frequent recitation and memorization. Nevertheless, the miniaturization of an earth-bound transcription of the "Word of God" as a small-scale codex only served to intensify the esteem granted to the book and reinforced its materiality, through the frequent handling that personal ownership allows.

An unexpected concordance: The maintenance of convention

Strikingly, the comparison of the *falnama* preserved in Adomeit C12 to a *falnama* contained in a Safavid Qur'an of normative dimensions uncovers strong concordances in composition and content. [9] This second *falnama* is

---

9. Defining "normative dimensions" in the Safavid period or any period is not an easy task, as the size of Qur'anic manuscripts naturally varied given their patron (namely, institutional or personal ownership) calligraphic script, place and location of production, and the possibility of trimming by later collectors. Nevertheless, a survey of the twenty-two Qur'ans assembled by David James in part II ("Qur'ans of sixteenth Century Iran under the Early Safavids") of his illustrious volume, *After Timur: Qur'ans of the 15th and 16th Centuries*, offers some insight. The Qur'ans range in date from 1490–1585, while their hypothesized or identified places of production range from Herat, Tabriz, Bukhara, Maraghah, and Shiraz to Karbala. All manuscripts are single-volume Qur'ans with the exception of entry 42, a single folio, and entry 49, the 21st *juz* (Ar. "part") of a thirty-part Qur'an. The two smallest Qur'ans measure 16.8 by 9.5 centimeters and 17.5 by 12 centimeters respectively. Eight Qur'ans measure between 20.5 by 13 and 27 by 18.5 centimeters. The majority of the Qur'ans, nine in total, measure between 32 by 20 centimeters and 38.8 by 24 centimeters, four of which are exceedingly close in size: 32 by 20 centimeters, 32 by 20.6 centimeters, 32.5 by 21 centimeters, and 32.5 by 23 centimeters. Only three Qur'ans exceed forty centimeters in height, measuring 41.4 by 29.4 centimeters, 42.5 by 25.2

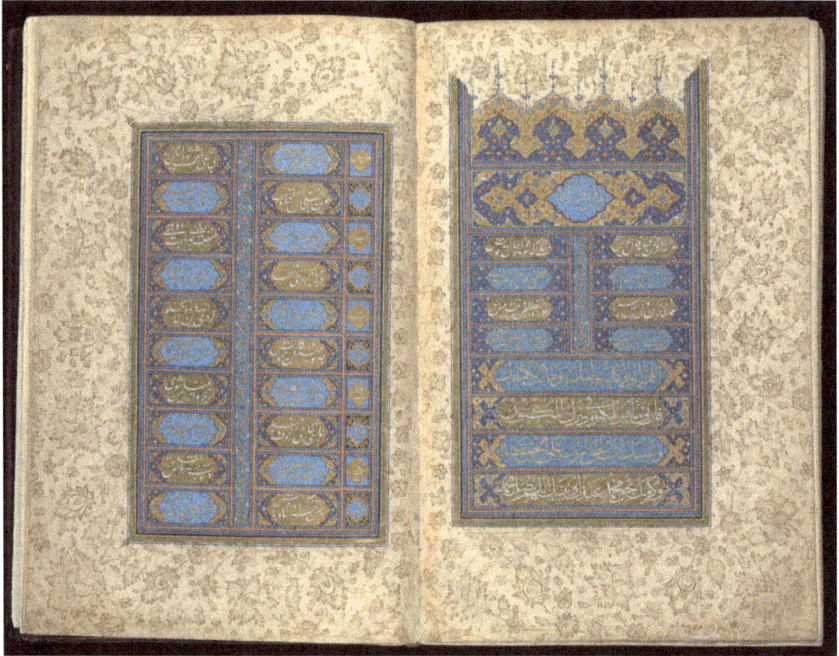

Figure 5.9: Initial folios of a *falnama* (instructions for divination and start of divination grid), Qur'an, probably Shiraz, Safavid Iran, 1560s-1570s, 36 by 24 cm, opaque watercolor, ink and gold on paper, MS 1548, folios 251v-252r. The Chester Beatty Library, Dublin. Credit: © The Trustees of the Chester Beatty Library, Dublin.

contained in MS. 1548 of the Chester Beatty Library in Dublin. The Qur'an manuscript is unsigned and undated but was likely made in Shiraz (Uluç 2006; for precedents, see Wright 2012) in the 1560s or 1570s (Arberry 1955–1966, no. 164; Farhad and Bağci 2009a, 86-87). Measuring 36 by 24 centimeters, its folios are substantially larger—almost six times larger—than the dimensions of Adomeit C12. Following a lavishly ornamented double-page selection of prayers on 250v–251r, the divinatory text commences with customary prefatory material atop 251v followed by the grid of the terminal *falnama* itself, which covers the remainder of folios 251v–253r (see Figure 5.9). The title *Min Kalam* ("Of the Word") is written on folio 251v in gold against a bright blue cartouche in the center of the *'unvan*, the upper-

centimeters, and 42.7 by 30 centimeters respectively. Somewhat unsurprisingly, it has been suggested that the largest Qur'an was produced for Shah Tahmasp himself. Among the single-volume Qur'ans, the number of calligraphed lines per folio therefore ranges from nine to seventeen, which is interrelated with the total number of surviving folios dedicated to the transcription of the Qur'an, which range from a relatively slim 203 to a whopping 718 folios (James 1992, entries 30–51, 11632).

most illuminated band surmounted by dark blue pointed lappets framed in gold containing finely drawn curling vines studded with tiny red and gold blossoms. The instructions for divination are written in Persian in *nasta'liq* script in four lines of paired, parallel cartouches. The script is written in oblong cartouches in white ink on a gold ground alternating with gold ink on a blue background. Here again, the seeker is advised to perform ablutions. He or she must then recite *Surat al-Fatiha* ("The Opening" 1:1-7) once and *Surat-al-Ikhlas*, the one hundred and twelfth *surah* of the Qur'an ("Unity" or "Purity" 112:1-4) three times. The seeker is then advised to recite the Arabic prayer transcribed below before randomly opening the book. Written in four lines of larger *muhaqqaq* script, the prayer reads:

> O God, I trust in you and take an augury from your book, so show me what is hidden in your innermost secret and knowledge of the unseen. You are the truth, and you sent down the truth, in your excellence and generosity through Muhammad, your servant and prophet. O God, pray [for] Muhammad. (Farhad and Bağci 2009a, 86)

Figure 5.10: Continuation of *falnama* (divination grid), Qur'an, probably Shiraz, Safavid Iran, 1560s–1570s, 36 by 24 centimeters, opaque watercolor, ink and gold on paper, MS 1548, folios 252v–253r. Credit: © The Trustees of the Chester Beatty Library, Dublin.

The Dublin divination grid begins on the opposite folio and is composed of two columns of distiches adjacent to the letters in the right margin, transcribed in white or gold ink against a gold or blue quatrefoil in a rubricated rectangle. For example, the outcome accompanying the letter *ha* reads "You will find good fortune through your relatives, and you will be free from the sorrow and fears of the heart." *Kha* is more ominous, and reads "[y]ou will not be free from fear and danger. Be with *Allah* [that is, be a believer], and avoid this task." *Jim* affirms the seeker to "[h]ave perseverance and effort in your task, because good fortune will be suddenly approaching you" (see Figure 10).[10]

The *falnama* of Adomeit C12 is obviously a miniaturized version of the Dublin Qur'an and similarly luxurious sixteenth-century Qur'ans, for which the inclusion of a *falnama* was so customary. The divinatory texts in both manuscripts are clearly in concert with one another in composition, instruction, and content. Despite obvious differences in their degree of illumination and decoration—compressed and relatively streamlined in Adomeit C12 versus the exhaustive intricacy of the Dublin Qur'an *falnama*—both offer the querent easily interpretable grids. Both *falnama*s exhort the seeker in Persian to recite the same *surah*s in preparation (*Surat al-Fatima* and *Surat al-Ihklas*), and to recite an Arabic prayer that beseeches Allah directly, emphasizing trust in the Qur'an and his revealed Word. Furthermore, the outcomes of letters regularly overlap in theme. Some portents are even occasionally identical all or in part. For instance, the letter *ba* in both manuscripts promises "comfort" in life or an immediate task, and that the seeker "will receive reward(s) from a Mighty Lord" (Coffey 2009a, 106). The concordance between the two manuscripts, and outright replication of content, is indicative of a degree of standardization governing these divinatory texts in mid-sixteenth century Persia which transcends scale altogether.

In addition to arguing for the ubiquity of *falnama*s within Safavid Qur'anic codices, including their extension to miniaturized Safavid versions, Adomeit C12's *falnama* suggests that small-scale Qur'anic codices, and by extension, miniaturized books writ large, do not automatically function as a platform for intense personalization or deviance from codicological convention, despite the fact that miniaturization facilitates a degree of intimacy, and even sustains possible secrecy, between the owner/user and the contents of the book against prying eyes. Diminutive volumes of religious texts need not strain or shirk orthodox practice by virtue of their discrete dimensions, nor solicit the semi-secretive or covert consultation characteristic of heterodox practices simply because their dimensions are well-suited to doing so. Rather,

---

10. I thank Sheida Riahi for her aid in translating these auguries.

miniaturized texts can replicate widespread devotional practice with remarkable fidelity. Yet is the divinatory text in Adomeit C12 merely a mechanical copy of those appended to Qur'ans of larger dimensions, rendering its reduced scale benign? How might the miniaturization of C12's *falnama* alter the divinatory experience? On a practical level, its minute scale offers the seeker ready accessibility and frequent, rapid consultation due to its portability. Recent research has also demonstrated that the cognitive load required to concentrate on and interpret very small texts, images, and micro-environments distorts the subject's experience of time, slowing its perception. Individuals consumed in the study of small things consistently overestimated the amount of time passed, as much as "six minutes perceived for every one minute actually elapsed" (Tilghman 2010–2011, 131 n135). In this altered state, a single minute is amplified, mimicking longer temporal increments. This psycho-sensory distortion only heightens the divinatory consultation of the little codex, by subsuming the seeker into a meditative state suited to lingering over the resulting letter and its associated prognostication. The owner of Adomeit C12 was then able to seek God's guidance twice over, amplifying devotional benefit: through the regular pious recitation of the Qur'anic text, and through the supplementary channel of consultation the *falnama* offered. The intersection of miniaturization and divination in C12 offered double protection from misfortune, wherein blessing (*baraka*) and guidance (*istikhara*) converge. The minutely rendered divination grid augmented the innate amuletic capacity of the Qur'anic text, which, when written in drastically reduced scale, intensified and expressed its protective force (Coffey 2009a, 101). Furthermore, the effort to untangle the outcome listed on the miniaturized *falnama* grid, semi-obscured by virtue of its own compression, transformed the seeker into the recipient of a personalized divine revelation from a revelatory text.

Along the bibliomantic spectrum:
(Micro) text versus (macro) image

The bibliomantic methods fashionable during Shah Tahmasp's reign also include large-scale illustrated *falnama*s that appear, at least initially, to be functionally and materially divorced from Adomeit C12's minute Qur'anic content. Specific to illustrated *falnama*s as a category is their oversized dimensions, which has led one scholar to accuse one surviving manuscript of "giantism" (Welch 1985, 94). The "giant" in question was completed in the mid-1550s to 1560s at the royal *kitabkhana* (book atelier) in the Safavid capital of Qazvin in Persia (Farhad 2015, 137). Now unbound and preserved among various international collections, the so-called Dispersed Falnama survives in thirty known folios (Farhad and Bağci 2009a, 43–52). Three other extant large-scale illustrated *falnama*s attest to this category of oversized divinatory practice in both Safavid and Ottoman territory. Dating from the later sixteenth and early seventeenth centuries, these include the Topkapi Persian Falnama (TSM H. 1702), the Dresden Falnama (SLUB E445), and the Falnama of Sultan Ahmed I commissioned as a gift for the Ottoman Sultan by the vizier Kalender Pasha (TSM H. 1703; Farhad 2015, 137; Farhad and Bağci 2009a, 41–75). Three to four smaller seventeenth-century illustrated *falnama*s also survive, which are treated as a distinct subgroup by scholars (Farhad and Bağci 2009b, 28 n7–9, 310). These date to the seventeenth century or later and are attributed to workshops in the Deccan or Ottoman and/or provincial Mughal ateliers.

The Dispersed Falnama is largely considered to be the last major commission of Shah Tahmasp's rule; as such it is relatively commensurate with Adomeit C12 in its date of execution. Each folio from this illustrated *falnama* is vertically oriented and measures an impressive 59 by 44.5 centimeters or almost two feet tall. Originally, its folios would have been even larger, but were separated from their surrounding margins at an uncertain date (Farhad and Bağci 2009b, 43) To put this in perspective, Adomeit C12's *falnama* measures only 6.3 by 5.7 centimeters. That is to say, each folio of the illustrated *falnama* is almost ten times larger in height and seventy-three times larger in surface area than each folio of Adomeit C12. The manuscript is so large that its folios are made of horizontal "fragments of paper that have been carefully glued together to create the desired size" (Farhad and Bağci 2009b, 312 n2). It has been suggested that such giant dimensions compensated for the Shah's failing eyesight, whether due to advanced age or the onset of a disease (Soudavar 1999; 51–52; Canby 2003b, 122). Alternatively, the manuscript may simply reflect the sheer abundance of materials, labor, and artistic skill available to a royal commission. Certainly, the scale of the volume—its weight and heft—may have required more than one person to open and close it, adding a performative dimension to its use, and ensuring it could accommodate collective viewing when desired without sacrificing legibility (Farhad and Bağci 2009a, 50, 314). Despite this seeming innate proclivity for display, each prognostication is individual in address, referring to the seeker in the singular, which likely reflects its royal patron, the Shah himself.

Large-scale illustrated *falnama*s are not appended to a Qur'anic text, and instead constitute fully independent manuscripts. Their alternate format must nonetheless be recognized as reactive adaptations to the prevalence of divination by means of a codex. This interrelationship is captured by the preparatory instructions to the Falnama of Sultan Ahmed I, which demands the recitation of *Surat al-Fatiha* three times followed by one recitation of *Surat al-Ikhlas* before posing a question (*niyat*) and turning to a random folio

(Farhad 2015, 139). The constituent folios nonetheless display an expanse of written text on one side and vibrant multicolored illustrations on the other. Each painting—which regularly consumes the entirety of the available paper surface—and its adjacent augury text, were created separately in the *kitabkhana* (book atelier) and pasted together to form the *recto* and *verso* of one folio (Farhad and Bağci 2009a, 312 n2). Whereas each parchment folio of the Tashkent Qur'an was extracted from the hide of a single animal, most of the folios are also constructed from multiple horizontal sections of paper that are carefully glued one atop the other to create a sheet of large dimensions. When the finished codex was bound, each painted image was "linked conceptually to the facing text" across the gutter of the manuscript as a double-folio divinatory mechanism that combined image and text (Farhad and Bağci 2009b, 43). These illustrated *falnama*s thus offered the seeker a distinct "experiential model" wherein they "were conceived to be opened randomly in order to view a single image and a self-contained unit of text" (Farhad and Bağci 2009b, 31), not to identify a single letter of the alphabet as an omen or sign. When seeking an augury, the manuscripts' other pictorial content was completely irrelevant to the querent, who focused on two adjacent folios only. Because Persian is a dextrosinistral language, that is, written and read from right to left, the paintings precede the text therefore enjoy a certain emphasis. Indeed, rather than "an unfolding narrative intermittently interrupted by illustrations" such as the lengthy pictorial cycles interlarded within the surviving manuscripts of Firdawsi's (d. 1019–1025) epic poem of 50,000–60,000 verses, the *Shahnama* ("Book of Kings") in Persian, "the images now appear at regular intervals and determine the meaning of the text, which lends them unprecedented importance" (Farhad 2015, 139). This pictorial primacy is intensified by the fact that the imagery commands the entire surface of the folio, and that the folios are usually devoid of text within the pictorial field.

As a Qur'anic manuscript, Adomeit C12 is devoid of anthropomorphic or zoomorphic imagery, despite its sumptuous illumination. In contrast, the surviving painted folios from Shah Tahmasp's illustrated *falnama* contain spirited depictions of diverse subject matter: Abrahamic prophets, scenes from the life of the Prophet Muhammad, 'Ali and his descendants, scenes inspired by the Qur'an, classical Arabic and Persian literature and poetry, and popular religious practices, signs of the zodiac, and astrological and eschatological content (Farhad and Bağci 2009a, 50; Farhad 2016, 137). The constituent paintings may be multi-figured arrangements or devoted to a single personage. They may be narrative compositions containing multiple spatial dimensions and vantage points or be relatively planar in structure. This arresting painting from Shah Tahmasp's *falnama*, entitled *The Footprints of Imam Riza*, is preserved in Geneva (Robinson 1974, no. 35; Jones and Mitchell 1976, no. 612a [attributed to the artist Aqa Mirak]; Welch 1985, no. 63; Robinson 1992, no. 90; Canby 2003b, 4.34 [attributed to Aqa Mirak]; Tokatlian 2007, no. 4 [attributed to Aqa Mirak]; Farhad and Bağci 2009a, no. 30, 136-137). Framed by lateral arches, lavishly illuminated footprints dominate the upper half of the composition and confront the viewer/seeker directly (see Figure 5.11). Ten worshippers honor the holy vestige in the lower half of the painting through various gestures and poses. Several raise their arms in prayer or gesture towards the footprints and two prostrate themselves before them. Their semi-circular devotion is augmented by the accoutrements of a mosque or place of veneration, such as the gilded lamp suspended above,

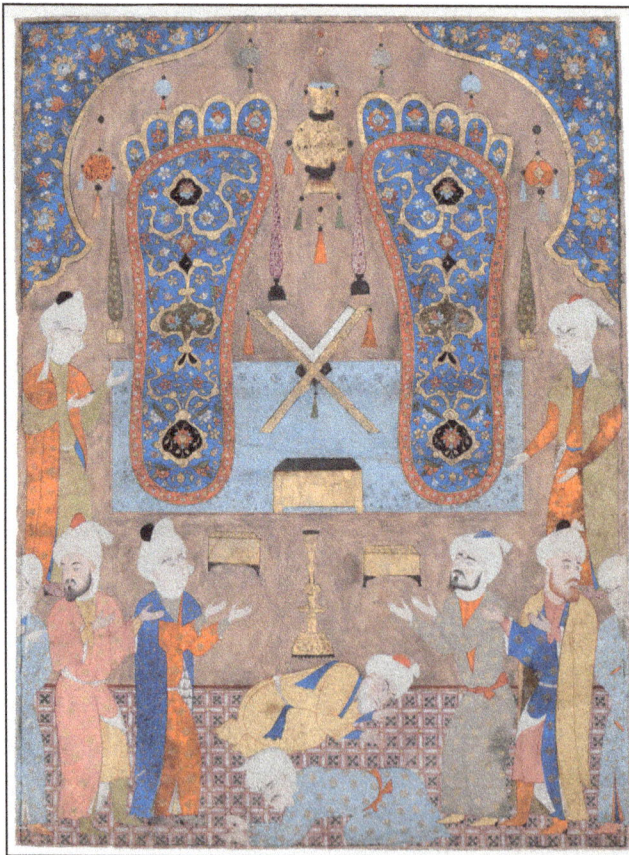

Figure 5.11: *The Footprints of Imam Riza*, attributed to Aqa Mirak. Folio from the Dispersed Falnama, attributed to the *kitabkhana* of Shah Tahmasp, Qazvin, Safavid Iran, mid-1550s–early 1560s, 59 cm by 44.5 cm, 1971-107/35. Musée d'art et d'histoire, Geneva. Credit: © Musées d'art et d'histoire. Ville de Genève.

the centrally-placed Qur'an on a folding stand, three chests (probably holding further volumes of the Qur'an) and a gilded candlestick. The illuminated imprints belong to Abu'l-Hasan, later titled Ali-al-Rida or Riza, the eighth Imam of the Twelver Shi'a (d. 818), and are painted renditions of surviving physical impressions of a relic attributed to the Imam. Multiple sanctuaries to the Imam were built throughout Persia, the most significant pilgrimage site being his *ghadamgah* (lit. "stepping stone") in Nishapur, near his tomb in Mashad (Farhad and Bağci 2009a, 136). The Imam was said to have halted there and left the imprint of his footprints on a stone. The veneration of the Imam's footprints, and their vestigial impression on a lithic surface, is an extension, within a Shi'i context, of a wider Islamic tradition surrounding the Prophet Muhammad himself, whose footprint was said to spontaneously impart whenever the Prophet stepped on a stone or rock, most famously upon the rocky outcrop preserved in the center of the Dome of the Rock in Jerusalem built by the Umayyad Caliph Abd al-Malik in 691 (Gruber 2013, 297, 299). This impression is now said to be contained in a reliquary, enveloped by a grille inlaid with silver and surmounted by a small pointed cupola, erected in 1609 by the Ottoman sultan Ahmed I (Gruber 2013, 300). Termed *qadam al-rasul* (Ar. "the foot[print] of the Messenger") and *al-qadam al-sharif* (Ar. "the noble foot[print]"), a number of footprints of the Prophet are said to be preserved in Mecca, upon Mount Abu Zubayda in al-Ta'if, and in Damascus, while other imprints were transported to locations such as Cairo and Istanbul. Still other imprints are said to be preserved in architectural shrines eponymously termed *Qadam Rasul* found in cities throughout the Indian subcontinent (Gruber 2013, 297; Hasan 1993, 35–43).

The lengthy augury originally adjacent to the painting is written in *nasta'liq* calligraphy preserved on the *recto* of a separate folio in New York (MMA 50.23.2). The masterful calligraphy has been attributed to the Qazvini calligrapher Malik al-Daylami (Tokatlian 2007, 37). Although no longer bound together, the pair of Persian distiches at the top of the folio identifies the subject of its companion image. The couplet reads: "Any place that Imam Riza sets foot/there hyacinth and basil always grow/With the fragrance of love is perfumed the nostril of anyone/Who smells the dust of the court of that king of truthful ones" (Farhad and Bağci 2009a, 263). The prognostication then continues, now in prose:

> O augury user, know that the footprint of the Lord of *Jinns* and Men, father of Hasan, son of Musa, Ali Riza, upon him be mercy and peace, has appeared in your augury. The augury indicates happiness, prosperity, contentment, and success in your affairs, and good fortune in both worlds. With every intent that you have, proceed, since your undertaking, with the blessing of the footprint of His Majesty the Imam, is progressing perfectly. Travel is very good,

and buying and selling will bring about increase of wealth. If you go to see someone important, state what you want, because it will turn out well, and if you are asking marriage, go ahead, since it is blessed. In summary, this augury is highly recommended for whatever you have opened it. Having put fear and distress from your mind, set out in complete devotion and be strong of heart, since His Majesty the Eighth Imam, the Guarantor, will keep you in the protection and safety of God, be he exalted, and you will attain your hopes and desires. (Farhad and Bağci 2009a, 263)

Oddly, there is relatively little overt resonance between the image and its subsequent prognostication, aside from the reference to the Imam near the beginning of the augury. The painting is not mentioned or described in the text, though its central subject matter is immediately identified. With the exception of the mention of travel, which is required to complete an act of pilgrimage, the augury seems initially discordant. It is not the seeker's potential courses of action represented in the painting, but rather the source of the beneficence governing those actions—the exalted Imam Riza, whose religious authority is embodied in the depiction of the miraculous footprints, offered here to the seeker for virtual veneration through the codex.

Comparing the divinatory experience engendered by Adomeit C12's miniaturized *falnama* against the divinatory machinery of the large-scale illustrated *falnama* reveals what might be termed an "inversive complementarity." Both manuscripts, small and large, require a formulaic manipulation of a codex and the completion of exceedingly similar preparatory processes. Adomeit C12 allows the seeker to meditate on the fundamental building blocks of the divine message: the Arabic letters themselves, against the creamy uncluttered expanse of the folio followed by pithy presages. Conversely, the large-scale *falnama* emphasizes grandiose pictorial content—here combining both anthropomorphic components with an overt corporeal symbol—with an oblique relationship to a longer augury text that must be slowly digested. Moreover, if the deciphering of micro-text indeed slows the mind, altering the subjective experience of time, the study of intricately detailed *oversize* painted compositions was perhaps similarly meditative. Furthermore, folios such as the *Footprint of Imam Riza* sanctions the practice of divination by its inclusion of religious figures, pilgrimage sites, and the depiction of devotional acts, thereby lauding divination as accepted religious practice by invoking an historical *Imam* and asserting Shi'i ideology, accentuating the legitimacy of Shah Tahmasp's own rule. Adomeit C12 then benefits from this authoritative recognition of bibliomancy. This authoritative recognition is further reinforced by the invocation of a second Shi'i personage in both manuscripts, Ja'far al-Sadiq (d. 765). In Adomeit C12, the sixth Shi'i Imam is explicitly named in the instructions to the querent preceding the divination grid on folio 278v

(Coffey 2009a, 96–104; Gruber 2011, 39). Conversely, the entirety of the text contained in the dispersed folios of the illustrated *falnama* has been credited to Ja'far al-Sadiq's inspired authorship (Farhad and Bağci 2009b, 31, 310 n21). The obvious discordance in date between his death in the eighth century and the textual and pictorial references to his grandson, Imam Riza, in the above folio, reveals the spurious nature of the attribution. Indeed, the addition of ahistorical ascriptions to manuscripts was a robust component of Safavid propaganda. An assortment of Qur'ans donated by one of Shah Tahmasp's successors, Shah Abbas I (r. 1588–1629), to the shrine of Imam Riza in Mashad (not Nishapur), where Imam Riza is in fact buried, feature signatures of Shi'i Imams who died in the seventh or eighth centuries, despite the fact that stylistic analyses of the Qur'ans in question date the codices to the ninth or tenth centuries, ensuring the inauthenticity of the autographs (Canby 2015, 97). The false signatures on these Qur'ans, which feature an unmistakably archaic aesthetic marked by evenly-spaced Kufic calligraphy on horizontal parchment, retroactively construct a visual and textual "chain of religious authority" from 'Ali, to several early Imams, and foreward to the Safavids themselves, underscoring the legitimacy of their theocratic rule for a subject population with a substantially Sunni component (Canby 2015, 101, 103–104). The attribution of both *falnamas* to Ja'far al-Sadiq was also undoubtedly motivated by his association with the esoteric sciences: in addition to having "performed several knowledge-based miracles," it was said that he penned several Sufi *tafasir* ("interpretations" in Arabic) of the Qur'an, and even authored a divination manual (Gruber 2011, 42–43 and 54, n51–55; see also Loebenstein 2003, 199–244; Gleaves 2008, 351–356).[11]

Finally, magnification is integral to both divinatory experiences. Whether standing or sitting, the owner of Adomeit C12 towers over the miniscule codex, and envelops it close to the body to peruse. Proximity to the codex literally magnifies the micrography, allowing consultation of the divine text

---

11. The attribution of divination texts to Ja'far al-Sadiq continues even in nineteenth-century Malay Qur'anic divination manuscripts. One such manuscript, MS 515(1), now preserved in the Perpustakaan Negara Malaysia (National Library of Malaysia) has been comprehensively studied by Majid Daneshgar. The manuscript, which contains tables, a circle or wheel diagram, and commentaries on verses from the Qur'an contained in the circle diagram, was written in 1891 CE by Abdulmajid ibn Hj Ibrahim from Rembau (Rimbu) in the village of Johol, then situated in Mecca and is dedicated to both the Prophet Muhammad and to the sixth Shi'ite Imam (see Daneshgar 2016, 123–144). The use of a circle or wheel diagram in nineteenth- and early twentieth-century Malay divinatory practices as a prognosticative genre has been further studied by Farouk Yahya (see Yahya 2017, 1–26).

and divinatory grid. In the case of the illustrated *falnama* produced in Shah Tahmasp's atelier, the situation is reversed: one might say that the divinatory codex is magnified in its entirety, towering over the seeker, who endeavors to hold the volume comfortably due to its mammoth proportions. This immerses the querent in the material presence of the manuscript, who, unless aided by another, is enveloped between the two covers of the open volume.

In conclusion, miniaturization proves once again to encompass monumental complexities (Coffey 2009a, 103). The appearance of miniaturization in the Islamic manuscript tradition in the ninth century prefigures the multiplication of miniaturized single-volume codices to come in later centuries. Comparing the miniaturized *falnama* of Adomeit C12 to a *falnama* contained in a Qur'an of conventional dimensions, and subsequently to a large-scale illustrated *falnama*, reveals the vicissitudes of scale and format governing Safavid bibliomantic practice, contextualizing the miniaturization of Adomeit C12 in the range of codicological responses to sixteenth-century prognostication. In so doing, it demystifies miniaturization, establishing it not as an aberration within Safavid book arts, but rather an equal participant in their mystical and divinatory dimensions.

Acknowledgements

I would like to extend warmhearted thanks to several individuals for invigorating discussions during the writing of this chapter, in physical and/or digital form, including Walid Saleh, Christiane Gruber, Nina Ergin, Kjeld von Folsach, Alexa Sand, Beate Fricke, Cornelius Berthold, Sheida Riahi, and Janet Rauscher. My deepest gratitude to both Kristina Myrvold and Dorina Parmenter for their generous commentary and criticism of this text in all stages of its development.

References

Al-Saleh, Yasmine. 2010. "Amulets and Talismans from the Islamic World." In *Heilbrunn Timeline of Art History*. New York: The Metropolitan Museum of Art. http://www.metmuseum.org/toah/hd/tali/hd_tali.htm

———. 2014. *"Licit Magic": The Touch and Sight of Islamic Talismanic Scrolls*. PhD dissertation, Cambridge: Harvard University.

Al-Saleh, Yasmine and Jonathan M. Bloom. 1994. *The Art and Architecture of Islam 1250-1800*. New Haven: Yale University Press. https://doi.org/10.1086/ahr/101.2.532

Arberry, Arthur J. 1955–1966. *The Chester Beatty Library: A Handlist of the Arabic Manuscripts*. Dublin: E. Walker.

Babayan, Kathryn. 2009. "The Cosmological Order of Things in Early Modern Safavid Iran." In *Falnama: A Book of Omens,* edited by Massumeh Farhad and Serpil Bağci, 245–255. Washington, DC: Freer Gallery of Art, the Arthur M. Sackler Gallery, Smithsonian Institution. https://doi.org/10.5479/sil.879423.39088017856642

Bağci, Serpil and Massumeh Farhad. 2009. "The Art of Bibliomancy." In *Falnama: A Book of Omens,* ed. Massumeh Farhad and Serpil Bağci, 19–25. Washington, DC: Freer Gallery of Art, the Arthur M. Sackler Gallery, Smithsonian Institution. https://doi.org/10.3202/caa.reviews.2010.110

Blair, Sheila S. 2006. *Islamic Calligraphy.* Edinburgh: Edinburgh University Press.

Bloom, Jonathan M. 2015. "The Blue Koran Revisited." *Journal of Islamic Manuscripts* 6: 196–218.

Canby, Sheila R. 2003a. "Safavid Illumination." In *Hunt for Paradise: Court Arts of Safavid Iran: 1501–1576,* edited by Jon Thompson and Sheila R. Canby, 134–153. Milan: Skira.

———. 2003b. "Safavid Painting." In *Hunt for Paradise: Court Arts of Safavid Iran: 1501–1576,* edited by Jon Thompson and Sheila R. Canby, 1–133. Milan: Skira.

———. 2015. "Early Qur'ans 'Signed' by the Shi'i Imams." In *People of the Prophet's House: Artistic and Ritual Expressions of Shi'i Islam*, edited by Fahmida Suleman, 97–105. London: Azimuth, Institute of Ismaili Studies, Department of the Middle East at the British Museum. https://doi.org/10.1353/mrw.2018.0006

Canaan, Tewfik. 2004. "The Decipherment of Arabic Talismans." In *Magic and Divination in Early Islam*, edited by Emilie Savage-Smith, 124–177. Aldershot: Ashgate.

Coffey, Heather. 2009a. "Between Amulet and Devotion: Islamic Miniature Books in the Lilly Library." In *The Islamic Manuscript Tradition: Ten Centuries of Book Arts in Indiana University Collections*, edited by Christiane Gruber, 78–115. Bloomington: Indiana University Press. https://doi.org/10.2307/j.ctt2005ssv.8

———. 2009b. "Miniature Manuscripts and Scrolls." http://www.indiana. edu/~i-uam/online_modules/islamic_book_arts/exhibit/miniature_manuscripts_and_scrolls/index.html

———. 1992. *The Abbasid Tradition: Qur'ans of the 8th to the 10th Centuries. The Nasser D. Khalili Collection of Islamic Art.* Volume 1. London and New York: The Nour Foundation, Azimuth, and Oxford University Press.

Daneshgar, Majid. "The Divinatory Role of the Qur'an in the Malay World." *Indonesia and the Malay World* 44(129): 123–144. https://doi.org/10.1080/13639811.2015.1044740

Déroche, François. 1983. *Catalogues des manuscrits arabes, Deuxième partie, Tome I/1: Les manuscrits du Coran. Aux origines de la calligraphie coranique.* Paris: Bibliothèque nationale de France. https://doi.org/10.1017/s0035869x00155017

Déroche, François. 2003. "Manuscripts of the Qu'ran." In *Encyclopaedia of the Qur'an,* edited by Jane Dammen McAuliffe, Volume 3, 254–274. Leiden, The Netherlands: Brill.

———. 2013. "Twenty Leaves from the Tashkent Qur'an." In *God is Beautiful and Loves Beauty: the Object in Islamic Art and Culture,* edited by Sheila Blair and Jonathan Bloom, 56–77. New Haven: Yale University Press, Qatar Foundation, Virginia Commonwealth University, and Virginia Commonwealth University School of the Arts in Qatar. https://doi.org/10.1086/ahr/101.2.532

Ekhtiar, Maryam D., Priscilla P. Soucek, Sheila Canby, and Navina Najat Haidar, eds. 2011. *Masterpieces from the Department of Islamic Art in the Metropolitan Museum of Art.* New Haven, NJ: Yale University Press. https://doi.org/10.3202/caa.reviews.2013.111

Fahd, Toufic. 1966. *La divination arabe: études religieuses, sociologiques, et folkloriques sur le milieu natif de l'Islam.* Leiden: Brill.

Farhad, Massumeh. 2015. "Between the Past and the Future: the *Fālnāma* (Book of Omens) in the 16th and 17th Centuries." In *People of the Prophet's House: Artistic and Ritual Expression of Shi'i Islam,* edited by Fahmida Suleyman, 137–145. London: Azimuth, Institute of Ismaili Studies, and Department of the Middle East at the British Museum. https://doi.org/10.1353/mrw.2018.0006

Farhad, Massumeh and Serpil Bağci. 2009a. *Falnama: A Book of Omens.* Washington, DC: Freer Gallery of Art, Arthur M. Sackler Gallery at the Smithsonian Institution. https://doi.org/10.5479/sil.879423.39088017856642

———. 2009b. "The Falnama in the Sixteenth and Seventeenth Centuries." In *Falnama: A Book of Omens,* edited by Massumeh Farhad and Serpil Bağci, 27–39. Washington, DC: Freer Gallery of Art, Arthur M. Sackler Gallery at the Smithsonian Insitution. https://doi.org/10.3202/caa.reviews.2010.110

Fodor, Alexander. 1990. *Amulets from the Islamic World.* Budapest: Eötvös Loránd University Chair of Islamic Studies.

Geoffroy, E. and F. Daftary. 2000. "Umm al-Kitāb." In *The Encyclopaedia of Islam,* second edition, edited by P. Bearman, Th. Bianquis, C. E. Bosworth, E. van Donzel, and W. P. Heinrichs. https://doi.org/10.1163/1573-3912_islam_com_1289

George, Alain. 2009. "Calligraphy, Colour and Light in the Blue Qur'an." *The Journal of Qur'anic Studies* 11: 75–125. https://doi.org/10.3366/e146535910900059x

———. 2010. *The Rise of Islamic Calligraphy.* London: Saqi.

Gleave, Robert. 2008. "Ja'far al-Sādeq ii. Teachings." In *Encyclopedia Iranica* 14(4): 351–356.

Graham, William A. and Navid Kermani. 2006. "Recitation and Aesthetic Reception." In *The Cambridge Companion to the Qur'an,* edited by Jane Dammen McAuliffe, 115–141. Cambridge: Cambridge University Press. https://doi.org/10.1017/ccol0521831601.007

Gruber, Christiane. 2006. "Divination." In *Medieval Islamic Civilization: an Encyclopedia,* ed. Josef W. Meri, 209–210. Abingdon: Routledge.

———. 2011. "The 'Restored' Shīʿī Mushaf as Divine Guide? The Practice of Fāl-i Qur'ān in the Safavid Period." *Journal of Qur'anic Studies* 13: 29–55.

———. 2013. "The Prophet Muhammad's Footprint." In *Ferdowsi, the Mongols and the History of Iran: Art, Literature, and Culture from Early Islam to Qajar Persia,* ed. Robert Hillenbrand, Andrew C. S. Peacock and Firuza Abdullaeva, 297–305. London: I.B. Taurus.

———. 2016. "From Prayer to Protection: Amulets and Talismans in the Islamic World." In *Power and Protection: Islamic Art and the Supernatural,* edited by Francesca Leoni, 33–52. Oxford: Ashmolean Museum.

Hasan, Perween. 1993. "The Footprint of the Prophet." *Muqarnas* 10: 35–43.

James, David. 1992. *After Timur: Qur'ans of the 15th and 16th Centuries.* The Nasser D. Khalili Collection of Islamic Art. Volume 3. London and New York: The Nour Foundation, Azimuth, and Oxford University Press.

Jeffrey, A. and I. Mendelsohn. 1942. "The Orthography of the Samarqand Qur'ān Codex." *Journal of the American Oriental Society* 62: 175–195. https://doi.org/10.2307/594134

Jones, Dalu and George Michell, eds. 1976. *The Arts of Islam.* London: Arts Council of Great Britain and the Hayward Gallery.

Kriss, Rudolf and Hubert Kriss-Heinrich. 1962. *Volksglaube im Bereich des Islam.* Volume 2: Amulette, Zauberformeln und Beschwörungen. Wiesbaden: O. Harrassowitz. https://doi.org/10.1017/s0041977x00065277

Leoni, Francesca. 2016. "Sacred Words, Sacred Power: Qur'anic and Pious Phrases as Sources of Healing and Protection." In *Power and Protection: Islamic Art and the Supernatural,* edited by Francesca Leoni, 53–68. Oxford: Ashmolean Museum.

Loebenstein, Judith. 2003. "Miracles in Šīʿī thought: A Case Study of the Miracles Attributed to Imām Gaʿfar al-Sādiq." *Arabica* 50: 199–244. https://doi.org/10.1163/157005803764778417

Lory, Pierre. 2016. "Divination and Religion in Islamic Material Culture." In *Power and Protection: Islamic Art and the Supernatural,* edited by Francesca Leoni, 13–32. Oxford: Ashmolean Museum.

Mavroudi, Maria. 2009. "Islamic Divination in the Context of its "Eastern" and "Western" Counterparts." In *Falnama: A Book of Omens,* edited by Massumeh Farhad and Serpil Bağci, 221–229. Washington, DC: Freer

Gallery of Art, Arthur M. Sackler Gallery at the Smithsonian Institution. https://doi.org/10.5479/sil.879423.39088017856642

Nasr, Seyyid Hossein. 1972. *Ideals and Realities of Islam*. Boston: Beacon.

Porter, Cheryl. 2018. "The Materiality of the Blue Qur'an: A Physical and Technological Study." In *The Aghlabids and their Neighbours: Art and Material Culture in Ninth-Century North Africa*, edited by Glaire D. Anderson, Corisande Fenwick, and Mariam Rosser-Owen, 575–586. Leiden: Brill.

Rauscher, Janet. 2009. "Ruth E. Adomeit: An Ambassador for Miniature Books." In *The Islamic Manuscript Tradition: Ten Centuries of Book Arts in Indiana University Collections*, edited by Christiane Gruber, 52–77. Bloomington: Indiana University Press. https://doi.org/10.2307/j.ctt2005ssv.7

Robinson, Basil, W. 1974. *Miniatures persanes: donation Pozzi, 29 juin au 6 octobre, Cabinet des estampes, Musée d'art et d'histoire, Genève*. Genève: Musée d'art et d'histoire. https://doi.org/10.3989/gladius.1969.172

———. 1992. *L'Orient d'un collectionneur: miniatures persanes, textiles, céramiques, orfévrerie rassemblés par Jean Pozzi: collections du Musée d'art et d'histoire, Genève, du Musée historique des tissus et du Musée des arts décoratifs-Lyon*. Geneva: Musée d'art et d'histoire. https://doi.org/10.1515/9783110972511.166

Ruska, Jan, Baron Carra de Vaux, and C. E. Bosworth. 2000. "Tilsam." In *Encyclopaedia of Islam*, second edition, edited by P. Bearman, Th. Bianquis, C. E. Bosworth, E. van Donzel, and W. P. Heinrichs. https://doi.org/10.1163/1573-3912_islam_sim_7553

Ruska, Jan and Mohamed Zakariya. 1996. *The Art of the Pen: Calligraphy of the 14th to the 20th Centuries*. The Nasser D. Khalili Collection of Islamic Art. Volume 5. London and New York: The Nour Foundation, Azimuth, and Oxford University Press. https://doi.org/10.1093/ww/9780199540884.013.u33028

Safwat, Nabil F. 2000. *Golden Pages: Qur'ans and other Manuscripts from the Collection of Ghassan I. Shaker*. Oxford: Oxford University Press. https://doi.org/10.3366/jqs.2003.5.2.129

Saleh, Walid. 2017. "British Library Or. 13002: A Qur'an for a Common Reader." Qur'an Plus workshop, organized by Christiane Gruber and Karla Mallette, 10 February. University of Michigan: Islamic Studies Program.

Savage-Smith, Emilie, ed. 1997. *Science, Tools, and Magic*. The Nasser D. Khalili Collection of Islamic Art. Volume 12. London and New York: The Nour Foundation, Azimuth, and Oxford University Press. https://doi.org/10.1017/s0025727300065893

———, ed. 2004. *Magic and Divination in Early Islam*. Aldershot: Ashgate.

Savory, Roger M., J. T. P. de Bruijn, Andrew J. Newman, Anthony T. Welch, and R. E. Darley-Doran, 1995. "Ṣafawids." In *The Encyclopaedia of Islam*, second edition, edited by P. Bearman, Th. Bianquis, C. E. Bosworth, E. van Donzel, and W. P. Heinrichs. https://doi.org/10.1163/1573-3912_islam_com_0964

Schmitz, Barbara, with contributions by Latif Khayyat, Svat Soucek, and Massoud Pourfarrokh. 1992. *Islamic Manuscripts in the New York Public Library.* Oxford: Oxford University Press and the New York Public Library. https://doi.org/10.1017/s0026318400028078

Shebunin, A. N. 1891. "Kufischeskij Koran Imperatorskoj Sankt-Petersbugskoj publichnoj biblioteki." *Zapiski Vostochnogo Otdelenija imperatorskogo russkogo arkheologicheskogo obstichestva* 6: 69–133.

Small, Keith E. 2011. *Textual Criticism and Qur'an Manuscripts.* Lanham, MD: Lexington.

Sobieroj, Florian. 2006. "Repertory of Suras and Prayers in a Collection of Ottoman Manuscripts." *Mélanges de l'Université Saint Joseph* 59: 365–386.

Soudavar, Abolala. 1999. "Between the Safavids and the Mughals: Art and Artists in Transition." *Iran* 37: 49–66. https://doi.org/10.2307/4299994

Spector, Buzz. 2009. "The Fetishism of the Book Object." *Art on Paper* 14(1): 76–79.

Stewart, Susan. 2001. *On Longing: Narratives of the Miniature, the Gigantic, the Souvenir, the Collection.* Durham and London: Duke University Press.

Tanindi, Zeren. 2016. "Illumination and Decorative Designs in Qur'anic Manuscripts." In *The Art of the Qur'an: Treasures from the Museum of Turkish and Islamic* Arts, edited by Massumeh Farhad and Simon Rettig, 99–117. Washington, DC: Arthur M. Sackler Gallery, Smithsonian Institution. https://doi.org/10.3202/caa.reviews.2018.130

Tilghman, Benjamin, C. 2010–2011. "Divinity in the Details: Miniaturization and Meditation in a Passion Cycle by Johannes Wierix." *The Journal of the Walters Art Museum* 68–69: 125–135.

Tokatlian, Armen. 2007. *Falnamah: livre royal des sorts.* Montreuil: Gourcuff Gradenigo.

Uluç, Lâle. 2006. *Turkman Governors, Shiraz Artisans and Ottoman Collectors: Sixteenth-Century Shiraz Manuscripts.* Istanbul: Türkiye İş Bankası. https://doi.org/10.1080/00210862.2011.586814

Welch, Stuart Cary, with Sheila R. Canby and Nora Titley. 1985. "The *Fālnāmeh* (Book of Divination) of Shah Tahmasp." In *Treasures of Islam*, edited by Toby Falk, 94–99. Secaucus, N.J.: Wellfleet.

Whelan, Estelle. 1990. "Writing the Word of God: Some Early Qur'an Manuscripts and Their Milieux, Part I." *Arts Orientalis* 20: 113–147.

Wright, Elaine Julia. 2012. *The Look of the Book: Manuscript Production in Shiraz, 1303–1452.* Washington: DC: The Freer Gallery of Art, Smithsonian Institution and Seattle: University of Washington Press.

Yahya, Farouk. 2017. "The Wheel Diagram in the Malay Divinatory Technique of the Fal Qur'an." *Indonesia and the Malay World* 45: 200–225. https://doi.org/10.1080/13639811.2017.1314636

6

Mite Qur'ans for Indian Markets:
David Bryce in the Late Nineteenth and Early Twentieth Century

Kristina Myrvold

Kristina Myrvold is Associate Professor of Religious Studies at Linnaeus University. She is the author and editor of numerous publications on Indian cultures, religions, and migration.

One of the perhaps largest publishers of miniature books in Europe during the late nineteenth and early twentieth century was David Bryce in Glasgow. With access to the latest printing technologies, he built up a business for mass-producing a substantial variety of small printed books for sale to the public. It has even been asserted that he "published more wee books than the total world production [of miniature books] up to that time" (Henderson 1928a, 3). Bryce took an early interest in the sacred writings of the world religions and printed tiny Christian books from the 1880s. This chapter explores how he from 1896 began issuing miniature editions of the Qur'an in Arabic script that were intended for markets in India and by what means he worked with the content, size, and appearance of the books.

Even though Bryce printed various miniature books in vast quantities for a global market, there are very few primary sources and little information available about him, his life, and his work (see Garbett 2011). One category of source material that can provide fragmentary glimpses into his book production, however, is the correspondence between him and Henry Frowde, the publisher at Oxford University Press and the manager of its Bible warehouse. Although the original letters from Bryce are not available to researchers, the archive of Oxford University Press has preserved the letters that Frowde issued to various recipients between March 1874 and 1913. This vast archival material includes 95 letters specifically addressed to Bryce and his wife. The letter books of Frowde have been used in previous research to map the history of Oxford University Press in Britain and India, and to examine the achievements of Frowde (see for example: Chatterjee 2004, 2006; Gilliver 2016;

Jaillant 2016), but not specifically for studies on the publishers' cooperation and production of miniature books over at least three decades. Based on
this source material, the chapter illustrates how Bryce worked together with
Frowde when producing editions of the "mite Koran" intended for India and
established an extensive transnational network of trade. The final section of
the chapter provides a few examples of how the miniature Qur'ans of Bryce
subsequently became linked with Orientalist narratives that tried to provide
cultural contexts of the books' uses by enmeshing them in Islamic amulet
traditions.

Qur'an and printing technologies

The Islamic world has a long history of reproducing small-sized Qur'ans,
especially in the various traditions of using talismans and amulets (*tawidh*)
for protective and curative purposes. Between the tenth and the fifteenth
centuries block-printed Arabic amulets (*tarshes*), usually strips of paper with
Qur'anic passages which were rolled and enclosed in metal cylinders, were
widely produced in the Arab world as charms to be worn by the users (Bulliet
1987, 438; Schafer 2002, 123). Another example is the Ottoman tradition
of so-called *sancak* Qur'ans, small handwritten octagonal "banner" Qur'ans
that were encased in boxes and attached to the shaft or the finial of military
standards when the Ottoman Army went into the field. In the battlefield
these small books could metonymically represent the sultan as a protector of
the Qur'an and in other contexts serve as talismans and amulets to be carried
by individuals on their bodies (Coffey 2010). It has been claimed that the
Topkapi Museum in Istanbul has preserved a collection of no less than 1,500
miniature manuscript Qur'ans, including sancak Qur'ans from the Ottoman
Empire (Blumenthal 1961, 12; Welsh 1987, 69).

Scholars have pointed out that printing technologies were not generally
used for producing Qur'ans in the Islamic world until the nineteenth century since the process of printing was considered disrespectful and violent to
the revealed words. Memorization and oral transmission were given a higher
value, and manuscript cultures with calligraphic art were considered to provide aesthetic acceptability to the sacred texts. The earliest printed Qur'ans
in Islamic countries were lithographed in Iran (Teheran, Schiraz, and Tabriz)
during the first half of the nineteenth century and in Cairo and Istanbul from
the 1860s and the 1870s (Aqeel 2009, 10; Bobzin 2002, 167; Wilson 2009).
In the Ottoman Empire books printed in the Arabic script were not officially
allowed to be circulated prior to 1588 and only Europeans and non-Muslims
were given permission to import non-religious books printed in Arabic from
this century. The printing of the complete Qur'an by Muslim publishers in
the Ottoman Empire was not given legal sanction by the sultan before the

1870s. The early Arabic editions of the Qur'an in print from the sixteenth century were thus European ventures, probably because there was a scholarly interest in Islam but also for the prospect of export to the Islamic world. Immigrants and Christian missionaries were also the first to establish printing presses in the Ottoman Empire during the eighteenth century. This restrictive attitude to print technologies changed in the nineteenth century when the sultan allowed and even gave support to printing presses for the purpose of producing state propaganda (Aqeel 2009, 12; Auji 2016, 26; Bobzin 2002, 153; Wilson 2009, 33, 38, 40).

A contributing factor to a wider acceptance of printed religious books was the technological developments of lithography and photomechanical reproduction of texts in the nineteenth century that enabled a strong resemblance to handwritten manuscripts. Printed Qur'ans in Islamic areas were generally produced by these techniques (Bobzin 2002, 167; Wilson 2009, 43, 66–67). Unlike letterpress printing that used moveable types and provided books with an aesthetically acceptable form according to European typographic conventions, the lithographic technique used limestone on which texts were inscribed directly or through transfer paper by scribes and thereby enabled a continuation of the manuscript culture. While the early Islamic books that were letterpress printed in Europe created an aesthetic appearance and orthography that did not possess authenticity in the calligraphic traditions of the Islamic world, the lithographic editions could bestow legitimacy. The photomechanical process that developed after the invention of photography in the nineteenth century further permitted the exact reproduction of old manuscripts that not only could preserve the original texts but also create clear and legible copies of various sizes. For instance, in the 1870s the state-supported press of Osman Zeki Bey in Istanbul, *Matbaa-i-Osmaniye*, made photographic reproductions of the seventeenth-century manuscript of the Qur'an prepared by the famous calligrapher Hafiz Osman and later, in the 1880s, also issued the scripture in miniature format (25 by 35 millimeters) with a tortoise-shell cover and a small magnifying glass attached (Kuran-Burcoglu 2007, 50; Roper 2013, 549). The sultan used printed copies of the Qur'an from this press as an emblem of his power and a political tool to impress and create bonds of loyalty with notables in other Muslim countries (Wilson 2009, 74, 77). Most of the printed miniature Qur'ans from the nineteenth and twentieth century were similarly produced by photomechanical reproduction and thus could make claims of tradition by being small facsimiles of much larger and historical handwritten manuscripts (Rauscher 2010, 75).

India under British rule showed a different scenario with the widespread popularity and use of print technologies. Some of the earliest printed editions of the Qur'an in India were issued in the 1830s in Calcutta, Serampore, and

Kanpur, and multiple translations were made into the various Indian languages from the early nineteenth century (Bobzin 2002, 167; Khan 2001). In the rapidly expanding business of cheap and mass-produced books, many publishers seem to have survived by adapting their production to the profitable market of religious books. When the vernacular press began to thrive in Northern India during the mid-nineteenth century a large part of the publishers' output was lithographic editions of religious books. In 1848, for example, the *Ussud-ol Akbhar Press* in Agra printed "pocket" Qur'ans (*hamail*) and two years later another reprint edition of 1,225 copies. Colonial reports revealed that the proprietor of the press, Mahomed Qamar-o-din Khan, decided to start with pocket Qur'ans for his "livelihood" because his newspaper had proved less profitable. Other Muslim presses in Agra and Delhi were similarly publishing pocket Qur'ans from the mid-nineteenth century (*Selections from the Records of Government* 1855, 240, 252, 266 268, 303). When reporting about the press in Northern India, a British administrator commented that religious books and especially "editions of the Qoran [Qur'an] appear to command the readiest sale" (*Selections from the Records of Government* 1855, 247). Nawal Kishore, the Hindu publisher who founded presses in the province of Punjab and the North-Western Provinces and Oudh, became famous for printing Muslim literature and issued lithographic versions of the Qur'an in multiple editions and sizes, including miniature versions (Stark 2009, 202, 205). Indian publishers appear to have printed religious books not only for the Muslim population in India but also for a transnational market of the larger Islamic world.

Publishers in Europe similarly realized the export potential of printed Qur'ans and during the nineteenth century extended the production and sale to small-sized editions. The firm Jan Steinbrener in Winterberg (Bohemia region), for instance, held a royal privilege to publish almanacs and a wide range of Catholic literature in different European languages for the Habsburg Empire. The publishing house was established in 1855 and made use of the technological advancements in photo-reduction for the production of small and artistic books. Among the firm's output by the turn of the century was a miniature Qur'an in Arabic with elaborate gilt leather binding and a tiny magnifying glass attached to the book with a cord. Steinbrener established a wide trade and distribution network that reached far beyond the Habsburg region and with warehouses in several European cities to supply "a market ranging from Manila to New York" (Dalbello 2002, 68–69). Another famous publisher of miniature books in Europe was David Bryce in Scotland, who by the end of the nineteenth century began producing small Qur'ans for Indian bazaars.

David Bryce & Son in Glasgow

In 1832 David Bryce (1808–1870) established the firm in Glasgow to operate as a bookseller and lend books from the family home.[1] He learned the
trade of books at the firm of Chalmers & Collins and soon became a leading
bookseller and lender in Glasgow with premises in Buchanan Street. The
"Bryce's Reading Club," established in 1841, provided subscriptions of books
and magazines in the city and "to any part of the Country" (*Glasgow Evening Post* 1970, 25 August). His son, also called David (1845–1924), took an
early interest in the firm and became a partner at the age of 17. When his
father died in April 1870, he continued the business as the sole proprietor
and developed it into a publishing house for literature and miniature books
of all kinds (*The Publishers' Circular* 1891, 279; Garbett 2011, 7–8; *Glasgow
Evening Citizen* 1870, 19 April). The firm was in the 1890s divided into a
publishing department under the name of David Bryce while the previous
library and bookselling business merged with another bookseller in Glasgow,
Thomas Murray & Son, to become Bryce & Murray Limited with David
Bryce as the managing director (*Dundee Advertiser* 1895, 8 April; Spielmann
1961, 274).

   A manuscript written by Bryce, which was discovered among his papers by
Adam L. Gowans and reprinted in the *News-letter of the LXIVMOS,* revealed
that he began reprinting the books of the world "in a new dress" (Bryce
1928a, 3) from 1876 and subsequently focused on miniature versions:

> Instead of developing works of a larger kind, I descended to the miniature,
> mite and midget size, producing a little dictionary, the smallest in the world,
> in a locket accompanied by a magnifying glass. I had many a scoff and jeer
> as to the absurdity of the production, nevertheless it at once appealed to Mr.
> Pearson of the notable weekly, who gave me a first order for 3,000 copies and
> its sales are now over 100,000. Other books followed and latterly a complete
> Bible. (Bryce 1928b, 2)

As Bryce underlined in his text, he transformed the firm from a local to a
global business venture:

> When I joined my father in 1857 in publishing, the consideration with him
> always seemed to be, how many copies would sell in Glasgow, and how many
> copies would sell in Edinburgh, and of course we would have to send a few
> copies to London for any stray inquirers. How different now when we have the
> pleasure and satisfaction of hearing from all parts of the world. (Bryce 1928b, 2)

---

1. In the Directory for Glasgow in 1837 he was recorded as a "bookseller" at 84
   Buchanan Street (*Pigot and Co.'s National Commercial Directory for the Whole of
   Scotland and of the Isle of Man* 1837, 534).

By the turn of the century Bryce had become quite wealthy from his business, but he seemed to have faced some financial and health-related problems prior to the First World War. The firm was taken over by Gowans and Gray, with whom he shared the premises, even if the trade name of David Bryce remained important until and beyond his death in 1924 (*Aberdeen Press and Journal* 1924, 15 April; Bondy 1981, 104; Garbett 2011, 10–11).

Bryce printed many of the books by letterpress printing and also used the new technology of photolithography. The earliest miniature publications by Bryce were letterpress printed and included the *Thumb English Dictionary*, which measured 57 by 44 millimeters (2 1/4 by 1 3/4 inches) and was printed by Glasgow University Press (Bondy 1981, 5, 104). As *The Publishers' Circular* noted in 1891, "[t]he 'Thumb Dictionary' [...] is one of his latest novelties, and one of the most useful, the first edition of 10,000 copies being exhausted in less than three months" (*The Publishers' Circular* 1891, 280). According Bryce himself, the small dictionary "took the public's fancy" and was issued in different editions and sold more than two million copies during the subsequent years (Bryce 1928b, 1). Like many other publishers Bryce realized the profitable market for religious books and soon began publishing Christian literature. Instead of utilizing letterpress print he made use of the latest technological advancements in photolithography and electroplates that were able to reduce larger original books to the smallest size with clarity and legibility of texts (Byrne 2016, 15).

Many of the miniature books published by Bryce were issued in close cooperation with Henry Frowde at Oxford University Press. Oxford was an important publisher of various miniature books bearing its own imprint, especially in the field of literature and Christian books (see for example Bondy 1981, 117, 131). From the early 1880s Bryce and Frowde discussed the joint venture of publishing the Sunday service book of the Church of England even if the book eventually turned out to be a failure from a business point of view (see for example: Letter from Henry Frowde to David Bryce 1883, 24 November; 1884, 10 January; 1884, 31 March; 1884, 29 July; 1885, 6 October). At the end of the 1880s they prepared a *Finger Prayer Book* that appears to have been issued at Oxford with Frowde paying royalties to the wife of Bryce for three years (Letter from Henry Frowde to Mrs. Bryce 1891, 8 June; 1892, 24 October; 1893, 14 January; *The Western Daily Press* 1889, 4 December). The contract proposals from Frowde suggest that the mass production of cheap books in editions no smaller than 10,000 copies was considered the key to profit and the two publishers arranged different deals for the production and sale. For the *Thumb Prayer Book* in the early 1890s, for instance, Oxford supplied paper and printed the books while Bryce took responsibility for the cloth binding since this work was considerably cheaper

in Glasgow. They divided the edition between each other with Bryce receiving 10,000 copies for his own business (Letter from Henry Frowde to David
Bryce 1893, 14 January; 1893, 31 March; 1896, 10 February). Similarly,
Oxford University Press provided the original texts for their joint publica-
tions printed with photo-reduction. *The New Testament of Our Lord Saviour
Jesus Christ* published in 1895 was a facsimile of the Pica 16mo New Testa-
ment of Oxford and measured only 19 by 16 millimeters. The complete Bible
issued the following year in 25,000 copies was a reproduction of the Oxford
Nonpareil 16mo Bible (see Parmenter this volume; Bondy 1981, 108, 111;
Kilgour 1928, 3; Metzger 1996, 9–10; Christie's 1979, 11, 70; Letter from
Henry Frowde to David Bryce 1894, 5 July).

An important factor behind Bryce's achievements with miniature books
was the access to the ultra-thin and opaque paper called "India paper" that
allowed clear print in neat editions (Smith 1913, 23). The paper was produced
at a mill in Wolvercote, which Oxford University Press under Frowde bought
in the 1870s and used with great success for Bible publications.[2] Oxford kept
the paper production secret and controlled the sale by not placing the paper
on the open market and only selling it to others for purposes approved by
the press (see for example Letter from Henry Frowde to E. Charansouney
1900, 11 December). Initially, Bryce seems to have been rather hesitant
about the paper because of the higher price, but began submitting orders
from the 1890s onwards while promising that it would only be used for specified undertakings approved by Frowde (Letter from Henry Frowde to David
Bryce 1893, 31 March; 1893, 3 May). Over the years Oxford experimented
with the paper to make it as thin as possible for books in smaller editions
(Letter from Henry Frowde to David Bryce 1894, 17 March). Frowde was
also very careful to have a credit line inserted in the books that used the India
paper and were printed at Oxford for other publishers (see for example: Letter from Henry Frowde to David Bryce 1909, 4 August; Bondy 1981, 111).

What became a trademark of Bryce's small books were the different accompanying cases and shelves that matched and protected the books. The tiny
editions of Scottish poetical works were, for instance, sold in wooden cases in

---

2. The legend behind the Oxford India Paper tells that in the 1840s a graduate
from Oxford returned from India with a small fold of thin paper and presented
it to the University Press. In 1842, 24 copies of small Bibles were printed from
it and attempts were made to trace the source of the paper. The search eventually
stopped until Frowde became the publisher in the 1870s and took over the
Wolvercote Mills where experiments with the paper started once again. In 1875
the first Bible printed on the Oxford India Paper was issued and became a huge
success (*The Oxford University Press 1468–1921* 1922, 10–11; *The Falkirk Herald
and Midland Counties Journal* 1900, 8 August; *The Herald* 1911, 18 March).

Figure 6.1: Steinbrener's miniature Qur'an from the 1920s. Photo by the author.

white or with a tartan cover. The volumes of Shakespeare's works were issued with a variety of boxes, cases, and stands in leather and wood (Bondy 1981, 115; Welsh 1987, 98). A peculiar accessory was a wooden lectern to which a miniature Bible was chained. This set was issued in 1911 to commemorate the tercentenary of the King James Bible (1611) and was to be a "memento" and facsimile of the "chained Bibles" in British churches, that is, Bibles accessible to anyone but guarded against theft with a chain (Bondy 1981, 109; *The Sphere* 1911, 15 April). The books in Bryce's "Midget series," including the Qur'an, the New Testament, and dictionaries, were sold together with plain or engraved lockets in silver and other metals with inset magnifying glasses in the center for reading the texts (Bondy 1981, 106, 111; Henderson 1928a, 5). The practice of enclosing miniature books in lids and attaching them with a magnifying glass was certainly not new or unique with the publications of Bryce but popular at different times and places. In the Islamic traditions, various metal cases were used for amulets containing handwritten Qur'anic verses as well as in the Ottoman practice of *sancak* Qur'ans (see for example: Coffey 2010, 82, 88; Roper 2013, 549). A small Qur'an from Teheran in the 1890s, for instance, was preserved in a wooden box wrapped in leather with space for a magnifying glass and a prayer stone (Bobzin 2002, 167, 489). In London in the 1830s and 1840s, Albert Schloss issued editions of the English Bijou Almanacs in cases with small magnifying glasses attached. By the end of the nineteenth century embossed metal covers with various patterns became increasing popular in Britain (Bromer and Edison 2007, 80–81, 96; Byrne 2016, 15). Bryce seems to have espoused these trends in order to aid the sale of his small books. As mentioned in the communication with Frowde, the books enclosed in lockets were considered much better for the sales carried out by the firm's traveling sellers in England and Scotland

(Letter from Henry Frowde to David Bryce 1894, 9 November). Preserved samples of the lockets among collectors and in museums indicate that some were from Samson Mordan & Co. in London, which at the time was a firm reputed for its smaller silver items and especially pencils, bookmarks, and letter openers with magnifying glass. Other lockets seem to have been made by Alfred Wigley of Birmingham, another silversmith known for supplying cases to watches.

Printing and selling Qur'ans for Indian markets

From the correspondence of Henry Frowde it appears that David Bryce began publishing miniature Qur'ans in Arabic by the beginning of 1896 with the intention to sell books in India. In a letter to the controller at Oxford University Press in December 1895, Frowde forwarded an order of forty reams of the thinnest India paper in the same size and weight that had been used for the "Mite Bible" and noted: "[h]e [Bryce] wants it this time for a tiny edition of the Koran, and I believe he has sold the whole edition to an Indian firm of Jewellers" (Letter from Henry Frowde to the Controller 1895, 16 December; see also Stone 1928, 1). Although the sources do not reveal the details of the venture in India, Bryce seems to have established transnational business links through the Parsi bookseller and publisher D.B. Taraporevala in Bombay, who resold the books to partners in India and Africa. In a letter to Bryce in October 1899, Taraporevala informed that he had visited his partners in the North Western Provinces in India to look after the sale of "locket Korans" and requested Bryce to withhold the supply for a few months because of decreasing sales due to the famine and plague that had hit the country during the year. As he further explained, the "Transval war" (the Second Boer War) had practically stopped the sale of miniature Qur'ans to South Africa:

> We used to supply thousands every month to a Mohamedan gentleman in Bombay to be shipped to Zanzibar, Natal and other places in Africa inhabited by the Mohamedans. We find this gentleman also does not like to take any more hereafter owing to the present serious affairs at Natal and other places of war. We would therefore suggest you to let the matter stand over for a short time and as soon as we find the Bazaar improving we will write you again to resume the supply of Korans only. (Letter from D.B. Taraporevala Sons & Co. to David Bryce 1899, 17 October)

As Taraporevala notified, they had instead arranged to send a man to Persia in order to find new markets for at least a few thousand Qur'ans every month. In the same letter he also drew attention to the lockets that were "not much liked by the Mohammedans, and are too costly for the price." Referring to their contract, which stated "Koran with or without lockets" and consequently obliged him to purchase only the books, he stated that he could try to sell a few thousand lockets but not any larger numbers (Letter from D.B. Taraporevala Sons & Co. to David Bryce 1899, 17 October). Even if Islamic traditions valued ornamental cases for copies or excerpts from the Qur'an, the British lockets were not considered marketable in India. Perhaps to meet these demands, Bryce seems to have issued editions of the Qur'an with book and slipcases that matched the morocco binding (see for example: Garbett 2011, 29; The Dog's Tooth n.d.).

Figure 6.2: David Bryce's miniature Qur'an from the early twentieth century. Photo by the author.

Based on the orders of India paper from Oxford University Press, it is possible to deduce at least two reprints of the miniature Qur'ans in 1899 and 1907 that slightly changed the appearance of the books. When the first reprint was under preparation Frowde suggested that a toned sheet was used instead of the earlier white and advised Bryce to be careful with the thickness of the volumes in case the large number of lockets became useless (Letter from Henry Frowde to David Bryce 1899, 21 February; 1899, 27 February; Letter by the Controller 1899, 27 February). It seemed like Bryce had some trouble getting the books to fit into the lockets and asked for thinner paper. Frowde suggested that his binder should try "to roll the sheets after folding, as by that means we are sometimes able to reduce the bulk of a particular book very considerably" (Letter from Henry Frowde to David Bryce 1906, 11 September). While testing the paper quality before the reprint in 1907, Frowde informed "that we have managed to get down to a lower eight and the paper is distinctly thinner than the last supplied, without I believe any loss in opacity" but it was at a considerably higher price. However, Frowde stated that he considered the production for the "Mite Koran" as "a curiosity rather than as a commercial product" and therefore promised Bryce to supply the improved paper at the same price as before (Letter from Henry Frowde to David Bryce 1907, 3 October; 1907, 11 November; 1907, 28 November).

From the copies of the Qur'ans that have been preserved by collectors, museums, and archives, it seems evident that Bryce experimented with millimeter dimensions and issued editions of various sizes – all from 31 by 22 to 23 by 17 millimeters. Many copies from the early twentieth century are in the format 26 by 19 millimeters (1 by 3/4 inches). In order to present them in an Oriental style, the bindings were richly gilt-stamped in red, green, brown or black morocco with gilt edges (see for example: Bondy 1981, 111; Bromer and Edison 2007, 87; Christie's 1979, 43; Spielmann 1961, 98). The Arabic text in most editions was printed without pagination in black with the opening pages and the headpieces for the *surah*s decorated. Bryce also seems to have tested various appearances of the books and even printed a few Qur'ans with golden text (Garbett 2011, 29). The details of how he procured a copy of the Qur'anic text remain unknown, but the books themselves provide information about which copy was used for the photolithographic reduction. The last page includes a certificate (*shehadetname*) in Ottoman Turkish that gives an official confirmation that the complete "copies of the noble Qur'an [...] was augmented by photo from the copy prepared by the late Hafiz Osman Efendi, a famous calligrapher in Hijri 1094" (1683 CE) and "there was no error in its any word" (see Figure 6.3). Although the Ottoman Empire assumed a restrictive position on the printing of Qur'ans, the calligrapher Osman Zeki Bey in Istanbul received in 1871 official permission to make a photographic reproduction. He analyzed the handwritten manuscript recorded by Hafiz Osman in the seventeenth century and got a group of learned Muslim scholars (*mullah*s) to examine and approve the proofs. This became the first legally printed version of the Qur'an in the Ottoman Empire and the year after, in 1872, the sultan authorized a free trade of the photographic copies that could be reproduced in various sizes (*The Daily Telegraph* 1871, 2 October; *Huddersfield Chronicle* 1872, 21 September; Kuran-Burcoglu 2007, 38; *The Star* 1896, 23 April; *Warder and Dublin Weekly Mail* 1871, 22 July; Wilson 2009, 62–63). Although the circumstances surrounding David Bryce's procurement of the text for his miniature Qur'ans are unclear, sources indicate that he established a large network of contacts that included the sultan (Garbett 2011, 9). The certificate inserted in the small Qur'ans from Glasgow made an appeal to Islamic traditions by attesting that the sacred text was an authoritative facsimile of the old manuscript recorded by the calligrapher Hafiz Osman and approved by the sultan and Muslim authorities. As Natalia K. Suit also illustrates in her study of publishing houses in Egypt, printed Qur'ans in different sizes included copies of a permission or certificate that attested the accuracy of the text since it was a punishable transgression to change the sacred text (Suit 2013, 200).

Figure 6.3: The Ottoman certificate in David Bryce's miniature Qur'ans. Photo by the author.

The correspondence between Bryce and Taraporevala further indicates that the publishers were planning both a Hindu and a Parsi "Prayer Book" for the transnational market, but for unknown reasons Bryce postponed the work (Letter from D.B. Taraporevala Sons & Co. to David Bryce 1899, 17 October). In Bombay Taraporevala had in 1899 issued both a miniature edition of the Khordeh Avesta, the Zoroastrian religious text, and "Holy Prayer book" in Gujarati and was exploring the possibility of having new editions printed in Britain (Henderson 1928b, 11; PDA Galleries 2016; Welsh 1989, 105). In the discussion with Bryce a disagreement emerged and Taraporevala informed that Frowde was instead willing to take up the job for these publications. Bryce therefore asked Frowde to confirm this. In the reply Frowde stated that he had not communicated with Taraporevala on the subject and the mentioning of his press "is enough to show he [Taraporevala] is utterly unreliable and untruthful" (Letter from D.B. Taraporevala Sons & Co. to David Bryce 1899, 17 October; Letter from Henry Frowde to David Bryce 1900, 28 March; see also Chatterjee 2006, 193–194). Regardless of this harsh judgment, Frowde stayed in contact with Taraporevala during the following years and invited him to Oxford (Letter from Henry Frowde to Mr. Vicaji

D.B. Taraporevala 1902, 10 June; Letter from Henry Frowde to Horace Hart 1902, 11 June; Letter from Frowde to Vicaji D.B. Taraporevala 1902, 30 December). In the correspondence from the summer of 1904 it is evident that Frowde prepared specimen blocks in two sizes from a book of Khordeh Avesta that Taraporevala had left with him and gave estimates of the costs for the blocks, printing, and paper (ordinary and Oxford India paper) for 3,000 to 5,000 copies. To provide an example of how the books could look he sent along sample copies in leather binding and requested six copies of the original books for the manufacture of blocks (Letter from Henry Frowde to Vicaji D.B. Taraporewala 1904, 27 June). This episode may indicate competition between Frowde and Bryce, but their correspondence rather suggests long-term business relations and friendship.[3] They revealed their publications plans to each other and even made deals to not publish the same books. When Bryce wished to print Burns' and Scott's poems in miniature size, for instance, Frowde promised that Oxford would not issue these works during the next coming years, but in return requested Bryce to leave "the field for portions of the Bible and Prayer Book and miniature reproductions of such devotional books" clear for him (Letter from Henry Frowde to David Bryce 1905, 23 January). Even if Oxford University Press certainly had market interests in religious books intended for Muslim readership,[4] the publishing and selling of miniature Qur'ans was reserved for Bryce.

The preserved letters do not elucidate what happened to the continued cooperation between Bryce and Taraporevala, but the publications from Bryce in the early twentieth century confirm that he took an interest in Indian religious scriptures and printed Khordeh Avesta in Gujarati as well as the Hindu Bhagavad Gita (Gita Pancha Ratna) from the Indian epic Mahabharata in Sanskrit (see for example: Bondy 1981, 112–113; Gita-Pancha-Ratna, RB.s.2749, Kordeh Avesta, FB.s.960). The copies of Bhagavad Gita seem to have been printed in sizes such as 24 by 21 and 25 by 19 millimeters with richly gilt-stamped covers similar to those used for the Qur'ans. The books also included 11 full-page illustrations and opened with the popular image of the chariot of Krishna and Arjuna in the battlefield of Kurukshetra (Bondy 1981, 112; Bromer and Edison 2007, 87; Spielmann 1961,

3. For example, Henry Frowde sent a gift to David Bryce's daughter and congratulated Bryce when his grandson was born (Letter from Henry Frowde to David Bryce 1906, 21 June; 1908, 14 April).
4. In May 1896 Henry Frowde wrote to the Orientalist and linguist Gottlieb Wilhelm Leitner, who had built the mosque in Woking in 1889, asking if he could help him to procure a copy of a hymnal book that had been "compiled for the use of the English speaking Moslems, who have recently built a Mosque at Liverpool" (Letter from Henry Frowde to Dr. Leitner 1896, 20 May).

58; Welsh 1987, 169).[5] Apparently, Bryce also had plans for publishing the Sikh scripture Guru Granth Sahib and made several test prints from a letterpress printed edition in the Gurmukhi script, though it seems like this printing project was eventually dropped. Similar to the large volumes used in Sikh worship, the test copies were printed in oblong format. One of them was bound in blind-stamped morocco with the title of the scripture in gold. Another had grapevine patterned paper binding in gold and pink with the title printed on a flower-patterned paper pasted on the front board.[6]

Undoubtedly, India presented an important market for small books. In February 1913 a newspaper reported that 3,000 miniature copies of the Qur'an had been sent to the "East" by a jeweler in London and each copy was enclosed in a metal case with a magnifying glass and ring by which the book could be hung around the neck. As the paper continued:

> The trade in miniature "Korans" is, it appears, at its highest during the season when pilgrims from every part of the East undertake their annual visit to Mecca, and ten thousand other copies are to be shipped to Bombay in the course of the next few weeks. The amulet is three-quarters of an inch by half an inch in size, and is sold at 1 s. 8 d. [1 shilling and 8 pence]. (*Lincolnshire Echo* 1913, 27 February)

The article did not confirm whether the books referred to were actually from Bryce's publishing house, but gave a glimpse of the profitable trade of miniature Qur'ans to India during seasons of religious pilgrimage and festivals. The small books apparently functioned as auspicious gifts and souvenirs for Muslims undertaking pilgrimage to Mecca (*hajj*) and India played an important role in providing these books for the Asian, African, and Middle-Eastern markets.

---

5. Miniature copies of the Bhagavad Gita were also printed in Bombay in 1903 and 1909 although the publisher is not mentioned (see Spielmann 1961, 11).

6. The National Library of Scotland has preserved two different test copies of *Guru Granth Sahib* that are from Bryce's personal collection. By mistake these have been catalogued and referred to by authors as Bhagavad Gita. These include test prints of pages 10 and 11 from the Sikh scripture that are organized in a two-column format on the pages. One of the test copies is enclosed in a rectangular silver box engraved with the text "David Bryce Jedburgh" (see Bhagavad Gita RB.s.2747; RB.s.2748).

Orientalist narratives

The tiny Qur'ans of Bryce became associated with various narratives from the First World War that attempted to provide cultural contexts for the books' admiration and use from Orientalist perspectives.[7] A popular anecdote in Lowell Jackson Thomas' famous book *With Lawrence in Arabia* from 1924 portrays how Lawrence during the war and his mission in Arabia discovered that an amulet worn by the Beduin Sheikh Auda Abu Tayeh was in fact a miniature Qur'an from David Bryce:

> Nearly all Arabs carry some sort of good-luck charm, and the belief in jinn or genii is still common. The talisman which Auda wore round his neck was probably one of the most extraordinary to be found in all Arabia. The amulet was a diminutive copy of the Koran about one inch square, for which he paid more than two hundred pounds. One day he displayed it with great pride, and Lawrence discovered it had been printed in Glasgow and, according to the price marked inside the cover, had been issued at eighteen pence. So far as we could make out, the only things Bedouin are afraid of are snakes, and they believe that the sole protection against them is such a charm worn round the neck. (Thomas n.d., 195)

This anecdote was popular and widely reproduced during the twentieth century, even transformed to give more agency to Lawrence and the British forces in the story (see for example Pearson 1937, 12 February). In Georgene O'Donnell's interpretation given in *Miniatura* of 1943, for example, it was Lawrence and the British who provided the Arabs with copies of the Bryce's Qur'an in a metal case in order to gain support and prevent them from joining the German side. As stated, this was well received since the Muslim soldiers believed that "wearing one of these little lockets containing the Koran assured them a place on the right side of Allah should they be killed" (O'Donnell 1943, 184–185). In an article by Joni Miller from 1988, Lawrence similarly gave each of his Muslim soldiers a miniature Qur'an from Bryce and "smuggled" the copies in small lockets with magnifying glasses (Miller 1988, 44).

Yet another anecdote that bears resemblance to the story about Lawrence of Arabia conveys how W.B. Seabrook, the American traveler and writer, visited Sheikh Mitkal of the Beni Sakhr tribe in the Sahara and upon his departure

---

7. In this context the notion "Orientalist perspectives" builds upon Edward Said's (1979) renowned understanding of Orientalism as a tendency among Western scholarship and worldviews to present the Eastern world as essentially dissimilar and inferior to Western culture. Representations of cultures and "natives" in the "Orient" are from these perspectives often portrayed as being more primitive, traditional, and exotic, in need of a cultural uplift and influence by Western ideas in order to reach the same civilized state as European cultures.

was given in an act of reverence a small Qur'an that was "a hollow amulet of heavy silver, in shape and size like a lump of domino sugar, containing an actual copy of the entire Koran, in Arabic characters so tiny that they can be distinguished only with the aid of a microscope" (Seabrook 2010, 47). Although the original text in Seabrook's travelogue *Adventures in Arabia* published in 1927 did not mention that it was a copy from David Bryce, later interpretations of the story made this connection clear (see Henderson 1928a, 4; Henderson 1933, 147).

The standard narrative that has been widely communicated by book collectors, libraries, museums, and others preserving and selling the small texts reiterates that the miniature Qur'ans from David Bryce were issued to Muslim soldiers fighting on the British side during the First World War in order to be used as charms and talismans and strengthen their loyalty (see for example: Bondy 1981, 112; Bromer and Edison 2007, 87; Hanebutt-Benz, Glass, and Roper 2002, 490; Henderson 1928a, 4; *Miniature Book News* 1966, 7). Embroidered legends even assert that the British government ordered no less than 500,000 copies of the miniature books that were distributed to the Muslim soldiers in British service, which had the effect of revitalizing the soldiers "to such an extent that they contributed in some small way to the defeat of the enemy" (Henderson 1933, 149). Assumptions that the Qur'ans of Bryce were published and distributed to soldiers in large numbers certainly lie close at hand considering the marketability of the books before the war and the various traditions of providing soldiers with religious books.

In this context it is perhaps noteworthy that Oxford University Press prepared in 1899 a pocket version of the Bible for British Christian soldiers, the so-called "Knapsack Bible" in khaki, for which Henry Frowde gave special care to the weight. After having presented the book to Queen Victoria for approval, the final version was printed in 80,000 copies and each weighed only 127 grams. The plan was to send the copies as New Year gifts to Christian British soldiers serving in South Africa, even if this was not realized because of delivery problems (Letter from Henry Frowde to Mrs. Vaughan Jackson 1899, 25 November; Letter from Henry Frowde to Major Digby du Boulay 1899, 25 November). At the beginning of the First World War in the fall of 1914, David Bryce issued *The Allies' Miniature Bible* that measured 44 by 28 millimeters and was bound in khaki with a magnifying glass attached. In addition to a small copy of the Oxford Nonpareil 16mo edition of the Bible, the book contained the national anthems of Britain, France, Belgium, and Russia, Rudyard Kipling's poem *Recessional*, and Neil Munro's *Evening Prayer of a People*, and was sold for a shilling. These examples illustrate the popularity of providing soldiers in the British Army small religious books and how Christian books were differently framed in national discourses. Unlike

Orientalist narratives about miniature Qur'ans, British newspapers described the small khaki Bible of Bryce as a "literary curiosity" and "pretty little curio" without mentioning how the Christian soldiers might have used the books in various ritual practices (*Birmingham Daily Post* 1914, 20 November; *Sheffield Weekly Telegraph* 1914, 19 December; *The Sphere* 1914, 5 December).

Available archival sources from the First World War confirm that significant numbers of Bryce's miniature Qur'ans were indeed procured by Indian and British individuals and associations to be distributed among Muslim soldiers at hospitals and convalescent centres for Indians (see Myrvold and Johansson in this volume). However, the small Qur'ans could also have been employed for other types of propaganda and were given or sold to soldiers by the allied German and Ottoman empires on the opposing side of the war. In a letter to the Under Secretary of State in August 1916, for instance, the publisher Evans Brothers in London informed British authorities that a German commercial house had made "extensive arrangements to exploit the sale of a Miniature Edition of the Koran throughout the Mohammedan population of the British Empire" and purchased large quantities of the small books to sell them in Egypt and other places at a lower price than their cost. Although the publisher did not inform the authorities about the producer, a specimen copy edition of the small Qur'an "in a locket with magnifying glass" was sent to them.[8] As indicated in an interview with the great-granddaughter of David Bryce, Mrs. Bridgie Unicume, the Qur'ans of Bryce might have been procured and distributed by the Ottoman sultan to Turkish soldiers in order to "improve morale" after the huge losses during the battle of Gallipoli in 1916 (Klyn 1969, 98).

In view of the historical sources available, it is presumable that tiny Qur'ans from Glasgow reached the Muslim world through various ways and means, primarily through the transnational trade of publishers and booksellers, and served many different functions, as novelty items, precious gifts, pilgrimage souvenirs, religious amulets, portable scriptures, collectables, and so on, depending on the intentions and purposes of the users. The Orientalist narratives that have been linked with these miniature books are however interesting since they provide an example of how the books, as material objects, have been invested with various iconic and performative meanings and functions. The tiny books do not only represent Muslim soldiers and Arabs entrenched

---

8. Evans Brothers requested the entire rights and names of firms in the British Empire that could drive the sale of Qur'ans. The Under Secretary of State replied that this information could not be supplied but advised the publisher to communicate with the government secretaries in each of the colonial areas with Muslim populations and the High Commissioner in London (*Miniature Edition of the Koran* 1916, 12 August).

in amulet traditions and index complex relationships between the British colonial rulers and their subjects, but they are also attributed the power to transform people, relationships, and even the course of history during a time when British security and honor were threatened. Giving and possessing the physical books in miniature size is presented in a way that evokes an instrumentality of a performative nature, which affects people and circumstances far beyond the textual confines of the books. As such, the miniature books make an interesting field for the study of material texts and especially how the physical forms of religious scriptures can influence and become sites of meanings in their own right.

Acknowledgments

I am grateful to many people for their kind assistance during the work for this chapter: Dr. Martin Maw and Mr. Michael Spurling at Oxford University Press, the staff at the Rare Books Collection at the National Library of Scotland, the staff at Asian and African Studies at the British Library, Mr. Ian Macdonald at Gleniffer Press, and Mr. Stephen Byrne and other members of the Miniature Book Society. I also want to direct special thanks to Dr. Rafah Barhoum, Lund University, and her student in Turkey for valuable help with the translation of Ottoman certificates in miniature Qur'ans. I am greatly indebted to Dr. Andreas Johansson, Linnaeus University, and Mr. Harpreet Singh who assisted me with the collection of archival material at the British Library and Oxford University Press. The work has been prepared with support from the *Swedish Research Council* (www.vr.se) under Grant 2014-956 and the *Crafoord Foundation* (www.crafoord.se) under Grant 20140550, and within the Centre for Concurrences in Colonial and Postcolonial Studies at Linnaeus University.

References

Primary sources

The British Library, UK

Selections from the Records of Government, North Western Provinces. 1855. Volume III, Part XII to XXI, Agra: Secundera Orphan Press.

The British Newspapers Archive, UK

Aberdeen Press and Journal. 1924. "Glasgow Publisher." 15 April.
Birmingham Daily Post. 1914. "Books Received." 20 November.
The Daily Telegraph. 1871. 2 October.
Dundee Advertiser. 1895. "Angling." 8 April.

The Falkirk Herald and Midland Counties Journal. 1900. "Oxford Bibles and India Paper." 8 August.

Glasgow Evening Citizen. 1870. "Death of David Bryce." 19 April.

Glasgow Evening Post. 1870. "Bryce's Reading Club." 25 August.

The Herald. 1911. "Oxford India Paper." 18 March.

Huddersfield Chronicle. 1872. "Miscellaneous News and Home Gossip." 21 September.

Pearson, G. W. 1937. "Books, Midgets and Monsters." *Dundee Evening Telegraph.* 12 February.

Sheffield Weekly Telegraph. 1914. 19 December.

The Sphere. 1911. "A Literary Letter: New Books on the Bible." 15 April.

The Sphere. 1914. "A Literary Letter: Christmas Presents and Prizes." 5 December.

The Star. 1896. "The Koran and Oriental Notions." 23 April.

Warder and Dublin Weekly Mail. 1871. "The Koran." 22 July.

The Western Daily Press. 1889. "The Publishing Season." 4 December.

The National Archives, UK

Miniature edition of the Koran: request for details of firms in the British Empire who could assist in its sale to the Mahommedan population. 1916. 12 August. CO 323 734 44.

The National Library of Scotland, UK

Bhagavad-Gita [Guru Granth Sahib]. RB.s.2747. http://main-cat.nls.uk/vwebv/holdingsInfo?bibId=4251582

Bhagavad-Gita [Guru Granth Sahib]. RB.s.2748. http://main-cat.nls.uk/vwebv/holdingsInfo?bibId=4256264

Koran. RB.s.2279. http://main-cat.nls.uk/vwebv/holdingsInfo?bibId=3401479

Kordeh Avesta. FB.s.960. http://main-cat.nls.uk/vwebv/holdingsInfo?bibId=4267168

Gita-Pancha-Ratna. RB.s.2749. http://main-cat.nls.uk/vwebv/holdingsInfo?bibId=4251577

Pigot and Co.'s National Commercial Directory for the Whole of Scotland and of the Isle of Man. 1837. 534. http://digital.nls.uk/85591012

Oxford University Press Archive, UK

Letter by the Controller. 1899. Letter book Volume 49. 27 February.

Letter from D. B. Taraporevala Sons & Co. to David Bryce. 1899. Letter book Volume 52, 17 October.

Letter from Henry Frowde to the Controller. 1895. Letter book Volume 37. 16 December.

Letter from Henry Frowde to E. Charansouney. 1900. Letter book Volume 54. 11 December.

Letter from Henry Frowde to David Bryce. 1883. Letter book Volume 12. 24 November.

Letter from Henry Frowde to David Bryce. 1884. Letter book Volume 12. 10 January.

Letter from Henry Frowde to David Bryce. 1884. Letter book Volume 12. 31 March.

Letter from Henry Frowde to David Bryce. 1884. Letter book Volume 13. 29 July.

Letter from Henry Frowde to David Bryce. 1885. Letter book Volume 14. 6 October.

Letter from Henry Frowde to David Bryce. 1893. Letter book Volume 29. 14 January.

Letter from Henry Frowde to David Bryce. 1893. Letter book Volume 30. 31 March.

Letter from Henry Frowde to David Bryce. 1893. Letter book Volume 30. 3 May.

Letter from Henry Frowde to David Bryce. 1894. Letter book Volume 33. 17 March.

Letter from Henry Frowde to David Bryce. 1894. Letter book Volume 34. 5 July.

Letter from Henry Frowde to David Bryce. 1894. Letter book Volume 35. 9 November.

Letter from Henry Frowde to David Bryce. 1896. Letter book Volume 37. 10 February.

Letter from Henry Frowde to David Bryce. 1899. Letter book Volume 49. 21 February.

Letter from Henry Frowde to David Bryce. 1899. Letter book, Volume 49. 27 February.

Letter from Henry Frowde to David Bryce. 1900. Letter book, Volume 52. 28 March.

Letter from Henry Frowde to David Bryce. 1905. Letter book Volume 67. 23 January.

Letter from Henry Frowde to David Bryce, 1906. Letter book Volume 71. 21 June.

Letter from Henry Frowde to David Bryce. 1906. Letter book Volume 71. 11 September.

Letter from Henry Frowde to David Bryce. 1907. Letter book Volume 75. 3 October.

Letter from Henry Frowde to David Bryce. 1907. Letter book Volume 75. 11 November.

Letter from Henry Frowde to David Bryce. 1907. Letter book Volume 76. 28 November.

Letter from Henry Frowde to David Bryce. 1908. Letter book Volume 77. 14 April.

Letter from Henry Frowde to David Bryce. 1909. Letter book Volume 81. 4 August.

Letter from Henry Frowde to Horace Hart. 1902. Letter book Volume 59. 11 June.

Letter from Henry Frowde to Dr. Leitner. 1896. Letter book Volume 38. 20 May.

Letter from Henry Frowde to Mrs. Bryce. 1891. Letter book Volume 25. 8 June.

Letter from Henry Frowde to Mrs. Bryce. 1892. Letter book Volume 28. 24 October.

Letter from Henry Frowde to Mrs. Bryce. 1893. Letter book Volume 29. 14 January.

Letter from Henry Frowde to Mrs. Vaughan Jackson. 1899. Letter book Volume 51. 25 November.

Letter from Henry Frowde to Major Digby du Boulay. 1899. Letter book Volume 51. 25 November.

Letter from Henry Frowde to Mr. Vicaji D.B. Taraporevala. 1902. Letter book Volume 59. 10 June.

Letter from Henry Frowde to Vicaji D.B. Taraporevala. 1902. Letter book Volume 61. 30 December.

Letter from Henry Frowde to Vicaji D.B. Taraporewala. 1904. Letter book Volume 66. 27 June.

Other

Bryce, David. 1928a. "Rigmarole Instances in My Publishing Career." *The News-letter of the LXIVMOS* No. 11. 15 October.

Bryce, David. 1928b. "David Bryce & Sons." *The News-letter of the LXIVMOS* No. 12, 15 November

The Publishers' Circular and Booksellers' Record. 1891. "Booksellers of To-day: Messrs. David Bryce & Son, Glasgow." No.1315, 12 September. London: Office of the Publishers' Circular.

The Publishers' Circular and Booksellers' Record. 1907. "David Bryce & Son's Publications." Vol. LXXXVI (January to June), 20 April. London: Office of the Publishers' Circular.

Smith, Willard F. 1913. "Characteristics of India Paper." *Paper*. Volume XIII(9): 23.

Secondary sources

Aqeel, Moinuddin. 2009. "Commencement of Printing in the Muslim World: A View of Impact on Ulama at Early Phase of Islamic Moderate Trends." *Kyoto Bulletin of Islamic Area Studies* 2(2): 10–21.

Auji, Hala, 2016. *Printing Arab Modernity: Book Culture and the American Press in Nineteenth-Century Beirut*. Leiden: Brill. https://doi.org/10.1163/9789004314351

Blumenthal, Walter Hart. 1961. "Octagonal 'Banner' Korans." *The Miniature Book Collector* 2(1): 10–13.

Bobzin, Hartmut. 2002. "From Venice to Cairo: On the History of Arabic Editions of the Koran." In *Middle Eastern Languages and the Print Revolution: A Cross-cultural Encounter,* edited by Eva Hanebutt-Benz, Dagmar Glass, and Geoffrey Roper, 151–176. Westhofen: WVA-Verlag Skulima.

Bondy, Louis W. 1981. "Miniature Books." *Antiquarian Book Monthly Review* 7(69): 2–7.

Bromer, Anne C. and Julian I. Edison. 2007. *Miniature Books: 4,000 Years of Tiny Treasures*. New York: Harry N. Abrams.

Bulliet, Richard W. 1987. "Medieval Arabic *Tarsh*: A Forgotten Chapter in the History of Printing." *Journal of the American Oriental Society* 107: 427–438. https://doi.org/10.2307/603463

Byrne, Stephen. 2016. "Miniature Books Bound to Impress." A Presentation given to the British Printing Society, Annual Convention, March.

Chatterjee, Rimi B. 2006. *Empires of the Mind: A History of the Oxford University Press in India under the Raj.* Oxford: Oxford University Press.

Chatterjee, Rimi B. 2004. "'Every Line for India': The Oxford University Press and the Rise and Fall of the Rulers of India Series." In *Print Areas: Book History in India*, edited by Abhijit Gupta and Swapan Chakravorty, 65–102. Delhi: Permanent Black.

Christie's. 1979. *The Collection of Miniature Books formed by Arthur A. Houghton, Jr.* London: White Bros.

Coffey, Heather. 2010. "Between Amulet and Devotion: Islamic Miniature Books in the Lilly Library." In *The Islamic Manuscript Tradition: Ten Centuries of Book Arts in Indiana University Collections,* edited by Christiane Gruber, 78–115. Bloomington: Indiana University Press.

Dalbello, Marija. 2002. "Franz Josef's Time Machine: Images of Modernity in the Era of Mechanical Photoreproduction." *Book History* 5: 67–103. https://doi.org/10.1353/bh.2002.0004

The Dog's Tooth. n.d. "Recent Acquisitions (2013): Miniature Books." https://lib-ldap.library.mun.ca/groups/thedogstooth/revisions/welcome/141/

Garbett, Michael. 2011. *An Illustrated Bibliography of Miniature Books Published by David Bryce and Son* (with an Historical Introduction by Ian Macdonald). Scotland: The Final Score.

Gilliver, Peter. 2016. *The Making of the Oxford English Dictionary.* Oxford: Oxford University Press. https://doi.org/10.1093/acprof:oso/9780199283620.001.0001

Hanebutt-Benz, Eva, Dagmar Glass, and Geoffrey Roper (eds). 2002. *Middle Eastern Languages and the Print Revolution: A Cross-cultural Encounter.* Westhofen: WVA-Verlag Skulima.

Henderson, James D. 1928a. "David Bryce & Son." *The News-letter of the LXIV-MOS*, No. 11. 15 October.

Henderson, James D. 1928b. "Gujarati." *The News-letter of the LXIVMOS*, No. 11. 15 October.

Henderson, James D. 1933. "A Lilliputian Library." In *The American Book Collector: A Monthly Magazine for Book Lovers,* 4(3–4): 145–150.

Jaillant, Lise. 2016. "'Introductions by Eminent Writers': T.S. Eliot and Virginia Woolf in the Oxford World's Classics Series." In *The Book World: Selling and Distributing British Literature, 1900–1940*, edited by Nicola Wilson, 52–81. Leiden: Brill. https://doi.org/10.1163/9789004315884_005

Khan, Mofakhkhar Hussain. 2001. *The Holy Qur'an in South Asia: A Bio-bibliographic Study of Translations of the Holy Qur'an in 23 South Asian languages.* Dhaka: Bibi Akhtar Prakasani.

Kilgour, R. 1928. "Scriptures in Miniature." *The News-letter of the LXIVMOS*, No. 8. 15 May.

Klyn, Doyle. 1969. "For Tiny Books, What else? Tiny Bookcases." *The Ottawa Journal.* 25 October.

Kuran-Burcoglu, Nedret. 2007. "Osman Zeki Bey and His Printing Office the *Matbaa-i Osmaniye.*" In *History of Printing and Publishing in the Languages and Countries of the Middle East,* edited by Philip Sadgrove and Colin Paul Mitchell, 35–58. New York: Middle East Studies Association of North America.

Metzger, Bruce M. 1996. "Some Curious Bibles." *Text* 9: 1–10.

Miller, Joni. 1988. "Small Wonders." *The Connoisseur: An Illustrated Magazine for Collectors* 218: 44.

Miniature Book News. 1966. "Miniature Books." 6 December.

O'Donnell, Georgene. 1943. *Miniatura: The World of Tiny Things.* Chicago: Lightner.

PDA Galleries. 2016. "Lot 170 of 500: Khordeh Avesta [Holy Prayer Books in Gujarat Language]." http://www.pbagalleries.com/view-auctions/catalog/id/390/lot/123496/Khordeh-Avesta-Holy-Prayer-Booksin-Gujarat-language?url=%2Fview-auctions%2Fcatalog%2Fid%2F390%2F%3Fpage%3D2

The Oxford University Press 1468–1921. 1922. Oxford: Clarendon.

Rauscher, Janet. 2010. "Ruth E. Adomeit: An Ambassador for Miniature Books." In *The Islamic Manuscript Tradition: Ten Centuries of Book Arts in Indiana University Collections,* edited by Christiane J. Gruber, 53–78. Bloomington: Indiana University Press.

Roper, Geoffrey. 2013. "The Muslim World." In *The Book: A Global History,* edited by Michael F. Suarez and H.R. Woudhuysen, 524–552. Oxford: Oxford University Press.

Said, Edward W. 1979. *Orientalism.* New York: Vintage.

Seabrook, W.B. 2010, *Adventures in Arabia: Among the Bedouins, Druses, Whirling Dervishes and Yezidee Devil-worshippers.* New York: Routledge.

Schafer, Karl. 2002. "Arabic Printing before Gutenberg: Block-printed Arabic Amulets." In *Middle Eastern Languages and the Print Revolution: A Cross-cultural Encounter,* edited by Eva Hanebutt-Benz, Dagmar Glass, and Geoffrey Roper, 123–128. Westhofen: WVA-Verlag.

Spielmann, Percy Edwin. 1961. *Catalogue of the Library of Miniature Books.* London: Edward Arnold.

Stark, Ulrike. 2009. *An Empire of Books: The Naval Kishore Press and the Diffusion of the Printed Word in Colonial India.* New Delhi: Orient Blackswan.

Stone, Wilbur Macey. 1928. "Polyglot." *The News-letter of the LXIVMOS*, No. 6. 15 April.

Suit, Natalia K. 2013. "Muṣhaf and the Material Boundaries of the Qur'an." In *Iconic Books and Texts*, edited by James W. Watts, 189–206. Sheffield: Equinox.

Thomas, Lowell, n.d. *With Lawrence in Arabia*. London: Hutchinson & Co.

Welsh, Doris V. 1989 [1965]. *A Bibliography of Miniature Books (1470–1965)*. New York: Kathryn I. Rickard.

———. 1987. *The History of Miniature Books*. Albany, New York: Fort Orange.

Wilson, M. Brett. 2009. *The Qur'an after Babel: Translating and Printing the Qur'an in Late Ottoman and Modern Turkey*. Doctoral dissertation, Department of Religion, Duke University.

7

Miniature Qur'ans in the First World War: Religious Comforts for Indian Muslim Soldiers

Kristina Myrvold and Andreas Johansson

Kristina Myrvold is Associate Professor of Religious Studies at Linnaeus University. She is the author and editor of numerous publications on Indian cultures, religions, and migration.

Andreas Johansson holds a PhD in History of Religion and is the Director of the Swedish South Asian Studies Network (SASNET), Lund University. His research interests include religion and politics in South Asia.

When Britain entered the First World War in 1914, one third of the British forces on the Western Front were Indians of the British Indian Army. In late September that year the first divisions of Indian troops arrived in France and were dispatched to the front. They were involved in several attacks on the Germans during 1915. Most units left Europe for other war theaters in late 1915 but at least two Indian cavalry divisions stayed on the Western Front until the end of the war in 1918 (Omissi 2012, 39). Statistics from the British War Office after the war showed that the number of men from India sent overseas to the different war theatres comprised a total of 1,381,050 men of all ranks (British and Indian). Out of these, 138,608 were Indian combatants (officers, warrant officers, and other ranks) and non-combatants serving in Europe (The War Office 1922, 777).[1]

Religion and regional belonging were important factors in the British recruitment of soldiers according to predominant essentialist ideas about "martial races." Many of the Indian soldiers who were recruited and fought

---

1. According to other government statistics, the number of personnel dispatched directly from India to the various expeditionary forces overseas (war theaters in France, East Africa, Mesopotamia, Egypt, Gallipoli, Salonika, Aden, and the Persian Gulf) from the outbreak of the war up to October 31, 1918, included 13,517 Indian officers and warrant officers, 538,794 Indian combatants of other ranks, and 391,033 Indian non-combatants, making a total of 943,344 people (Authority of the Government of India 1923, 96–97).

for the British Army during the war were Muslims and Sikhs from the northern part of India, as they were considered particularly warlike because of their
histories and religious traditions. In particular, men from rural areas of the
north-western province of Punjab were associated with stereotypes of military
prowess. From the latter part of the nineteenth century the British recruited
almost half of the army from this province (Omissi 1998, 4, 6; 2012, 37; Tai-
Yong 2005, 70). Of the 282,171 combatants recruited for the war from Punjab (including Delhi) between 1915 and 1918 the Muslims constituted 55.4
percent, which equaled to 156,308 men (Leigh 1922, 44). In addition to
groups termed "Punjabi Muslims," other Muslims considered to be "martial
races" and mobilized for the war were Pathans of Afghani origin and "Hindustani Muslims," that is, Muslims from other provinces and areas in India
(Authority of the Government of India 1923; Roy 2013, 1340). Military service was associated with indigenous ideals of honor (*izzat*) and prestige, and
because of unproductive farming many Muslims enlisted to supplement their
income (Omissi 1994, 49–52; Morton Jack 2006, 335–336). The British
authorities displayed a bias in favor of the dominant and landowning castes
and tribes of Muslims since they were deemed more suitable for warfare, even
if their loyalty was occasionally questioned after Ottoman Turkey joined the
war on the opposing side and German propaganda urged mutiny and *jihad* in
the Middle East (Morton Jack 2006, 353; Omissi 1998, 110–111; Roy 2011,
17; Tai-Yong 2005, 74–75).

This article explores the significance of religious scriptures during the First
World War and especially the provision of miniature editions of the Qur'an
to Muslim soldiers from India. Since religion was attributed the power to
affect the Indian loyalty towards the colonial power, the religious needs of the
Indian soldiers became a matter of concern for military authorities, charities,
and different influential individuals in Europe and India. As the first section
of the article illustrates, British authorities attempted to identify the religious needs through various measures, such as communication with officers
responsible for the Indian troops, field trips to the Western Front, and regular
checks of the soldiers' letters, which underwent military censorship. Many of
the letters written by Muslim soldiers to relatives and friends in India, France,
and England included specific requests for Qur'ans, protective amulets, and
ritual services like recitations of the Qur'an. The article further examines
how a British charity such as the Indian Soldiers' Fund, which was established especially for the purpose of aiding sick and wounded Indian soldiers,
worked as a key agent to obtain miniature copies of the Qur'an, cooperated
with organizations and individuals in Britain and India to consolidate donations of religious scriptures and artifacts, and arranged for the distribution
to the soldiers at hospitals and at the front. The research presented in this

article is based on archival material of the Indian Soldiers' Fund, the papers of Walter Lawrence, and copies of letters from soldiers in the reports of the censor of Indian mails that are preserved at the British Library, as well as British newspaper articles and other colonial material from the time of the war.

Religious comforts and needs

In order to provide clothing and comforts for the sick and wounded Indian soldiers at hospitals and at the front, the Order of St. John of Jerusalem in Britain inaugurated the Indian Soldiers' Fund in the fall of 1914 with King George V as the royal patron. The Fund became an important charity to consolidate donations from the public and different prominent people in Britain and India, and also operated as a principal agent for the provision of religious artifacts to the soldiers until the end of the war (Omissi 2012, 40). A committee for the Fund was formed by 35 notable male and female members, including the Indians Maharani of Bharatpur, His Highness Aga Khan, and Mr. Ratan Tata, and with John P. Hewett as the chairperson (*Report of the First Six Months' Work* 1914–1915, 1). As another objective was to assist and maintain hospitals for the Indian wounded, the Fund operated closely with Walter Lawrence who had been appointed by the Secretary of State for War, Lord Kitchener, as the commissioner for the welfare of the Indian troops with responsibility to arrange hospitals in existing buildings (*The Sphere* 1916, 26 February).

For the purpose of maintaining discipline and avoiding public unease in India, the military authorities, together with charities such as the Indian Soldiers' Fund and the staff of the Indian Medical Service, tried to satisfy the soldiers' religious needs in various ways. At the different hospital ships, convalescent centers, and hospitals for Indian soldiers in England and France, separate kitchens, slaughterhouses, water taps, washrooms, lavatories, and other facilities were adjusted to the soldiers' different religions and castes.[2] At the Royal Dome and Pavilion Hospital in Brighton, for example, there were nine separate kitchens for the various food restrictions of the soldiers. Pork and beef were forbidden within the premises of the hospital and the wards had separate water taps for Muslims and Hindus to avoid ritual pollution. At the hospital premises separate areas were also arranged for Muslim, Sikh, and Hindu worship (*Report about the Pavilion Hospital* 1915–1916; Omissi 2007, 378–379; Robinson 1996, 43; Robinson 2015). The Muslim

---

2. According to the report of the Indian Soldiers' Fund in 1915, the medical facilities for Indian soldiers were: nine hospital ships, seven hospitals in England, five hospitals and convalescent depots in Boulogne, one hospital in Rouen, five hospitals and depots in Marseilles, three clearing hospitals in France, and two hospitals in Egypt (*Second Report of the Indian Soldiers' Fund* 1915, 12–13).

soldiers were given *halal* meat, that is, non-pork meat slaughtered according to Islamic traditions, and were allowed to observe Ramadan and other religious practices. At Lady Hardinge Hospital in Brockenhurst, which functioned between January 1915 and March 1916 with support from the Indian Soldiers' Fund, the wards, drinking taps, and washrooms were arranged with respect to religion and a separate room was provided for the Muslim soldiers for the reading of the Qur'an (*The Lady Hardinge Hospital* 1916, 5; Morton Jack 2006, 357). The Muslim regiments at the front had their own *mullah*, educated in Islamic traditions, to lead worship, and military authorities considered arranging and sending for a separate *mullah* from India for the Indian hospitals in England, even if this was never implemented (Letter from J. P. Hewett to Walter Lawrence 1915, 6 April; Meeting of the General Committee 1915, 3 March). In France, temporary mosques were built in the coastal

Back View of the Mahomedan Mosque

The semicircular recess represents the direction of Mecca. towards which all the Faithful turn in their prayers. This mosque was built for the wounded Indians on the French sand dunes. It measured about 30 ft. by 12 ft.

Figure 7.1: A Mosque built for wounded Muslim soldiers in France. Source: *The Sphere* 1916, 26 February. Photo: © Mary Evans Picture Library Ltd.

town of Hardelot as well as at the Indian Convalescent Depot in Boulogne, funded by donations from the Imperial War Fund, while marquees were built and functioned as mosques in the Flanders (Basu 2015; Report from John P. Hewett 1915, 27 July).

One of the reasons why the Indian Soldiers' Fund began providing religious symbols and literature to Indian soldiers was a concerned telegram from the British government in India. In early 1915 the Viceroy Lord Hardinge informed the Indian Soldiers' Fund that the numerous Indian soldiers who had been removed from military service in Europe had arrived in India without turbans and religious symbols. Anticipating criticism of the British government in India, he asked if the Fund could be of help and supply some "essentials" before the men started their journey home (Letter from the Indian Soldiers' Fund to Walter Lawrence 1915, 2 February). In a letter to Walter Lawrence the Viceroy explained that the kindness shown to the Indian soldiers in England was of "priceless value" because it "tends to increase our prestige in this country, and also the attachment that the lower classes have to the Sircar [the government]. This war should also help a great deal to bring British and Indian soldiers closer together." While estimating the situation in India as "on the whole satisfactory," he admitted that there was "a great deal of anxiety" due to Afghani attacks on the frontier and "the renewed activities of the anarchists and of bands of revolutionaries" when the military situation was weak because of the many troops overseas (Letter from Viceroy Hardinge to Walter Lawrence 1915, 14 April). In another attempt to avoid discontent, the Viceroy decided to give each returning sick and wounded soldier a cash amount of 50 rupees when landing at Bombay. As he wrote, "[i]t puts him in a very good honor and he goes back to his village full of money" (Letter from Viceroy Hardinge to Walter Lawrence 1915, 8 June; Report from Walter Lawrence to Kitchener 1915, 21 July). The different strategies were in September 1915 deemed as fairly successful. The Viceroy informed Walter Lawrence that "the attitude of the men has partly changed" and the Sikhs especially were satisfied while the Muslims were still rather "sulky," probably because some had been influenced by "the Jehad feeling" (Letter from Viceroy Hardinge to Walter Lawrence 1915, 14 September).

Representatives of the Indian Soldiers' Fund conducted regular field trips to assess the operative work and requirements of the hospitals for the Indian sick and wounded, and collected information about the expressed needs of the soldiers at the front. When Walter Lawrence returned from field visits to the hospitals at the front in early January 1915, he reported about the need for religious literature and suggested the Fund equip the various hospitals for Indian wounded with libraries and recreation rooms in which books could be stored (Letters from officers of the Indian Soldiers' Fund 1914–1915). He proposed that these should store books such as the Qur'an, as well as games and stationery. This was discussed during a meeting with the committee of the Fund in January 1915 when the chairman John P. Hewett also pointed out the difficulty of finding such literature in England. He had therefore been in contact with the India Office, the St. John Ambulance Association in India, and Sirdar Jogendra Singh, a member of the Viceroy's Executive Council in India (Meeting of the General Committee 1915, 6 January).

Military authorities made use of letters copied by the military censor between 1914 and 1918 in order to evaluate the Indian soldiers' morale, loyalty, and needs during the war. A special Indian Base Post Office was set up first in Rouen and later in Boulogne to check incoming and outgoing mails in the Indian languages and the censor provided regular reports with extracts from the soldiers' letters translated into English. Since writing letters was the primary means of communication with family, friends, and colleagues in India and Europe, this vast material included various issues related to their appalling conditions at the front, the situation at home in India, and reflections on life and people in Europe (see Omissi 1999, 2007; Vankoski 1995). The letters also voiced concerns about religion, such as worries about losing their faith when staying in a non-Muslim context, and wishes for religious scriptures, practices, and artifacts.

Among the different religious favours which Muslim soldiers asked for from relatives and friends in India were visits to mosques and Sufi shrines (see Letter from Palak Khan to Zawar Khan 2015, 23 September), readings of particular prayers (see Letter from Abdullah Khan to Haidar Shah 1915, 19 September), and recitations from the Qur'an for protection and victory in the war (see Letter from Ali Khan to Pawam Ali 1915, May; Letter from an Oraksai Pathan to a friend 1915, 26 February). The letters illustrate the importance of the Qur'an among the soldiers and especially how those stationed at the front requested their colleagues remitted to Indian military hospitals and convalescent centers in England to procure and send copies of the scripture. A soldier in the infantry regiment 40th Pathans serving at the front wrote to friend of the same regiment who was hospitalized in England:

> Please make enquires very carefully about the matter which I have written below. By all means get me a Holy Qur'an of the same pattern as your own, even if it costs ten rupees, and send it to me. You can send it by the hand of any man who is coming to the front or by parcel post. [...] Make every effort to get me a Holy Qur'an. Never mind the price; I will pay it. (Letter from unknown Pathan to Sepoy Bahram Khan 1915, 31 October)

Another soldier, reported to be a "Pathan or Punjabi Musalman [Muslim]" at Lady Hardinge Hospital in Brockenhurst, informed a friend in the 40th Pathans that he had been able to obtain a Qur'an as a gift:

> The best thing here, in my judgment, is that which I have got for you both, my brothers, and that is the Holy Qur'an, like (the one that) Segar Sahib gave to Subedar Ghulam Ali. If I return to the regiment or go home, this thing is yours. (Letter from Rahm Ali Khan to Choudhri Khan 1915, 30 December)

Copies of the Qur'an were available in London and the soldiers on duty or convalescing at various places in England were able to send for these and forward them to their colleagues stationed in mainland Europe (see for example Letter from Sohbat Khan to Sabar Amin 1915, 28 October). As a soldier hospitalized in Brighton wrote to a friend in France:

> Tell Mehr Gul that Sher Muhammad has written to me to say that he is sending him a Holy Qur'an. But it is difficult (to keep) the Holy Qur'an in the trenches, because it is usually raining. [...] It is difficult to say the prescribed prayers in the trenches. I will send for a Holy Qur'an, and will leave one with Juma Khan for you. If you live, it will be useful at home. [...]When I get well, I will send (for the Qur'an) and despatch [sic] it to you. They can be got in London not in Brighton. (Letter from Naik Sher Muhammed Khan to Sepoy Khan Badshah 1915, 11 November)

Some of the soldiers seem to have made severe efforts to assist their friends. A Pathan of the Afridi tribe at Kitchener Indian Hospital in Brighton notified a friend in France: "I have sent you twelve Qur'ans" and two of them were for other people but "the rest you can yourself make use of" (Letter from Sub. Mir Dast to Jem. Yar Guhlam 1915, 14 October). The same individual wrote to another colleague in the 40th Pathans, confirming that he had sent twenty-four copies of the Qur'an to "your company, No. 7" in two parcels (Letter from Sub. Mir Dast to Sepoy Abdul Rahim 1915, 16 October). Another Pathan at the Indian Military Depot in Milford likewise informed a colleague at the front: "I have had your two copies of the Holy Qur'an done up in leather and am sending them to you today by post. Let me know as soon as they reach you" (Letter from Talib Husain to Abuzar Khan 1915, 24 September). However, not all soldiers were able to satisfy these requests and wrote about their difficulties in obtaining scriptures (see for example Letter from Maulvi Sarir Din to Razi Khan 1915, 2 October). A Punjabi Muslim soldier at the Pavilion Hospital in Brighton wrote to a friend at the Indian Convalescent Home in Boulogne:

> As to your request to send you a copy of the Qur'an, I have already written and told you that I cannot get one here. What is the use of repeating it? If I could get one here, I would send it. You say the Qur'an can be got in London, but London is 52 miles from here and we do not go there. (Letter from Khadim Ali to Jabar Khan 1915, 17 October)

The letters further indicate an interest in small portable Qur'ans and the soldiers' awareness of the availability of these books at different locations. A

Punjabi Muslim serving at the front in France requested a doctor at the Pavilion Hospital in Brighton to obtain a copy for him in London:

> I have a request to make. Please send me a Holy Qur'an – a very small one,
> such as can be had in London. It will be very kind of you. (I want) a Holy
> Qur'an which is kept like a locket—that is a very small one. (Letter from
> Shah Nawaz Khan to Doctor Sahib Khan 1915, 22 October)

Another Punjabi Muslim in France requested a friend in India to send a
pocket Qur'an together with the copies of *Ganj-ul-Arsh*, that is, a *du'a* or
prayer for protection against enemies (see for example Gardet 2012):

> Please buy and send me a small Qur'an which will go into the pocket together
> with the Ganj-ul-Arsh. Send them by parcel post without payment. I will
> regard this as a great kindness on your part. I used to say my prayers at the
> proper times, but somebody took away my Ganj-ul-Arsh and left me empty.
> Please send me these things quickly. (Letter from Firoz Khan to Jem. Said
> Muhammad Khan 1915, 13 October)

Similarly, a soldier of the Dehra Dun Brigade wrote to a friend stationed in
Egypt and asked him to acquire a scripture that seems to have been in miniature size: "My dear friend, do send me a little Koran, printed in Egypt which
can go inside a little box, the sort of thing that I can keep in my pocket. Mind
you send this" (Letter from Said Ali to Faqir Khan 1915, 5 October).

Furthermore, the voiced religious needs in the soldiers' letters were not
restricted to requests for books with the complete text of the Qur'an but also
included specific excerpts and chapters from the scripture. As a Pathan at
Kitchener Indian Hospital in Brighton wrote to a friend in Jalandhar (India):

> I have a request to make. You remember the five SURAS (chapters of the
> Qur'an) which I had in our mosque, and of which, when I came away, I asked
> you to take care. If you still have them please make a parcel of those five Suras
> and of another which is a little shorter than they are and send them to me
> here. For I am in great need of them. That will be very kind of you. Whatever
> you will spend on this you can take from my pay. I am in great need. (Letter
> from Akbar Khan to Hav. Yakub Khan 1915, 22 September)

The soldiers also contacted various persons and shrines at home for religious
artifacts. A preference among the religious objects seems to have been various
protective amulets (*tawiz*), some of which may have included quotes from
the Qur'an (see Letter from a friend to Shah Jahan Khan 1915, 12 September). A Punjabi Muslim at the front, for instance, wrote directly to Pir Mehr
Ali Shah, a Sufi master of the Chishti order in Golra near Rawalpindi, for a
personal letter and an amulet with a promise to serve the *pir* if he returned
safely home (Letter from Waris Khan to Pir Sahib Mehr Ali Shah 1915, 20
September). Another Punjabi soldier requested the *pir* Lal Badshah in Jhelum
to "[b]e constant in prayer for me and wrap up an amulet of some kind in

writing paper and send it to me" (Letter from Bakhsh Khan to Pir Sahib Lal Badshah 1915, 4 October). The correspondences suggest that the senders of the letters attributed these amulets with supernatural powers. In a letter to a friend in India a Punjabi Muslim wrote from Brighton about another soldier who had been hospitalized and lost his *tawiz*. Because of this, he had "begun to be possessed and subject to seizure at intervals" (Letter from Nizam-ud-Din to a friend 1915, 28 April).

Following the interceptions of these requests, the British military authorities, charities such as the Indian Soldiers' Fund, and various individuals in India and Britain made several efforts to satisfy the religious needs of the Indian Muslim soldiers at hospitals in England and France by procuring and distributing Qur'ans, including scriptures in miniature size.

Procuring and distributing Qur'ans

From the beginning the Indian Soldiers' Fund cooperated with several individuals, charities, and governmental authorities in Britain and India to gain assistance with acquisitions and purchases of articles that were not procurable in Europe, as well as with the transfer and shipping of gifts given by different prominent people in India. Regarding religious comforts for the soldiers, one of the challenges for the Fund was access to religious literature in Britain. For this reason, the Fund early on involved the London Moslem League and especially Ameer Ali who had founded the league in 1908 and became its president (Visram 2016, 99; *Wellington Journal* 1908, 9 May). Originally from the Indian state of Oudh and with a background as a judge of the court in Calcutta, Ameer Ali settled in England in the early twentieth century and became a prominent political leader and voice for the British Muslim community. As well as playing an important role for mosques in and around London, he was the first Indian to sit as a member of the Judicial Committee of the Privy Council and received an honorary doctoral degree in law at Cambridge (*East Anglian Daily Times* 1909, 10 December; *Cambridge Independent Press* 1910, 17 June). When the Indian Soldiers' Fund was in need of assistance he personally aided with purchases.

In March 1915 Ameer Ali sent Walter Lawrence a list showing the availability and prices of miniature copies of the Qur'an. He informed him that Luzac & Co, an Oriental bookseller and publisher located opposite the British Museum, had "miniature Korans bound in leather in gilt cases at 2/- [shilling] each, in white metal case at 1/3 [one shilling and three pennies] each, in white metal case bound in paper 10d [pennies] each" (Letter from Ameer Ali to Walter Lawrence 1915, 23 March). On request, the bookseller sent copies of the miniature volumes to the Fund for examination but they decided not to place an order. As John P. Hewett explained in a letter to Walter Lawrence, "[w]e came to the conclusion that the print is so very diminutive that it was not a good business to purchase them, and I personally do not feel at all satisfied that the whole of the Qur'an is reprinted in these miniature volumes." Instead the Fund acquired all the "reasonable sized Qur'ans" in stock with Luzac & Co (Letter from J. P. Hewett to Walter Lawrence 1915, 26 March).

During the first six months of the Fund, from October 1914 to the end of March 1915, 200 copies of the Qur'an were purchased in London and forty or fifty more copies were procured from the library of the India Office (*Report of the First Six Months' Work* 1914–1915, 11). The General Committee of the Fund was informed in February 1915 that 203 of these Qur'ans had been supplied to different hospitals but no more copies were available in England. Consequently, the Fund contacted Pardey Lukis, the director general of the Indian Medical Service and the chairman of the St. John Ambulance Association in Simla, who was sending 200 additional copies from India with consent from the Viceroy and had been asked to send more (Meeting of the General Committee 1915, 17 February; Letter from J. P. Hewett to Pardey Lukis 1915, 5 February; 1915, 18 February; Telegram from the Viceroy 1915, 30 January).

Even if the members of the Indian Soldiers' Fund had strong support from the British government in India, they were confronted with different opinions and considerations as to whether it was proper to submit religious scriptures and artifacts to the Indian soldiers. In a letter to Walter Lawrence in April 1915, John P. Hewett wrote that a Mr. Harley had visited the Fund's office and expressed his aversion to the sending of copies of the Qur'an and Guru Granth Sahib to him in the field. Hewett confirmed that the demand for religious books was indeed enormous and the Fund had received a large supply from India. But, as he continued, "I am not sure whether we should go too far in supplying them, as the native of India, if he gets too religiously inclined, is apt to become a bit sulky" (Letter from J. P. Hewett to Walter Lawrence 1915, 22 April).

Colonel Strachey at the India Office expressed a contrary position to that of Hewett when he reported in August 1915 that the censor of Indian mails in Boulogne had taken notice of a letter from a Sikh soldier in France who had expressed that he received plenty of "everything" except for religious symbols and, therefore, was forced to relax his religious obligations. Although the letter concerned a Sikh, Strachey suggested a larger distribution of religious items, and especially literature, for all in the Indian ranks based on the following statement from Captain Evelyn Berkeley Howell, the chief censor of Indian mails:

> It is suggested that steps might be taken to expend more of the money collected for the Indian Soldiers' Fund on things to which the Indian soldier attaches reli-

gious importance, and less on personal comforts and indulgences. The Indian soldiers, like most Orientals, value the minute observation of their religions far above
anything else, and a few rupees expended on Qur'ans, extracts from the Granth,
Kirpans, Brahmanical threads and the like would give more pleasure than a great
deal of sweetmeats and tobacco. Expert advice, however, would of course be necessary in selecting such objects, and in making up the parcels. (Indian Mail Censor 1915, 9 August; Meeting of the General Committee 1915, 18 August)

In response to this, John P. Hewett provided the India Office with a detailed
description of all the measures that had already been taken by the Fund to
satisfy the religious needs of the soldiers, including the dispatch of scriptures
and symbols, and also pointed out the responsibility of officers to request
comforts for the soldiers (Letter from J. P. Hewett to Colonel Strachey 1915,
27 August).

As a general rule throughout the war, the Fund consulted and followed the
instructions of the officers responsible for the Indian forces, and especially the
recommendations and orders of James Willcocks, the Lieutenant General for
the Indian Corps in France, with whom they stayed in contact through tele-
grams (Meeting of the General Committee 1915, 18 August). When Indian
medical officers at the hospitals in Brighton in July 1915 discussed the question whether Muslim patients should be allowed to fast during the month
of Ramadan, for example, Walter Lawrence initially consulted Aga Khan in
India, the Imam of the Nizari Ismaili community and one of the founders of the All India Muslim League, but eventually decided to follow James
Willcocks' example, who had made arrangements and provided the Muslim
soldiers at the front with a special rest period during Ramadan based on
an order from the War Office regarding the observance in England (Report
from Walter Lawrence to Kitchener 1915, 21 July). Consequently, the hospitals let the Muslim soldiers observe Ramadan. At Kitchener Indian Hospital,
for instance, a committee of Muslim officers decided which patients were fit
enough to fast and between sunset and sunrise gave cooked rations to those
who were fasting (*A Report on Kitchener Indian Hospital Brighton* 1915).

Following Willcocks' advice, the Fund supplied religious books only to
hospital institutions and depots "where they could be suitably housed, so as
to avoid the possibility of injury through their being left about uncared for by
the men at the front." Willcocks stated in April 1915 that he was unwilling to
present any bound volume of a religious nature to the men at the front since
they "could not be readily scrapped" (Meeting of the General Committee
1915, 18 August). Although the Fund entered into different types of cooperation with other war funds, charities, and stores, it carefully protected the
distribution of articles in order to not hurt any religious feelings. When supply systems were discussed in October 1915, Hewett emphasized the impor-

tance for the Fund to maintain control and prevent incidents of ignorance, giving as an example the distribution of toothbrushes made of pig bristles to Muslim soldiers which subsequently created rumors about religious offenses and mistreatment (Meeting of the General Committee 1915, 20 October).

The initial hesitancy to acquire miniature editions of the Qur'an due to the diminutive print also transformed when it became known that the tiny scriptures were appreciated by Muslim soldiers as talismans to bring good luck and avert harm (*Second Report of the Indian Soldiers' Fund* 1915, 23). During a meeting in August 1915, the General Committee of the Fund approved the expenditure of one pound, eleven shillings and four pence for "40 miniature Qur'ans in lockets for the men at the Indian Convalescent Home, Barton, New Milton." The officer in command of the Convalescent Home had requested books especially for celebration of the *Id al-Fitr* and Ameer Ali at the Moslem League had sent the copies termed "lockets." As the General Committee concluded, "...though these miniature Qur'ans were not quite what had been asked for, they had been greatly appreciated by the men" (Meeting of the General Committee 1915, 18 August; *The Graphic* 1915, 27 August). In the subsequent months the Fund therefore purchased more miniature copies. The second report of the Indian Soldiers' Fund informed that between April and November 1915 the Fund had purchased 440 miniature Qur'ans of which all were distributed to the hospitals. An additional number of these "lockets" had been presented by unnamed "private Indians" (*Second Report of the Indian Soldiers' Fund* 1915, 23, 35–36). The third report similarly stated that between November 1915 and November 1916 the Fund had bought 156 miniature Qur'ans, of which 150 were distributed to hospitals and 6 to the front (*Third Report of the Indian Soldiers' Fund* 1915–1916, 26–27). The Fund noted that the small editions were procurable in England at a very low cost and were enclosed in metal cases to form lockets. Since the print was miniscule the lockets had small magnifying glasses for legibility (*Second Report of the Indian Soldiers' Fund* 1915, 23). The reports did not name the producer of the books but the description seems to indicate that these were miniature Qur'ans from David Bryce & Son in Glasgow.

Many of the miniature editions of the Qur'an purchased for the soldiers by the Fund were distributed through the Ladies' Committee at the Indian Gift House in Brighton. The Gift House started in December 1914 to cope with the numerous gifts for the war hospitals and was formed by reputable ladies with the Countess of Chichester as the president. They secured a small house in Brighton and regularly received gifts and comforts from different societies and funds, including the Indian Soldiers' Fund, which were packed and marked before being dispatched to the soldiers. In January 1916 the Indian Soldiers' Fund sent 100 miniature Qur'ans to the Ladies' Committee for the Indian troops at the general hospitals (John Stanley's vouchers 1916, 26 January). In December 1916 it was further recorded that during the previous month the Fund had purchased an additional 100 miniature Qur'ans in cases with yellow edges from the firm Luzac & Co., which were distributed to the Indian Gift House (Order book No. 1 1916, 29 December). An overview of the work of the Ladies' Committee between December 1914 and December 1916 specified that the Gift House had received in total forty-eight Qur'ans and 350 miniature editions from the Indian Soldiers' Fund. All of the larger copies were distributed to the Indian General Pavilion Hospital (30) and the Kitchener Indian Hospital (18) in Brighton, while twenty-six miniature Qur'ans were given to the Pavilion and 224 to Kitchener (Report of the Ladies' Committee 1916). Apparently, the latter hospital had assumed the practice of distributing miniature Qur'ans to the Muslim soldiers who returned to military duties after their stay in hospital. In a report by Bruce Seton of the Indian Medical Service it was admitted that the Kitchener Indian Hospital could not fulfill all the religious needs of the soldiers, such as constructing a permanent building of a mosque, but a temporary place of worship was erected and "[t]hrough the generosity of the Indian Soldiers' Fund and many private donors in India, religious works in the vernacular, Hindu and Musulman [Muslim,] were distributed among patients and personnel and all Musulmans [Muslims] returning to the Front were given miniature Korans" (*A Report on Kitchener Indian Hospital Brighton* 1915, 10). It appears the soldiers become aware of these religious gifts and also sent them to their friends at the front, even if some had to wait for their copies. As a soldier at the Kitchener Indian Hospital wrote to a friend in France:

> You wrote and said that small copies of the Holy Qur'an would be supplied to this hospital. My brother, as yet none has been given. I will do my best, but I have not yet got one myself. What can I do? If they are given out I will send you one. (Letter from Ashraf Khan to Mira Khan 1915, 10 October)

Religious gifts from India

As the news about harsh conditions and large casualties at the front spread during the fall of 1914, people in India donated an enormous amount of clothes, comforts, and cash in support of the Indian soldiers, while authorities and various charities and war funds made concerted efforts to convey comforts and gifts to the units at the front and the wounded at war hospitals (see for example: Pati 1996; Authority of the Government of India 1923). In acts of loyalty to the British Crown, the native Indian rulers responded to King George's request in the fall of 1914 to contribute to the imperial war effort (*India and the War* 1915, 39–41). The governmental statistics for Punjab alone reported that cash contributions to war funds and charities in the British districts during the war amounted to 5,171,328 rupees, while the Indian native states in Punjab donated 16,943,173 rupees.[3] The war loans given by the British districts and the Indian states in Punjab were 26,027,817 rupees (Leigh 1922, 79, 81–82). The donations included a large amount of material gifts that were especially suited to the soldiers' religious and caste traditions. The state of Patiala in Punjab, for example, donated a large set of religious symbols for the Sikhs, including 10,919 combs (*kangha*s), 13,200 undergarments (*kaccheras*), 5,219 small swords (*kirpans*) and 2,000 religious books (*Patiala and the Great War* 1923, 67). The neighboring state of Malerkotla sent 100 copies of "the Sacred Books of the Muhammadans and Sikhs" (Leigh 1922, 95). The Maharani Nundkanvarba of Bhavnagar provided 345 copies of the Bhagavad Gita, 300 copies of Ramayana, and 5,000 bead rosaries for the Hindu soldiers as well as 1,500 "Brahmanical threads" (*janeu*) to high caste Hindus. The Indian Soldiers' Fund was an important mediator for many gifts and received aid from the St. John Ambulance Association in Simla in response to requests to find clothes and comforts in India that were not procurable in Europe (*Report of the First Six Months' Work* 1914–1915, 7).

The Fund had already noted during the first part of 1915 that an additional supply of Qur'ans from England was not required because of the many gifts that were received from India (Letter from J. P. Hewett to Walter Lawrence 1915, 26 March). An important donor of religious literature for the sick and wounded Muslim soldiers was Sultan Kaikhusrau Jahan, who ruled the princely state of Bhopal in central India and went under the name Her Highness the Begum of Bhopal. During the nineteenth century the state of Bhopal had established its own printing press to promote education. Except for newspapers and literature, the press also published editions of the Qur'an and became well known among scholars for printing with great care and accuracy (Her Highness Nawab Sultan Jehan Begum 1926, 89–90). In March 1915 the Indian Soldiers' Fund reported that "a very large and indeed almost embarrassing supply of copies of the 'Qur'an' has been received. 1,000 volumes have already been delivered or are in course of delivery" along with other religious books (*Report of the First Six Months' Work* 1914–1915, 11–12, 19). The subsequent reports indicated that the state of Bhopal had presented 900 copies of the Qur'an and 1,400 Muslim tracts that were sent by different shipments (Meeting of the General Committee 1915, 4 April; *Second Report of the Indian Soldiers' Fund* 1915, 22; Letter from J. P. Hewett

---

3. The war funds included in this statistic were Punjab Aeroplane Fund, Imperial Indian Relief Fund, Hospitals, Ambulance and Red Cross Fund, Comforts Funds, Recruiting Funds, and "Other Funds." The Indian states were Patiala, Bahawalpur, Jind, Nabha, Kapurthala, Mandi, Sirmur, Faridkot, Chamba, Suket, Kalsia, Pataudi, Lohari, and Dujana (Leigh 1922, 79).

to Colonel Strachey 1915, 27 August). The consignment of these books illustrates how Indian nobility was able to put pressure on British authorities in a war situation by referring to religious sentiments while simultaneously displaying loyalty to the colonial power. In the case of the Begum of Bhopal, the donation of religious books for soldiers in the British forces seems to have functioned as an expression of loyalty at a time when Ottoman Turkey joined the war on the side of the central powers and Muslims in India were perceived to have a more "questionable loyalty" (see for example: Morton Jack 2006, 353; Omissi 1994, 120 ff.; Roy 2011, 17).[4]

In correspondence with the St. John Ambulance Association in India in early 1915, the Begum of Bhopal advised that she was arranging to send 500 Qur'ans to the War Gifts Depots in Bombay for the sick and wounded Muslims in Europe. By referring to "the extreme reverence in which the Holy Koran is held by Mussalmans [Muslims]" and emphasizing "that the entire Mussalman community will highly appreciate the thoughtful efforts of your Association to provide for the spiritual as well as the bodily needs of our gallant troops," she requested that three conditions were to be fulfilled when dispatching the books: Firstly, none of the copies sent were to be issued to men leaving hospitals for the front since she feared that they may not be able to take care of the books if wounded in action. Secondly, the copies were not to be sent with other packages but with either a Muslim or a European officer going to England who "should take these copies of the Koran with him with great care and attention." Thirdly, she informed that she would arrange to have the copies properly packed in India and asked the St. John Ambulance Association to send instructions for how the books were to be received on arrival in England. A specific wish was to not have the boxes containing the Qur'ans marked with signs for the Red Cross (Letter from Sultan Jahan of Bhopal to Major R.J. Blackhan 1915, 19 January).

In response to these requests, the St. John Ambulance Association informed the Army Department in Delhi and the Indian Soldiers' Fund that the 500 Qur'ans should be sent to Britain by an early convoy and in the charge of an officer (Letter from Pardey Lukis to J. P. Hewett 1915, 4 February; Letter

---

4. The Berlin "Lokalanzeiger" claimed in October 1914 that the Begum was delegated by the Indian Muslims to proceed to Constantinople for the purpose of informing the Caliph of "the real feeling" prevailing among the Muslims in India. Upon hearing this, the British authorities arrested the princess and her son (*Daily Record* 1914, 21 October). On November 6, 1914, the Begum addressed her people in the public durbar and stated that she would remain loyal to the treaties, which were binding upon her, not only as a ruling chief under the protection of the British government, "but also as a follower of Islam, which enjoined upon all its followers the sanctity of a promise" (*Dundee Courier* 1914, 12 November).

from Pardey Lukis to the Secretary to the Government of India 1915, 27 January). The government of India further contacted the India Office in London to advise that "an Army Despatch [*sic*]" of the Qur'an would be transmitted in due course (Letter from Major Spencer to the Under Secretary of State for India 1915, 8 February). Together these different bodies arranged for a special consignment that would comply with the conditions of the Begum of Bhopal. At first the books were to be sent by the hospital ship *Loyalty* with the medical officer in charge of the vessel, Major J. W. Watson, who was given responsibility to take personal care of the parcels and deliver them to the India Office (Letter from Pardey Lukis to the Secretary to the Government of India 1915, 27 January; Letter from P.G. Agnew to the Assistant Military Secretary 1915, 15 March).[5] The Viceroy Lord Hardinge later advised that the Qur'ans had instead been sent by hired transport with the ship *Neuralia* on March 4 and were under the personal care of Captain Stack from the Royal Army Medical Corps who would hand them over them to P.D. Agnew, the secretary of the Indian Soldiers' Fund (Telegram for the Viceroy 1915, 6 March). According to the invoices sent through the shipping firm Musgrave & Co. in London, the parcel included four cases (Letter from P.D. Agnew to the Under Secretary of State of India 1915, 22 March).

On the British side the Fund made arrangements for the proper reception and distribution of the Qur'ans in consultation with Ameer Ali and the Moslem League in London (Letter from P.D. Agnew to the Assistant Military Secretary 1915, 15 March). When the scriptures arrived, the secretary of the League and the *maulvi* of the mosque at Woking housed them in the mosque and assisted with packing and distribution under the instructions of the Fund (Meeting of the General Committee 1915, 4 April; 1915, 18 August). In compliance with the requests of the Begum of Bhopal and on the advice of James Willcocks, the volumes were dispatched to various war hospitals and depots "where they could be suitably housed, so as to avoid the possibility of injury through their being left about uncared for by the men at the front" (Letter from J. P. Hewett to Colonel Strachey 1915, 27 August). Meanwhile, the press in India and Britain circulated news to the public about the impressive royal gifts of Qur'ans that were distributed under special arrangement in order to pay due religious respect (see for example: *Western Mail* 1915, 12 April; *Liverpool Daily Post* 1915, 12 April). The scriptural gifts for Muslim soldiers were even mentioned in the House of Commons (Sastri 1916, xlii-xliv).

---

5. Indian chiefs provided the hospital ship *Loyalty* for the use of returning Indian invalid soldiers. The Begum of Bhopal, together with the Maharaja of Gwalior, covered the expense of converting the ship into a hospital with 500 beds (see *Surrey Mirror* 1915, 12 January; *Judicial and Public Department Files* 1914).

Another contribution from India that received attention was the donation from Mirza Hairat Ali, the editor of the Urdu paper *Curzon Gazette* in Delhi, who sent 500 "handsome and useful" Qur'ans as well as 100 "amulets" (*Third Report of the Indian Soldiers' Fund* 1915–1916, 11). Since the Fund had received many Qur'ans, the new books were initially kept in stock for "issue as required" and in September 1916 they were sent to Muslim soldiers serving in the Mountain Batteries in Salonika (*Second Report of the Indian Soldiers' Fund* 1915, 22). Another donation that emanated from an interest in the miniature Qur'ans published by David Bryce in Glasgow and articulated curiosity for the reception of the books came from Alfred Ezra. He belonged to the renowned Jewish Sassoon family in Calcutta and had moved to England in 1912. With an interest in aviculture and ornithology, he became a member of and worked for the London Zoological Society (Delacour 1956, 135–136). The Ezra family seems to have been involved in different charitable work during the war. Alfred Ezra's sister, Mrs. Rachel Elliot, for instance, asked for permission to visit the wounded Indians at the Pavilion Hospital in Brighton, which was approved since she had "discretion" and spoke Urdu well (General correspondence 1914–1916).

In the fall of 1915 Alfred Ezra visited the Indian hospitals in England and procured at least 3,000 miniature Qur'ans and a similar number of copies of the Bhagavad Gita that were given to Muslim and Hindu soldiers at hospitals through the assistance of the Indian Soldier's Fund (Report from Walter Lawrence to the Secretary of State for War 1916, 8 March). Bryce's books had attracted Ezra's attention when he read a review about the tiny Qur'ans in a London paper and decided to purchase copies for the soldiers (*Publishers' Circular and Booksellers' Record* 1915, 584). As a newspaper reported, they were "eagerly asked for by the Indian soldiers as they come in batches from the Glasgow firm which is kept well employed producing them" (*The Sphere* 1915, 30 October). The books were presented as small amulets to be worn:

> Each of these Scriptures is an inch long, three-quarters of an inch broad, and one-third of an inch deep. They are enclosed in small metal cases glazed in front, and with ring attached to enable them to be worn on the person. (*Edinburgh Evening* 1915, 8 October)

Other newspapers reported with similar fascination the appearance of the small books and the Indian soldiers' expressed gratitude to Ezra for supplying them for use in hospitals (see for example: *Birmingham Daily Post* 1915, 29 December; *Evening Express* 1915, 13 October*)*. When the books had been distributed Ezra wrote a letter addressed to David Bryce in Glasgow to communicate how especially the Qur'ans were received by the soldiers in ritual practices:

You will be pleased to hear that the mite "Korans" have been a huge success with our Mohammedan soldiers, and nothing I have given the men has been appreciated half so much as these exquisite little books. On receiving one, the man will stand up, put the book over his head and touch each eye with it, and then kiss the book with reverence. They nearly all wear them round their necks, and say that this protects them from all harm. I am sure it must be most gratifying to you to hear that your books have been so much appreciated. Yours faithfully, Alfred Ezra. (*Publishers' Circular and Booksellers' Record* 1915, 584; *The Moslem World* 1916, 204)

The letter was published in full in magazines to illustrate how the Qur'ans functioned as amulets for the sick and wounded in "Oriental" practices. It is perhaps noteworthy that during the same period the British press printed anecdotes telling about the distribution of Qur'ans to Turkish soldiers as gifts from the Ottoman Sultan to "improve the morale" after the terrible losses at Gallipoli and how the wounded soldiers would hang the Qur'ans around body parts that were hurt and in pain (for example: *Birmingham Daily Post* 1915, 26 October; *The Burnley News* 1915, 11 September; *The Liverpool Echo* 1915, 10 September).

Concluding remarks

It is challenging to acquire first-hand sources that can reveal how the Indian Muslim soldiers responded to these religious gifts and in particular how they used the small and large versions of the Qur'an in various religious practices during the war. The Indian Soldiers' Fund regularly received letters of thanks from officers of the Indian units, and a few short excerpts of these were rendered in the reports, but generally the gratitude for gifts was brief and sometimes included comments about how the religious items had boosted the soldiers' "morale" (see for example: *Fifth Report of the Indian Soldiers' Fund* 1918–1919, 17–19; Letter from James Willcocks to Headquarters Indian Corps 1915, 4 April). These notes, along with common presumptions that religion permeated the lives of Indian soldiers in more articulated ways, were also a part of underlying Orientalist and colonial perspectives. As the Fund explained in a report, "[h]is [the Indian soldier's] religion is very close to the heart of the Oriental, and the Indian Soldiers' Fund has always borne this fact in mind" (*Second Report of the Indian Soldiers' Fund* 1915, 21). The letters by the soldiers which went through the military censor seem to have voiced a wide spectrum of positions towards the religious provision by British authorities and charities—ranging from those who expressed a high appreciation for the arrangements to those who condemned the provision (see for example: Letter from Sabir Din to Hafiz Sadir Din 1915, 22 September; Letter from Gulbadin to Huzrat Shah 1915, 14 September). For instance, as a Pathan on the appreciative side wrote to his uncle in France: "While I was in Netley I was given a small printed Qur'an. I am reading it. It is the grace of God that I went to Netley from France (Letter from Raba-ud-Din to uncle 1915, 23 April).

The Koran in Little for the Indian Soldiers in the Field   A Case which Contains Either the Koran or the Bhagavad Gita   The Bhagavad Gita, or Divine Song of the Mahabharata

Figure 7.2: Photographs of the miniature books given to Indian soldiers by Alfred Ezra. Source: *The Sphere* 1915, 30 October. Photo: © Mary Evans Picture Library Ltd.

Several scholars have suggested that religion and the use of sacred books and amulets among soldiers in the First World War did not merely serve as ritual means for protection and consolation during the most challenging circumstances, but were also used as religious strategies to cope with suffering and fears and to maintain connections with the civil life beyond the trenches (see for example Van Osselaer 2014, 245). From the perspective of James W. Watts' theory about ritualization of texts along the semantic, the performative, and the iconic dimensions (Watts 2006), the provision, possession, and use of miniature Qur'ans as religious objects could certainly have played a significant role for the soldiers on different levels and would have attributed various performative functions believed to evoke powerful spiritual and material forces and effects on the soldiers. While the soldiers might have utilized the books for a variety of purposes—readings of the texts, as religious stimulus, as mobile amulets or talismans, as mementos of civil life, or perhaps as exquisite gifts and collectibles to bring home—the British and Indian acts of giving books also invested the material objects with strong iconic functions to represent religions, collective identities, and complex relationships. By means of the various efforts to procure and distribute Qur'ans for Muslim soldiers, the books traveled across seas and national borders through imperial and military networks, and created bonds between colonial authorities and the Indian subjects at a time when the British power was dependent on Indian loyalty and troops.

Acknowledgments

We are grateful to David Omissi at the University of Hull for guidance, the helpful staff at Asian and African Studies at the British Library, and Mr. Harpreet Singh for assistance with the collection of archival material. The work has been prepared with support from the Swedish Research Council (www. vr.se) under Grant 2014-956 and the Crafoord Foundation (www.crafoord. se) under Grant 20140550, and within the Centre for Concurrences in Colonial and Postcolonial Studies at Linnaeus University.

References

Primary sources

British Library, UK

A Report on Kitchener Indian Hospital Brighton by Col. Bruce Seton, I.M.S. 1915. Mss Eur F143/82.

General correspondence about matters relating to Indian hospitals in England, 1914–1916. Mss Eur F143/66.

Fifth Report of the Indian Soldier's Fund, for the period 1st January, 1918, to July, 1919. Mss Eur F120/10.

Indian Mail Censor, Indian Expeditionary Force (A), France. 1915, *Reports of the Censor of Indian Mails in France,* Volume 1, June 1915–August 1915, 9 August. IOR/L/MIL/5/825/4.

John Stanley's vouchers. 1916. 26 January. Mss Eur F120/84.

Judicial and Public Department Files. 1914. File 4031, The European War. IOR/L/PJ/6/1327.

Letter from an Oraksai Pathan (France) to a friend (India). 1915. *Reports of the Censor of Indian Mails in France,* Volume 1, December 1914–April 1915, 26 February. IOR/L/MIL/5/825/1.

Letter from Abdullah Khan (France) to Haidar Shah (Campbellpore). 1915. *Reports of the Censor of Indian Mails in France.* Volume 1, September 1915–October 1915, 19 September. IOR/L/MIL/5/825/6.

Letter from Akbar Khan (K.I.H., Brighton) to Hav. Yakub Khan (Jalandhar). 1915. *Reports of the Censor of Indian Mails in France.* Volume 1, September 1915–October 1915, 22 September. IOR/L/MIL/5/825/6.

Letter from Ali Khan (K.I.H., Brighton) to Pawam Ali (Rawalpindi). 1915. Copies of extracts from censored Indian mails, March–June, May. Mss Eur F143/83.

Letter from Ameer Ali to Walter Lawrence. 1915. 23 March. Mss Eur F143/67.

Letter from Ashraf Khan (K.I.H, Brighton) to Mira Khan (France). 1915. *Reports of the Censor of Indian Mails in France.* Volume 1, September 1915–October 1915, 10 October. IOR/L/MIL/5/825/6.

Letter from Bakhsh Khan (at the front) to Pir Sahib Lal Badshah (Jhelum). 1915. *Reports of the Censor of Indian Mails in France*, Volume 1, September 1915–October 1915, 4 October. IOR/L/MIL/5/825/6.

Letter from a friend (Paharpur) to Shah Jahan Khan (France). 1915. *Reports of the Censor of Indian Mails in France,* Volume 1, September 1915–October 1915, 12 September. IOR/L/MIL/5/825/6.

Letter from Firoz Khan (at the front) to Jem. Said Muhammad Khan (Jhelum). 1915. *Reports of the Censor of Indian Mails in France*. Volume 1, September 1915–October 1915, 13 October. IOR/L/MIL/5/825/7.

Letter from Gulbadin (France) to Huzrat Shah (Kohat). 1915. *Reports of the Censor of Indian Mails in France*, Volume 1 September 1915–October 1915, 14 September. IOR/L/MIL/5/825/6.

Letter from James Willcocks to Headquarters Indian Corps. 1915. 4 April. Mss Eur F120/15.

Letter from J. P. Hewett to Colonel Strachey, India Office. 1915. 27 August. IOR/L/MIL/7/17264.

Letter from J. P. Hewett to Pardey Lukis. 1915. 5 February. Mss Eur F120/16.

Letter from J. P. Hewett to Pardey Lukis. 1915. 18 February. Mss Eur F120/16.

Letter from J. P. Hewett to Walter Lawrence. 1915. 26 March. Mss Eur F143/67.

Letter from J. P. Hewett to Walter Lawrence. 1915. 6 April. Mss Eur 143/67.

Letter from J. P. Hewett to Walter Lawrence. 1915. 22 April. Mss Eur F143/67.

Letter from Khadim Ali (Pavilion Hospital, Brighton) to Jabar Khan (Indian Convalescent Home, Boulogne). 1915. *Reports of the Censor of Indian Mails in France*, Volume 1, October 1915–November 1915, 17 October. IOR/L/MIL/5/825/7.

Letter from Major Spencer to the Under Secretary of State for India, India Office. 1915, 8 February. IOR/L/MIL/7/17264.

Letter from Maulvi Sarir Din (K.I.H., Brighton) to Razi Khan (Marseilles). 1915. *Reports of the Censor of Indian Mails in France*, Volume 1, September 1915–October 1915, 2 October. IOR/L/MIL/5/825/6.

Letter from Naik Sher Muhammad Khan (Pavilion Hospital, Brighton) to Sepoy Khan Badshah (France). 1915. *Reports of the Censor of Indian Mails in France*, Volume 1, October 1915–November 1915, 11 November. IOR/L/MIL/5/825/7

Letter from Nizam-ud-Din (Brighton Pavilion) to a friend (Punjab). 1915. Copies of extracts from censored Indian mails, March–June 1915, 28 April. Mss Eur F143/83.

Letters from officers of the Indian Soldiers' Fund, subcommittee of the Order of St. John of Jerusalem, mainly about providing comforts for Indian hospitals, 1914–1915. Mss Eur F143/67.

Letter from Palak Khan (K.I.H., Brighton) to Zawar Khan (South Waziristan). 1915. *Reports of the Censor of Indian Mails in France.* Volume 1, September 1915–October 1915, 23 September. IOR/L/MIL/5/825/6.

Letter from Pardey Lukis to J. P. Hewett. 1914. 4 February. Mss Eur 120/16.

Letter from Pardey Lukis to the Secretary to the Government of India, Army Department. 27 January. IOR/L/MIL/7/17264.

Letter from P.D. Agnew to the Under Secretary of State of India. 1915. 22 March. IOR/L/MIL/7/17264.

Letter from P.D. Agnew to the Assistant Military Secretary, India Office. 1915. 15 March. IOR/L/MIL/7/17264.

Letter from Raba-ud-Din (hospital in England) to his uncle (France). 1915. *Reports of the Censor of Indian Mails in France*, Vol. 1, Apr 1915–May 1915, 23 April. IOR/L/MIL/5/825/3.

Letter from Rahm Ali Khan (Lady Hardinge Hospital, Brockenhurst) to Choudhri Khan. 1915. *Reports of the Censor of Indian Mails in France*, Volume 2, December 1915–Jan 1916, 30 December. IOR/L/MIL/5/826/1.

Letter from Sabir Din (K.I.H., Brighton) to Hafiz Sadir Din (at the front). 1915. *Reports of the Censor of Indian Mails in France.* Volume 1, September 1915–October 1915, 22 September. IOR/L/MIL/5/825/6.

Letter from Said Ali to Faqir Khan (Egypt). 1915. *Reports of the Censor of Indian Mails in France,* Volume 1, October 1915–November 1915, 5 October. IOR/L/MIL/5/825/7.

Letter from Shah Nawaz Khan (at the front) to Doctor Sahib Khan (Pavilion Hospital, Brighton). 1915. *Reports of the Censor of Indian Mails in France.* Volume 1, September 1915–October 1915, 22 October. IOR/L/MIL/5/825/7.

Letter from Sohbat Khan (K.I.H., Brighton) to Sabar Amin (Boulogne). 1915. *Reports of the Censor of Indian Mails in France.* Volume 1, September 1915–October 1915, 28 October. IOR/L/MIL/5/825/7.

Letter from Sub. Mir Dast (K.I.H., Brighton) to Jem Yar Guhlam (France). 1915. *Reports of the Censor of Indian Mails in France.* Volume 1, September 1915–October 1915, 14 October. IOR/L/MIL/5/825/6.

Letter from Sub. Mir Dast (K.I.H., Brighton) to Sepoy Abdul Rahim (France). 1915. *Reports of the Censor of Indian Mails in France.* Volume 1, October 1915–November 1915, 16 October. IOR/L/MIL/5/825/7.

Letter from Sultan Jahan of Bhopal to Major R.J. Blackhan, C.I.E., V.H.S. Joint Secretary, St. John Ambulance Association, Delhi. 1915. 19 January. IOR/L/MIL/7/17264.

Letter from Talib Husain (Ind. Mil. Depot, Milford) to Abuzar Khan (at the front), 1915. *Reports of the Censor of Indian Mails in France*, Volume 1, September 1915–Oct 1915, 24 September. IOR/L/MIL/5/825/6.

Letter from the Indian Soldiers' Fund to Walter Lawrence. 1915. 2 February. Mss Eur F143/67.

Letter from unknown Pathan (at the front) to Sepoy Bahram Khan (hospital in England). 1915. *Reports of the Censor of Indian Mails in France.* Volume 1, September1915–October 1915, 31 October. IOR/L/MIL/5/825/7.

Letter from Viceroy Hardinge to Walter Lawrence. 1915. 14 April. Mss Eur F143/73

Letter from Viceroy Hardinge to Walter Lawrence. 1915. 8 June. Mss Eur F143/73.

Letter from Viceroy Hardinge to Walter Lawrence. 1915. 14 September. Mss Eur F143/73.

Letter from Waris Khan (at the front) to Pir Sahib Mehr Ali Shah (Golra, Rawalpindi). 1915. *Reports of the Censor of Indian Mails in France.* Volume 1, September 1915–Oct 1915, 20 September. IOR/L/MIL/5/825/6.

Meeting of the General Committee. 1915. Proceeding of the General Committee, Book No. 1, Indian Soldiers' Fund. 6 January. Mss Eur F120/1.

Meeting of the General Committee. 1915. Proceedings of the General Committee, Book No. 1, Indian Soldiers' Fund. 17 February. Mss Eur F120/1.

Meeting of the General Committee. 1915. Proceedings of the General Committee, Book No. 1, Indian Soldiers' Fund. 3 March. Mss Eur F120/1.

Meeting of the General Committee. 4 April 1915. Proceedings of the General Committee, Book No. 1, Indian Soldiers' Fund. Mss Eur F120/1.

Meeting of the General Committee. 1915. Proceedings of the General Committee, Book No. 2, Indian Soldiers' Fund. 18 August. Mss Eur F120/2.

Meeting of the General Committee. 1915. Proceedings of the General Committee, Book No. 2, Indian Soldiers' Fund. 20 October. Mss Eur F120/2.

Order book No. 1. 1916. Indian Soldiers' Fund. 29 December. Mss Eur F120/46.

Report about the Pavilion Hospital by Major C.L. Williams. 1915–1916. Mss Eur F143/81.

Report from J. P. Hewett of the Convalescent Depots after his visit to the front in France. 1915. 27 July. Mss Eur F143/67.

Report from Walter Lawrence to Kitchener. 1915. 21 July. Mss Eur F143/65.

Report from Walter Lawrence to the Secretary of State for War, *Arrangements made for Indian Sick and Wounded in England and France.* 1916. 8 March. Mss Eur F143/65.

Report of the First Six Months' Work [Indian Soldiers' Fund], for the period 1st October, 1914, to 31st March, 1915. 1915. Mss Eur F120/6.

Report of the Ladies' Committee, report by Gertrude A. Brailey. 1916. Indian Gift House, Brighton. Mss Eur F143/81.

Second Report of the Indian Soldiers' Fund, for the period 1st April, 1915, to 20th November, 1915. 1915. Mss Eur F120/7.

Telegram for the Viceroy. 1915. 6 March. IOR/L/MIL/7/17264.

Telegram from the Viceroy. 1915. 30 January. Mss Eur F120/16.

The Lady Hardinge Hospital, report by Lt. Colonel F.F. Perry. 1916. Mss Eur F120/14.

Third Report of the Indian Soldiers' Fund, for the period 21st November, 1915, to 30th November, 1916. 1916. Mss Eur F120/8.

British Newspaper Archive, UK

Birmingham Daily Post. 1915. "A Mission Hospital in Turkey." 26 October.

Birmingham Daily Post. 1915. "The King and the Indian Army." 29 December.

The Burnley News. 1915. "Turks' Terrible Losses." 11 September.

Cambridge Independent Press. 1910. "Cambridge Moslim Association." 17 June.

Daily Record. 1914. "Begum of Bhopal." 21 October.

Dundee Courier. 1914. "Indian Chief's Loyalty and Devotion." 12 November.

East Anglian Daily Times. 1909. "Mr. Ameer Ali and the Privy Council." 10 December.

Edinburgh Evening. 1915. "Waistcoat Pocket Korans." 8 October.

Evening Express. 1915. "Waistcoat Pocket Korans." 13 October.

The Graphic. 1915. "His Majesty's Moslem Subjects in England: The Woking Gathering for the Eid-ul-Fatr Festival." 27 August.

Liverpool Daily Post. 1915. "From India's Coral Strand." 12 April.

The Liverpool Echo. 1915. "Koran Distributed to Raise Morale of Turks." 10 September.

Surrey Mirror. 1915. "The Hospital Ship 'Loyalty'." 12 January.

The Sphere. 1916. "Wounded Indians in France and England." Newspaper-cuttings relating to the First World War. 26 February.

The Sphere. 1915. "Sacred Books of the East for Indian Soldiers." 30 October.

Wellington Journal. 1908. "Indian Moslems." 9 May.

Western Mail. 1915. "Princely Gifts." 12 April.

Other

The Moslem World: A Quarterly Review of Current Events Literature, and Thought among Mohammedans and the Progress of Christian Missions in Moslem Lands. 1916. "The Koran at the Front for Moslem Troops." Volume VI. Number 1. London: The Nile Mission Press.

The Publishers' Circular and Booksellers' Record. 1915. "'The Koran' at the Front: A Glasgow Edition Welcome by Our Moslem Troops," Volume 103 (July to December). London: Office of thePublishers' Circular.

Secondary sources

Authority of the Government of India. 1923. *India's Contribution to the Great War*. Calcutta: Superintendent Government Printing.

Basu, Shrabani. 2015. *For King and Another Country: Indian Soldiers on the Western Front, 1914–1918*. New Delhi: Bloomsbury.

Delacour, J. 1956. "Obituaries: Alfred Ezra." *Ibis* 98: 135–136.

Gardet, L. 2012. "Du'ā'." In *Encyclopaedia of Islam*, edited by P. Bearman, Th. Bianquis, C.E. Bosworth, E. van Donzel, and W.P. Heinrichs. http://reference-works.brillonline.com/entries/encyclopaedia-of-islam-2/dua-COM_0195

Her Highness Nawab Sultan Jehan Begum. 1926. *Hayat-I-ShahJehan: Life of Her Highness the Late Nawab ShahJehan Begum of Bhopal, C.I., G.C.S.I.* (Translated by B. Ghosal). Bombay: The Times Press.

India and the War, with an Introduction by Lord Sydenham of Combe, 1915. London: Hodder and Stoughton.

Leigh, M.S. 1922. *The Punjab and the War*. Lahore: Superintendent, Government Printing.

Morton Jack, George. 2006. "The Indian Army on the Western Front, 1914–1915: A Portrait of Collaboration." *War in History* 13(3): 329–362. https://doi.org/10.1191/0968344506wh344oa

Omissi, David E. 2012. "Sikh Soldiers in Europe During the First World War, 1914–1918." In *Sikhs Across Borders: Transnational Practices of European Sikhs*, edited by Knut A. Jacobsen and Kristina Myrvold, 36–50. London: Bloomsbury.

———. 2007. "Europe Through Indian Eyes: Indian Soldiers Encounter England and France, 1914–1918." *English Historical Review* 122(496): 371–396. https://doi.org/10.1093/ehr/cem004

———. 1999. *Indian Voices of the Great War: Soldiers' Letters, 1914–1918*. Basingstoke: Macmillan. https://doi.org/10.1007/978-1-349-27283-9

———. 1998. "'Martial Races': Ethnicity and Security in Colonial India 1858–1939." In *Recruiting, Drafting and Enlisting: Two Sides of the Raising of Military Forces*, edited by Peter Karsten, 101–128. New York: Routledge.

———. 1994. *The Sepoy and the Raj: The Indian Army, 1860–1940*. London: Palgrave Macmillan. https://doi.org/10.1007/978-1-349-14768-7

Pati, Budheswar. 1996. *India and the First World War*. New Delhi: Atlantic.

Patiala and the Great War: A Brief History of the Services of the Premier Punjab States. 1923. London: Medici Society.

Robinson, Catherine. 2015. "Indian Soldiers on the Western Front: The Role of Religion in the Indian Army in the Great War." *Religions of South Asia* 9(1): 43–63. https://doi.org/10.1558/rosa.v9i1.23964Robinson, Catherine. 1996. "Neither East nor West: Some Aspects of Religion and Ritual in the Indian Army of the Raj." *Religion* 26: 37–47. https://doi.org/10.1006/reli.1996.0003

Roy, Kaushik. 2013. "Race and Recruitment in the Indian Army: 1880–1918." *Modern Asian Studies* 47(4): 1310–1347. https://doi.org/10.1017/S0026749X12000431

Roy, Kaushik, ed. 2011. *The Indian Army in the Two World Wars.* History of Warfare Number 70. Leiden: Brill.

Sastri, V.S. Srinivasa. 1916. *Self-Government for India under the British Flag.* Allahabad: Servants of Indian Society.

Tai-Yong, Tan. 2005. *The Garrison State: Military Government and Society in Colonial Punjab, 1849–1947.* London: Sage.

Van Osselaer, Tine. 2014. "Missing in Action? Religion in the Great War: A Historiographical Survey of Belgium and the Netherlands." *Trajecta* 23: 239–254.

Van Koski, S. 1995. "Letters Home, 1915–16: Punjabi Soldiers Reflect on War and Life in Europe and Their Meanings for Home and Self." *International Journal of Punjab Studies* 2(1): 43–63.

Visram, Rozina. 2016. *Ayahs, Lascars and Princes: The Story of Indians in Britain 1700–1947.* New York: Routledge.

The War Office. 1922. *Statistics of the Military Effort of the British Empire during the Great War.* London: His Majesty's Stationery Office.

Watts, James W. 2006. "The Three Dimensions of Scriptures." *Postscripts: The Journal of Sacred Texts and Contemporary Worlds* 2(2–3): 135–159.

8

Size Matters!
Miniature *Mushafs* and the Landscape of Affordances

Jonas Svensson

Jonas Svensson is a Professor in the Study of Religions at Linnaeus University. His current research focusses on integrating the cognitive science of religion into the academic study of Islam.

This chapter explores the question of why miniature copies of the Qur'an are desirable objects. That the answer to this question is by no means simple may be illustrated with an example taken from the large (over 110,000 members and approximately seven million posts in total) online UK registered, but in practice transnational Muslim discussion group, *ummah.com*. In a posting dated December 23, 2010, the user Ibrahim-70 wrote:

> So there I was in the most beautiful Islamic bookshop in the world [...] and I saw something similar to this [image of a miniature Qur'an] on the counter [...] yes thats [*sic*] right, a mini Qur'an. So I bought it not really knowing what I was going to do with it. Took the Qur'an out of its little covering case and there is a gold chain inside it. Is this for wearing around the neck? Is this permissible in Islam to wear a mini-Qur'an around the neck? I look forward to your replies inshallah. (Ibrahim-70 2010, December 23)

Most of the sixty-three responses, posted in the following three days, answered the specific question "Is this permissible?" in the negative. Several users wrote that it is *haram*, forbidden, to use the Qur'an as a talisman by hanging it around the neck, since Islam shuns amulets in general.[1]

Other commentators shared their personal experiences with miniature Qur'ans. Some claimed that people hang them in their cars. One person

---

1. The comments as well as the orginal posting by Ibrahim-70 are no longer publicly available on ummah.com. A printout of the whole conversation resides with the author. Comments cited were made by users Umm La'y (2010, December 23), straigthpath (2010, December 23), yassin' (2010, December 25), 1MuslimByChoice (2010, December 23), AvenueToPeace (2010, December 23), Abu.Rambo (2010, December 23) and Shamil (2010, December 23).

reported having seen people reading from miniatures in the Great Mosque in Makka and Madina. Yet another had put the miniature Qur'an on a shelf.

In a later posting Ibrahim-70 asked, "So what do I do with it then? It is too small to read, so where should I hang it, or stand it?" And then again, in a later post: "Its [*sic*] not for reading, and I have another 4 'normal' szie [*sic*] Qur'ans in the house already lol. I just bought it cause . . . ok, i dont know why I brought [*sic*] it (!) but it looked nice.

Why, indeed, did Ibrahim-70 buy a miniature version of the Qur'an (priced at £4.95), apparently without having any idea of what to do with it? This chapter will provide some avenues for possible answers to this question, and I will return to this specific case in the conclusion.

As Kristina Myrvold notes, Qur'ans, or *mushafs* (copies of the Qur'anic text in the form of codices),[2] have been produced in miniature since at least the seventeenth century (Myrvold this volume). Miniatures of the premodern era were rare hand-made luxury items, examples of exemplary craftsmanship, procured by rulers and dignitaries.

It was not, however, until the late nineteenth century that miniature *mushafs* became objects of mass production, more affordable and more available. Publishers, such as David Bryce, who started mass-producing miniature Qur'ans, evidently did so because they envisaged a global market for them (Myrvold this volume). This is an activity that continues up to this date.

Today, miniature *mushafs* still constitute seemingly marketable commodities, as is shown by the example at the beginning of this chapter. I have myself bought several at the pilgrimage site Eyüp in Istanbul. Here, they are marketed both in souvenir shops and by the street vendors, and in several different forms. Very small *mushafs* are enclosed in lockets with a complementary neck chain and other, larger ones, but still miniatures (four by five centimeters), are enclosed in plastic imitation-leather miniature cases. They are found alongside other religious paraphernalia, such as refrigerator magnets with the *basmala*, *miswak* toothbrushes (wooden sticks of a type claimed to have been used by Muhammad), bottled water from the sacred *zamzam* well in Makka, and digital rosaries in the form of an electronic finger counter. Miniature *mushafs* are found in the street stalls alongside clearly non-religious gadgets and children's toys (see Figure 8.1).

Anyone with access to the Internet can browse online Islamic gadget stores and discover miniature *mushafs* in the form of key chains, rear-view mirror and car door ornaments, lockets for necklaces, and other similar items.

---

2. I here use an anglicized plural form of *mushaf*. The Arabic word in singular is *mushaf*, and the correct plural form is *masahif*.

Figure 8.1: A photo taken of a street stall in Eyüp featuring toys and miniature Qur'ans. Photo by the author.

The very fact of their existence in the contemporary marketplace suggests that miniature *mushafs,* in different shapes and sizes, are desirable artifacts. The question is of course why? Referring mainly to the miniature *mushafs* produced by David Bryce in the late nineteenth century, Kristina Myrvold (this volume) suggests that those "served many different functions, as novelty items, precious gifts, pilgrimage souvenirs, religious amulets, portable scriptures, collectables, and so on, depending on the intentions and purposes of the users." In the following, I will expand on Myrvold's suggestion, and focus mainly on the apparent desirability of contemporary, mass-produced, and generally inexpensive miniature *mushafs.* I will not dwell upon the appeal of miniature *mushafs* as antique collectables or as examples of intricate pre-modern workmanship. Furthermore, while miniature *mushafs* may have been novelty items in the late nineteenth and early twentieth century, they are no longer so, but evidently they still remain attractive.

Furthermore, I will suggest explanations that further add to those Myrvold provides, mainly with reference to the "intentions and purposes of the users." As the introductory example indicates, miniature *mushafs* may be desirable objects for consumers who have no idea what makes them sought after. This points to a more general and methodological problem. Even if we have reports from purchasers of miniature *mushafs* concerning "intentions and purposes," how can we be sure that these are not *post hoc* rationalizations? We do know from research on human decision making that people are not always particularly good at providing correct accounts of the *causes* of their behaviour, but are good at rationalizing it, or providing *reasons* for their actions (Haidt 2001; Kahneman 2011; Lewis 2013). This fact merits also looking beyond reasons given by informants, however sincere those utterances may be.

In searching for answers to the question of the desirability of miniature *mushafs*, I will address religio-cultural conceptions of the Qur'an as a sacred scripture, and practices related to those conceptions. I will also discuss what can be termed the social aspects of the handling and use of miniature *mushafs*. Lastly, I will look beyond these more or less socially situated and culturally specific contexts and approach the issue at hand from a perspective that takes into account more general human proclivities. The conceptual framework used to connect these different approaches is one of "affordances."

Affordances: Some theoretical remarks

The concept of affordances stems from the academic discipline of ecological psychology and from the psychologist James Gibson, who devoted a chapter in his book *The Ecological Approach to Visual Perception* to "the theory of affordances" (Gibson 1986, 127–146). Gibson puts forward the view that objects, in a wide sense, host what can be seen as *action possibilities* or *potentialities*. These, however, are not inherent in the objects themselves, but arise as a result of the encounter between the object and a potentially acting subject, an organism. The affordances of an object vary with the organism, and are thus relational in nature.

Since affordances are relational, they are provided and constrained, but not determined, by the physical properties of the object. A chair, for example, has the affordance of being "sitable" in relation to a particular human being. It also shares this affordance with a stone in the woods. However, in relation to an organism not having a backside to lean on, or being too large to fit on the chair, the chair does not have the affordance of being "sitable."

The concept of affordances, following Gibson, has been used in such diverse fields as archaeology (Knappett 2012), anthropology (Ingold 2000), evolutionary biology (Withagen and van Wermeskerken 2010) and, more recently, the study of religions (Davidsen 2016; Taves 2013). It can be seen as particularly revealing in relation to artifacts, that is, human-made objects. These are usually produced with particular affordances in mind, but may actually have other, not anticipated, affordances in practice. An author may write and publish a book with the intention of it having the affordance of being "readable" to a particular subset of the species *Homo sapiens*; for example, those who are literate and understand the language in which the book is written. But an actual physical copy of the book has a wide range of other affordances that diverge from, and at times may be directly opposed to, the affordances intended by its author or publisher. It may have the affordance of being "door stoppable" in relation to humans, or even "edible" in relation to certain insects. For the following, it is important to note that affordances are not just a matter of *potentialities* (that expand affordances) but also of *constraints* (that limit affordances) (Knappett 2005, 52–54).

Affordances are, according to James Gibson, given by the physical properties of the object (being solid, of a particular size or form, opaque, etc.) in relation to the physio-psychological properties of the organism. These affordances are, in the words of archaeologist Carl Knappett, in a sense direct, or "transparent" (2005, 46). Knappett, however, voices some criticism of Gibson's original theory. In many cases, and perhaps particularly in the case of artifacts, affordances are indirect and contingent upon, or at least mediated by, culture: beliefs, values, and standardized behavior within a group, transmitted (at least metaphorically so) horizontally and vertically within that group (*cf.* Knappett 2005, 46). Such beliefs, values, and practices in a particular context may both limit and expand the set of affordances of a particular object compared to other contexts.

In addition, Carl Knappett makes yet another remark concerning affordances, closely related to the importance of culture, particularly in the context of humans: the social aspect. The affordance of the object may not only be a question of the relationship between the object and *one* organism (in this case a human being) but of several human beings in interaction and the object, and that the inter-individual interactions and relations also affect the range of affordances of the object (Knappett 2005).

In the following, I shall apply the concept of affordances to the phenomena of miniature *mushaf*s as desirable artifacts. I start with the mediating role of (religious) culture, proceed to the notion of affordances and sociality (without losing sight of the cultural context) and conclude with what could, perhaps, be termed affordances related to more general, less culture specific, pan-human psychological proclivities.

Three dimensions of sacred texts

It is important not to lose sight of the fact that miniature *mushaf*s contain the Qur'anic text in full, albeit in very small lettering. In this, they differ from those miniatures that are representations, reproductions, or models of full-scale objects (such as miniature cars as toys, miniature railways, or miniature plastic dinosaurs). As miniatures go, they are rather like Japanese *Bonsai* trees, which are still fully within the category of trees, just very much smaller than what could be termed "prototypical" trees (Foxhall 2015).

The concept of prototypes, which will be used henceforth, is taken from research into human categorization and concept formation, particularly in everyday life. This research indicates that when humans categorize, so to say, "on the hoof," they do not generally reason in sufficient and necessary conditions for membership in a category, but instead use as a starting point often implicit notions of what constitutes the *typical* example within the category, or the "prototype" (Rosch 1978). An important advantage of this take on categorization is that it allows for an analysis of diversity and change. It can also account for many instances of inter-human conflict and confusion over what a particular linguistic term "really" denotes. Hence concepts such as "tree" or "bird" will produce different images of a prototypical bird or a prototypical tree in the minds of people in different geographical contexts and perhaps different historical periods, given the particularities of the local flora and fauna, not to mention individual experience.

I suggest that miniature *mushafs* are a particular set within the larger category of *mushafs*, not primarily because they correspond to (or rather fall short of) a specific height, width or length, but because they, due to their minuteness, deviate in their affordances in relation to prototypical *mushafs*. In order to substantiate this suggestion, I utilize James W. Watts' notion of dimensions in the use of sacred scriptures as material objects: the semantic, the performative, and the iconic. The semantic and performative dimensions relate to a book that affords *reading*, of containing ink-on-paper signs that may be read, decoded or verbally reproduced. In these dimensions, the book, or rather the content of the book—the written text—can be a source of information, or in the case of the performative dimension, form a part of worship. In contrast, the iconic dimension concerns the uses of scriptures as special material objects: to be displayed in public as signs of devotion, as sources of divine power, or as objects to be treated in a particular manner, revered and respected (Watts 2013, 13–14).

Addressing these three dimensions and at the same time considering the physical properties of a *mushaf* is revealing. It is possible to argue that in relation to a prototypical *mushaf*, all dimensions potentially apply equally. However, as a particular *mushaf* deviates from the prototype, affordances related to one dimension may be more accentuated, while other affordances relating to another dimension may be diminished (*cf.* Foxhall 2015; Knappett 2012).[3]

---

3. Size might actually not be the only thing that matters. For a discussion on the effects of other forms of deviation from prototype *mushafs*, particularly concerning rules on purity, see Suit 2013.

The semantic dimension

James W. Watts' semantic dimension concerns the scripture's affordance of *decipherability* in search of information on beliefs and norms. Since miniature *mushaf*s, as far as I know, are all printed in the Arabic script, they lack this particular affordance for those individuals who do not master that language. This would include the majority of the world's Muslims. This particular limitation in affordances is of course shared with prototype-sized *mushaf*s in Arabic. In addition, however, the physical minuteness of miniature *mushaf*s constrains this particular affordance further. Although some versions of miniature *mushaf*s have been produced with magnifying glasses attached, it is difficult to see how this particular dimension can be a major factor in explaining the desirability of the objects.

Miniatures have the affordance of being highly portable, more so than prototype-sized *mushaf*s, but so do larger, but still small, pocket versions of the text, with increased decipherability affordance compared to miniatures. In addition, modern technology has today made it possible to transport the Qur'anic texts for the purposes of information mining in other media than the printed book, as stand-alone small gadgets, but perhaps more likely as mobile phone applications. It is quite revealing that in an advertisement for a particular miniature *mushaf* available for purchase online it is explicitly stated that it "is very small and not for reading purpose [*sic*]" (Amazon 2017). If you want a portable Qur'an to read from, there are better alternatives than a miniature *mushaf*.

In the mystical search for hidden information in the text, the hard-to-read character of the text could enhance the reader's concentration and meditation. However, as far as I am aware, there are no indications that divination constitutes a specific context for contemporary uses of miniature *mushaf*s.

The performative dimension

There are both similarities and differences between James W. Watts' semantic and performative dimensions. Both relate directly to the *content* of the sacred text, rather than focusing on the book (the physical artifact) that contains the text. However, in the semantic dimension, the focus is on information related to beliefs, values, and norms, while in the performative dimension, the focus is on the text as part of a ritual performance, such as a public recitation or personal meditative practice. In the Islamic tradition, such performances abound. Reciting certain *surah*s (chapters) or excerpts from verses in the Qur'an is a mandatory part of daily prayers, but recitation is also an important ritual, both communal and private (Gade 2009).

Recitation does not require the presence of a material piece of text. In daily prayers, recitation is performed from memory. Basic religious training, or education, has traditionally focused on children memorizing selected parts of the text: the introductory chapter *al-Fatiha*, some shorter *surah*s towards the end of the Qur'an, and some selected excerpts from other chapters. Being able to read and articulate the Arabic script of the Qur'an, but not necessarily to understand what the text means—much like a computer running text-to-speech software—is a competence that many Muslims have, since it is a part of early religious education. It would appear that a miniature *mushaf*'s affordance of being recitable is reduced in a similar manner as its affordance of being *decipherable* compared to a prototype-sized *mushaf*. This, however, may not always be the case.

Kristina Myrvold and Andreas Johansson report how the British authorities at one time, for a limited period, distributed miniature *mushaf*s to their Muslim soldiers during the First World War in order to cater to the latter's "religious needs" (Myrvold and Johansson this volume). What those needs were exactly is not altogether clear. Even though this activity was short-lived, Myrvold and Johansson note how Muslim soldiers, in private letters, expressed a desire to possess such artifacts. While the interpretation of this desire, at the time, was with reference to an "Oriental" perception of the utility of the Qur'anic text as a talisman, there is a possible alternative, that to my knowledge has not been explored: the act of reciting the Qur'an is a devotional practice that does not require the presence of a physical text if the text has been memorized. However, as Islamic studies scholar Josef Meri notes, Muslim religious scholars in history have stated that it is religiously commendable to have a physical copy present, holding it and gazing upon the text during recitation, regardless of whether the text is actually read or not (Meri 2001). Miniature *mushaf*s could, at least potentially, have fulfilled such a devotional function, and particularly in a situation where their portability affordance was important. The minuteness of the script itself need not have constituted a constraint in relation to its affordance of recitability.

Whether or not Muslims used miniature *mushaf*s in this manner during wars and in other contexts is still an open question, but, as mentioned in the introductory example from *ummah.com*, there is anecdotal information of contemporary similar practices. In a reply to the original posting, the user Abu.Rambo claims to know a *hafiz* (that is, one who has memorized the whole of the Qur'an) using a miniature "every day" for reciting purposes.

The iconic dimension

As James W. Watts notes, "[b]ooks and other written texts usually draw our attention to their verbal contents, but smaller-than-average books and

non-standard sizes of fonts, pages and bindings draw our attention to the
book's material form" (Watts this volume). In a similar manner, These observations could be rephrased by combining James W. Watts' dimensional classifications with James Gibson's concept of affordances: downsizing (as well
as upsizing) a *mushaf* compared to the prototype, leads to a shift in affordances from those connected with the semantic (and perhaps performative)
dimension towards those related to the iconic dimension, or of the scripture
primarily as a material object.

Perhaps the most recurring explanation for the existence and desirability
of miniature *mushaf*s is that they are used as talismans, as objects containing power that can protect and bring health and wellbeing. The notion that
the Qur'anic text, due to its divine origin, is a source of tangible power or
"blessing" (*baraka*) upon contact is widely held among Muslims, in history
as well as today. It informs a variety of practices. Verses from the Qur'an may
be written on pieces of paper, or with chalk on tablets, and the text (ink or
chalk) is then dissolved in water, thereby turning the liquid into a powerful
medicine. There are, despite the above-mentioned criticism of some religious
scholars, plenty of examples where amulets are produced by writing verses of
the Qur'an on a piece of paper (or other material) and enclosing it in a container to be worn around the neck or the wrist for good luck or protection.
Cutlery with engraved verses and clothes embroidered on the inside with
Qur'anic verses are similar examples of a perception of benefit from physical
contact with the Qur'anic texts (for these and other examples, see Meri 2001;
Svensson 2010).

Against this background it would appear reasonable to conclude that miniature *mushaf*s small enough to be worn around the neck, for example, and
accompanied by small cases that clearly afford such use, are in fact talismans.
This holds true for both contemporary miniature *mushaf*s available today,
as well as those produced by David Bryce in the late nineteenth century. As
Kristina Myrvold and Andreas Johansson note, the talismanic use was the
standard colonial explanation for the desirability of miniature *mushaf*s during
the First World War (Myrvold and Johansson, this volume). It is well attested
that humans tend to resort to magical thinking particularly in times of distress and when they experience lack of control (Keinan 2002). However, the
conclusion that the use of Qur'anic text as a means for receiving protection
and blessing is the major explanation for the desirability of miniature *mushaf*s
may be drawn too hastily. Such a conclusion could be tainted by ethnocentric
and Orientalist preconceptions about the "Other" as entirely "different" and
"exotic," perhaps also combined with a value judgment of the "Other" being
"irrational" and "superstitious." As noted above, there are alternatives available to using complete *mushaf*s as amulets (for example, enclosed excerpts).

As far as I know, there is no justification for assuming that believing Muslims view complete *mushaf*s as having greater affordance in this respect than excerpts.

There may be other aspects of the Qur'an within the iconic dimension, apart from the scripture as a source for *baraka* and protection, to be considered that are affected by differences in size and the changes in affordances those differences produce. The *mushaf* is an object of veneration, an object that merits respect, love, and adoration. This can be seen in the practices of kissing *mushaf*s, elevating them above the head, wiping them over the face and the eyes, and gazing at them (McAuliffe 2009, 410–411; Meri 2001; Suit 2013). Given its increased affordance of portability, it would follow that a miniature *mushaf* should provide more opportunities for such particular practices, all of which are independent of its decreased affordance of being readable.

The iconic dimension and social affordances

There is one important part of James W. Watts' notion of iconic dimension that merits particular attention: the use of scriptures in "public displays." While Watts notes this function mainly in relation to persons in political power displaying scriptures as part of claims to legitimacy (Watts 2013, 22–23), the potential is wider, and increases with diminished size, making miniature *mushaf*s particularly interesting. It is also possible to place this particular function in a wider theoretical context.

Human beings are prone to advertising to others the content of their unobservable "inner worlds" in terms of beliefs, values, and aesthetic preferences, and experience satisfaction in doing so with the help of conspicuous cultural markers such as clothing, facial hair, turbans, badges, tattoos, and so on. Previous research has suggested that this is connected to human "coalitional instincts" (Toby 2017), which in turn can be explained by our unrivaled ability for large-scale cooperation with non-kin, or reciprocal altruism. Cultural markers advertise commitment and willingness to cooperate with whomever shares that commitment, and contribute to divisions between "us" and "them." The potency of cultural markers to promote emotions of love and solidarity between members of the perceived in-group (and animosity towards the out-group) has been repeatedly shown in experimental research (Greene 2013; Tajfel 1970; 2010).

Miniature *mushaf*s, to a larger extent than prototype-sized *mushaf*s, have the social affordance of being easily "displayable" in public due to size and portability, and even wearability. While the talisman hypothesis may be relevant in relation to a subset of miniature *mushaf*s (those with the affordance of being "wearable"), the sign hypothesis covers more cases that, unlike prototype-sized *mushaf*s, are small enough to carry around and put (or hang) in strategic places, such as from the rear-view mirror of a car, as advertisements of the owner's piety and devotion, and suitability as a coalition partner.

There is yet another conceivable social function of miniature *mushafs*, mentioned by Kristina Myrvold, that merits attention: they have an increased affordance, compared to prototype-sized *mushafs*, of being "give-awayable." The literature on the social significance of gifts and gift giving is extensive (Komter 2007). Some general considerations are relevant to the issue at hand. Gifts can establish or confirm social bonds between people, both through the act of giving, and the corresponding act of accepting the gift given. The perceived value of the gift is important. A gift of low value can easily be interpreted by the receiving party not as a confirmation of a social bond, or an attempt at establishing such a bond, but as a direct insult and even a hostile act. It may be a highly delicate act for a giver to select a suitable gift. This is where contemporary miniature *mushafs* may be considered a perfect option, at least in a social relationship between two believers.

Many believing Muslims consider *mushafs* to be suitable gifts for special occasions. This is evidenced by the availability of deluxe "gift editions" of the text, with richly embellished covers and in highly ornamented cases, priced at several hundred dollars. Such *mushafs* are popular, for example, as wedding gifts. However, it is not necessarily the forms of the *mushaf* given as gifts that matter the most but rather their symbolic value. The Qur'an is spiritually valuable, regardless of its form. For believing Muslims, it is the most valuable text imaginable. This adds an important aspect to presenting a *mushaf* as a gift. It would be difficult, perhaps impossible, for a believer to refuse to accept it, or feel insulted, even if the actual copy has a low market value. This is what, at least in theory, provides miniature *mushafs* with the affordance of being particularly "give-awayable." They are easily transported and, in addition, the mass-produced versions, such as those available in souvenir shops, are inexpensive.

Therefore, when the British authorities gave away not only miniature *mushafs*, but also larger-sized ones, to the Muslim soldiers during the First World War, the explicit motive might have been altruistic: a concern for the religious needs of those fighting for the empire. In addition, however, the gift from the authorities to the Muslim soldiers was one that made it possible for the colonial masters to force a social relationship on the soldiers at a relatively low cost, and in a manner that was difficult for the recipients to refuse.

In addressing the affordances of miniature *mushafs* in social signaling and gift giving, I have to a large extent referred to theoretical frameworks of a more generally human, and less culturally specific, Muslim character. One could also, following Carl Knappett, describe this as a move from less transparent to more transparent affordances. To recapitulate: transparent affordances (in relation to human beings) relate to the fact that the miniature *mushaf*s are small, making them more portable, wearable, and placeable, but also less readable than prototype-sized *mushaf*s. Less transparent affordances are dependent on cultural understandings of the text and codex, and their power, value, and meaning. In the following, I will suggest three additional answers to the question of why miniature *mushaf*s are desirable objects, and will continue on this trajectory from less to more transparent affordances, from the particularly Muslim, to the generally human.

Miniature *mushaf*s as souvenirs

As previously mentioned, my primary encounter with miniature *mushaf*s has been during visits to the pilgrimage site in Eyüp, Istanbul. Here visitors from different parts of the Muslim world gather to partake in the blessings present at the grave of one of Muhammad's companions, Abu Ayyub. The centre of the pilgrimage site is the grave, and the adjacent mosque. But at the site, which is easily reachable by both bus and boat, there are also all the facilities that the tourist could ask for, such as restaurants, gift shops, and street vendor stalls. In the latter, one finds many of the same souvenir items that are available in the Grand Bazaar and along the streets in central Istanbul, but the ratio of particularly religious items is conspicuously higher.[4]

From existing research on souvenirs it becomes clear that the practice of procuring (by buying or stealing) items from sites that one visits has a long history, and is culturally widespread (for an overview, see Swanson and Timothy 2012). The standard explanation for this practice is that the objects thus attained serve as tangible, material reminders of particular experiences tied to an event and a place, and are thus invested with a symbolic value that often transcends their market value.[5]

Here, I suggest, hypothetically, that miniature *mushaf*s belong to a category of items with a high affordance of being "procurable as souvenirs," particularly in contexts of religious tourism or pilgrimage. This affordance is dependent upon the particular context that promotes certain mindsets and emotional states. The pilgrimage site of Eyüp is a sacred place, in the sense that it is "set apart" from other places. Many who visit do so in a particular mindset of devotion, and perhaps experience emotional arousal. If the practice of obtaining souvenirs is indeed tied to the motive (conscious or not) of preserving a particular experience, items with specific religious connota-

---

4. The potential function of miniature *mushaf*s as "pilgrimage souvenirs" also occurs in Kristina Myrvold's list cited above.

5. For alternative explanations about the function of pilgrimage items, see Paraskevaidis and Andriotis 2015.

tions increase in the affordance of being procurable as souvenirs, especially if they also are of low cost. This would hold true for mass-produced miniature *mushafs*, but also other low cost religious items such as the ones mentioned above (like key chains, refrigerator magnets featuring the *basmala*, digital as well as analog rosaries, etc.).

Admiration and control

While miniature *mushafs* are phenomena particular to a Muslim religious context, miniatures in general are not. Archaeologists can show that miniature versions, as well as miniature reproductions of objects (artifacts, people, plants, animals, natural objects), have existed for a long time in human history, and in diverse cultural settings (see articles in *World Archeology* 2015). Miniatures continue to be produced today, and attract attention in forms such as miniature railways, miniature food dishes, or miniature reproductions of celebrities. There appears to be a widespread human fascination with miniatures in general.

Referring to miniature books in particular, James W. Watts ties the fascination to an admiration for the production process (Watts this volume; for similar views, see Olmsted 1993). The miniatures prompt us to ask the question "How did they do it?" While perhaps relevant in some cases, it would appear less of a factor in explaining the fascination for mass-produced items. Another explanation claims that miniatures, due to their size, provide those interacting with them with a pleasant sense of overview, control or even omnipotence (Millhauser 1983). While discussing miniature figurines manufactured in Hellenistic Babylonia, the archaeologist Stephanie M. Langin-Hooper suggests that one of the reasons why human beings are attracted to miniatures is that the reduced scale in relation to the prototype (and to the human body) promotes a sense of empowerment and control in the individual who interacts with the object. This is particularly relevant for miniatures of objects that in real life are "more powerful – physically, cosmically, politically or socially – than the human user. Such miniatures make the stressful realities of life in the full-size real world more manageable by shrinking intimidating forces to tiny, controllable proportions" (Langin-Hooper 2015, 68).

Langin-Hooper's suggestion could be relevant in the case of miniature *mushafs*. Being the word of God, and an object of awe and respect, the Qur'an is potentially overwhelming and perhaps even intimidating to believers. In this context, miniature *mushafs*, compared to prototype-sized ones, have increased affordances of being "controllable," which may influence their affordance of being desirable possessions. If this interpretation is correct, we could expect miniatures in general to be more attractive to individuals who, due to the surrounding environment or a particular social position, experience lack of control in their everyday life. If, for example, miniature *mushafs* indeed were particularly popular among soldiers participating in the First World War, this could perhaps be an indication in this direction.

Cute Qur'ans

One last suggestion as for why miniature *mushafs* are desirable items could be put forward, which may have a special advantage above the ones already discussed. All these assume that the attractiveness of miniatures lies in their potential *functions,* whether anticipated or not by those harbouring the desire to own them. But perhaps parts of the desirability affordance of miniature *mushafs* is not at all connected to actual or perceived functions, but to aesthetics related purely to size.

This way of approaching the basic question of this paper attaches itself to the emerging field of "cute studies," exploring what literature studies scholar Joshua Paul Dale names the "Aaw factor" in human-human, human-animal, and human-artifact relations, or a tendency to mobilize certain positive emotions of love, affection, and attraction in the presence of objects identified as "cute" (Dale 2016; see also Buckley 2016). Cuteness is a general term in English, but perhaps, as psychologist Hiroshi Nittono claims, the Japanese word *kawaii* is more apt, because it connotes not only cuteness, but also adorableness, loveliness, and prettiness (Nittono 2016, 89). Furthermore, while cuteness is mainly an issue in human-human and human-animal interaction—and cuteness of inanimate objects is conceived of as an extension of this—*kawaii* encompasses, at least in standard definitions, also the *kawaii* of inanimate objects. Nittono quotes a contemporary Japanese dictionary with the following subentry of the term *kawaii* "(of things and shapes) attractively small, small and beautiful" (Nittono 2016, 81). While the concept has been used mainly in a Japanese cultural context, Nittono, with reference to a wide range of behavioral research, claims that it is useful as an analytical concept since it has deep roots in terms of pan-human psychological proclivities (Nittono 2016).

For a long time there have been scholarly discussions on the human tendency to invest objects with cuteness, stretching back to Charles Darwin's work on emotions, and in particular Konrad Lorentz's notion of a "baby schema" as an evolved mental disposition activated by certain stimuli, stimuli that are present in young children (so-called neotenous features such as smallness, rounder features, proportionally larger eyes etc. in relation to adults). Put in an evolutionary psychological context, it has been argued that these dispositions have evolved because they have promoted caretaking behavior, and hence increased survival rates of children whose parents have such a disposition, and who, then, are more likely to pass these dispositions on genetically to the next generation (Gould 1979). The "baby schema" has also been used to explain attractiveness of particular artifacts based on their appearance, from toys to alarm clocks, to cars (Cho 2012; Cho *et al.* 2011). Attractiveness of inanimate objects based on the appraisal of *kawaii* is here then construed as an accidental by-product of a human proclivity being applied outside of its original domain (caretaking). While there have been some suggestions for modification in terms of the ultimate explanations for this tendency or why it has evolved (Sherman and Haidt 2011), few question that it exists and has real effects.

Returning to miniature *mushafs*, the cited research does appear to provide an additional possible explanation for the affordance of these objects as "desirable": a *kawaii* affordance purely due to physical size. Miniature *mushafs* become desirable to some because they are unconsciously construed as "baby Qur'ans," hence activating the same emotions of attractiveness that small children activate. Since miniature *mushafs* are not merely representations of prototype-sized *mushafs,* but *mushafs* in their own right, the effect can be assumed to be even stronger. In addition, as I have argued elsewhere, most of the beliefs and practices related to the iconic dimension of the Qur'an make sense if we assume that in the minds of believers, *mushafs* are, unconsciously, construed as persons, as containing a "life force essence" otherwise mainly reserved for human beings. This could, at least in theory, be a factor that promotes a conception of miniature *mushafs* as "baby Qur'ans" and prototype-sized Qur'ans, consequently, as adults.

Conclusion

The possible explanations for the desirability affordance of miniature *mushafs* that have been suggested above are at this stage highly tentative. All have to be further substantiated with the help of empirical research using a diverse range of methods, including archival research, ethnography, and perhaps even experiments. Nevertheless, it is possible, as has been done occasionally in the course of this text, to make some initial comparison between alternatives. For example, it is highly unlikely that miniature *mushafs* are desirable because they are viewed as portable sources of information on the will of God. Their readability affordance is simply too low.

It should be stressed that some relevant issues connected to miniature *mushafs* as cultural phenomena have been left out of the discussion, issues that merit further theoretical and empirical research. One major issue, that has only been slightly touched upon, is the consequences the size of the *mushaf,* and it potential uses, have on behavior related to norms on how to handle a Qur'anic codex, particularly norms relating to purity and impurity. Deviations from the prototype may have consequences in this context, and warrant further examination.

One ambition in this text has been to stress the importance of looking beyond the culturally specific when searching for explanations for the desirability of miniature *mushafs,* towards more general human psychological proclivities and their possible role in affecting cultural beliefs and practices. I believe such a perspective may be highly fruitful, which can be exemplified through returning to the case of Ibrahim-70.

Why did Ibrahim-70 purchase a miniature *mushaf* during a visit to an Islamic bookshop? It was obviously not for the purpose of having a portable Qur'an for reading or for performing particular rituals of recitation, since the text was too small to easily afford that, and Ibrahim-70 already had several *mushafs* with a higher affordance in this respect. The affordance of being wearable as an amulet or as a portable sign of belonging only presented itself after the object was more closely examined and found to contain a golden (or more likely a gold imitation) chain. Obviously, Ibrahim-70 did not have a preconceived idea of where to place the artifact, which indicates that is was not bought with the intention of being displayed to others. Neither was it bought as a gift for someone else. Hence, it would appear that those less transparent affordances that miniature *mushafs* may have in accordance with the outline above are of less relevance in this case. Other more transparent affordances fare at bit better, perhaps.

The purchase of the miniature was made in a place that Ibrahim-70 describes as special, as "the most beautiful Islamic bookshop in the world." If this is taken literally, it testifies to an emotional arousal, with religious undertones, that could promote an inclination to obtain a souvenir from the event. A fairly inexpensive item such as a miniature *mushaf* would be suitable. The very fact that Ibrahim-70 posts a query on what to do with the item purchased could be an indication of a general uncertainty concerning religious norms, which fits well with the suggestions that a need for control may underlie the attractiveness of miniature *mushafs.* Lastly, the reason explicitly given does open up for the final suggestion above: the miniature *mushaf* was procured because it "looked nice," that is, it had a quality that caught the buyer's attention and promoted a desire of ownership. And that quality was its very tininess.

References

Amazon. 2017. "Al-Ameen Muslim Gift Islamic Car Mirror Hanging Decoration Ornament Mini Al-Qur'an Keychain Keyring (Silver)." https://uedata. amazon.com/Al-Ameen-Decoration-Ornament-Al-Qur'an-Keychain/dp/ B01LFCLU1E/

Buckley, Ralf C. 2016. "Aww: The Emotion of Perceiving Cuteness." *Frontiers in Psychology* 7: 1740. https://doi.org/10.3389/fpsyg.2016.01740

Cho, Sokyung. 2012. Aesthetic and Value Judgment of Neotenous Objects: Cuteness as a Design Factor and its Effects on Product Evaluation. Doctoral dissertation. University of Michigan.

Cho, Sokyung, Richard Gonzales, and Carolyn Yoon. 2011. "Cross-Cultural Difference in the Preference of Cute Products: Asymmetric Dominance Effect with Product Designs." In *Diversity and Unity: Proceedings of IASDR2011*, edited by N.F.M. Roozenburg, L.L. Chen, and P.J. Stappers, 1–7. IASDR: Deft.

Dale, Joshua P. 2016. "Cute Studies: An Emerging Field." *East Asian Journal of Popular Culture* 2: 5–13. https://doi.org/10.1386/eapc.2.1.5_2

Davidsen, Markus A. 2016. "The Religious Affordance of Fiction: A Semiotic Approach." *Religion* 46: 521–549. https://doi.org/10.1080/0048721X.2016.1210392

Foxhall, Lin. 2015. "Introduction: Miniaturization." *World Archaeology* 47(1): 1–5. https://doi.org/10.1080/00438243.2015.997557

Gade, Anna M. 2009. "Recitation." In *The Blackwell Companion to the Qur'an*, edited by Andrew Rippin, 481–493. Oxford: Wiley-Blackwell.

Gibson, James J. 1986. *The Ecological Approach to Visual Perception*. New York: Psychology Press.

Gould, Stephen J. 1979. "Mickey Mouse Meets Konrad Lorenz." *Natural History* 88: 30–36.

Greene, Joshua D. 2013. *Moral Tribes: Emotion, Reason, and the Gap Between Us and Them*. New York: Penguin Press.

Haidt, Jonathan. 2001. "The Emotional Dog and Its Rational Tail: A Social Intuitionist Approach to Moral Judgment." *Psychological Review* 108: 814–834. https://doi.org/10.1037/0033-295X.108.4.814

Ingold, Tim. 2000. *The Perception of the Environment: Essays on Livelihood, Dwelling and Skill*. London: Routledge.

Kahneman, Daniel. 2011. *Thinking: Fast and Slow*. New York: Farrar, Straus and Giroux.

Keinan, Giora. 2002. "The Effects of Stress and Desire for Control on Superstitious Behavior." *Personality and Social Psychology Bulletin* 28: 102–108. https://doi.org/10.1177/0146167202281009

Knappett, Carl. 2005. "The Affordances of Things: A Post-Gibsonian Perspective on the Relationality of Mind and Matter." In *Rethinking Materiality: The Engagement of Mind with the Material World*, edited by Elizabeth Demarrais, Christopher Gosden, Lord Colin Renfrew, 43–51. McDonald Institute for Archeological Research: Cambridge.

———. 2012. "Meaning in Miniature: Semiotic Networks in Material Culture." In *Excavating the Mind: Cross Sections through Culture, Cognition and Material-*

ity, edited by Mads Jessen, Niels Johanssen, and Helle Juel Jensen, 87–109. Aarhus: Aarhus University Press.

Komter, Aafke. 2007. "Gifts and Social Relations." *International Sociology* 22: 93–107. https://doi.org/10.1177/0268580907070127

Langin-Hooper, Stephanie M. 2015. "Fascination with the Tiny: Social Negotiation Through Miniatures in Hellenistic Babylonia." *World Archaeology* 47: 60–79. https://doi.org/10.1080/00438243.2014.991803

Lewis, David. 2013. *Impulse: Why We Do What We Do Without Knowing Why We Do It.* Cambridge: Belknap. https://doi.org/10.4159/harvard.9780674729902

McAuliffe, Jane D. 2009. "Exegetical Sciences." In *The Blackwell Companion to the Qur'an*, edited by Andrew Rippin, 403–419. Oxford: Wiley-Blackwell.

Meri, Josef W. 2001. "Ritual and the Qur'an." In *Encyclopaedia of the Qur'an* [online edition], edited by Jane D. McAuliffe. Leiden: Brill.

Millhauser, Steven. 1983. "The Fascination of the Miniature." *Grand Street* 2: 128–135. https://doi.org/10.2307/25006539

Nittono, Hiroshi. 2016. "The Two-Layer Model of 'Kawaii'": A Behavioural Science Framework for Understanding Kawaii and Cuteness." *East Asian Journal of Popular Culture* 2: 79–95. https://doi.org/10.1386/eapc.2.1.79_1

Olmsted, A.D. 1993. "Hobbies and Serious Leisure." *World Leisure & Recreation* 35: 27–32. https://doi.org/10.1080/10261133.1993.10559138

Paraskevaidis, Pawlos and Konstantinos Andriotis. 2015. "Values of Souvenirs as Commodities." *Tourism Management* 48: 1–10. https://doi.org/10.1016/j.tourman.2014.10.014

Rosch, Eleanor. 1978. "Principles of Categorization." In *Cognition and Categorization*, edited by Eleanor Rosch and Barbara B. Lloyd, 27–48. Hillsdale: Erlhaum.

Sherman, Gary D. and Jonathan Haidt. 2011. "Cuteness and Disgust: The Humanizing and Dehumanizing Effects of Emotion." *Emotion Review* 3: 245–251. https://doi.org/10.1177/1754073911402396

Suit, Natalia K. 2013. "Mushaf and the Material Boundaries of the Qur'an." In *Iconic Books and Texts*, edited by James W. Watts, 189–206. Sheffield: Equinox.

Svensson, Jonas. 2010. "Relating, Revering, and Removing: Muslim Views on the Use, Power, and Disposal of Divine Words." In *The Death of Sacred Texts: Ritual Disposal and Renovation of Texts in World Religions*, edited by Kristina Myrvold, 31–53. London: Ashgate.

Swanson, Kristen K. and Dallen J. Timothy. 2012. "Souvenirs: Icons of Meaning, Commercialization and Commoditization." *Tourism Management* 33: 489–499. https://doi.org/10.1016/j.tourman.2011.10.007

Tajfel, Henri. 1970. "Experiments in Intergroup Discrimination." *Scientific American* 223: 96–102. https://doi.org/10.1038/scientificamerican1170-96

———. (ed.) 2010. *Social Identity and Intergroup Relations*. Cambridge: Cambridge University Press.

Taves, Ann. 2013. "Non-Ordinary Powers: Charisma, Special Affordances and the Study of Religion." In *Mental Culture: Classical Social Theory and the Cognitive Science of Religion*, edited by Dimitris Xygalatas and William W. McCorkle, 80–97. Durham: Acumen.

Tooby, John. 2017. "Coalitional Instincts." *Edge*. 2017: What Scientific Term or Concept Ought to be More Widely Known? https://www.edge.org/response-detail/27168

Ibrahim-70. 2010. "Wearing the Qur'an Around the Neck. Permissable?" Web page no longer accessible. Orginal print out with author.

Watts, James W. 2013. "The Three Dimensions of Scriptures." In *Iconic Books and Texts,* edited by James W. Watts, 9–32. Sheffield: Equinox.

Withagen, R. and M. van Wermeskerken. 2010. "The Role of Affordances in the Evolutionary Process Reconsidered: A Niche Construction Perspective." *Theory & Psychology* 20: 489–510. https://doi.org/10.1177/0959354310361405

9

Gitamahatmya!
Paratexts in Miniature Bhagavad Gitas
with Special Reference to Pictures and Gender

Jon Skarpeid

Jon Skarpeid is Associate Professor of Religious Studies at Stavanger University. His research interests include religion and aesthetics.

This paper examines miniature Bhagavad Gitas from the perspective of four publishers: Nightingale, Gita Press, Khemraj Shrikrishnadass, and Mini-books. The sacred text of such editions rarely stands alone; other texts are included in the bound books, such as prefaces, interviews, and advertise-ments. In his *Paratexts: Threshold of Interpretation*, Gérard Genette calls these texts "paratexts," a term that also incorporates illustrations and other aspects of a book's format: "The most all-embracing aspect of the product of a book—and thus the materialization of a text for public use—is doubtless the choice of *format*" (1997, 17). When the materialization is given in the form of a miniature, it may influence the readability of the book. Thus, it becomes interesting to investigate how far the publishers are willing to go in mini-mizing the letters and how the size may influence the readability. Is the text primarily meant for reading, or is it the appearance in miniature format that really counts? The paratexts created by the publishers—such as prefaces, illus-trations, and blurbs—may affect the reception of the book. Philippe Lejeune claims that the paratexts are "a fringe of the printed text which in reality controls one's whole reading of the text" (Lejeune 1975, 45). This might push the argument too far, but the paratexts certainly influence the perception and reception of books in several ways. This paper investigates the priorities and ideologies of the publishers of miniature editions of the Bhagavad Gita and demonstrates that some paratexts consist of mantras, which indicate that these books are specifically produced for ritual worship. The act of reciting the mantras is considered to generate performative powers, and most of the publishers believe that the very presence of the Bhagavad Gita, even in the smallest version, provides positive energy. All the four publishers include illustrations in their editions of the Bhagavad Gita, and these are also important components in the formation of the ideology. Although pictures and illustrations are part of Genette's concept of paratexts, he does not elaborate on this element. I will therefore include ideas from Roland Barthes' "Rhetoric of the Image" (1977) in order to analyze how cultural constructions are displayed as something natural. Even gender hierarchies are portrayed as being natural, for example, in the forms of "function ranking" and "ritualization of subordination" (Goffman 1979). A gendered perspective is also present in the inclusion or exclusion of gender-problematic verses from the Bhagavad Gita and when the paratexts include the prescription of activities such as rituals that are meant only for males. According to my knowledge, there exist very few, if any, explicit studies of paratextuality in the Bhagavad Gita, be it miniatures or other formats. In addition to the comparison of the four miniatures, paratexts of other formats will be taken into account for a comparative perspective.

Editions and definitions

Although numerous Bhagavad Gitas have been printed during the last two hundred years in India and elsewhere, miniature versions are rare. One of the earliest was printed in Gorakhpur by The Indian Industrial Company in 1853 (Weber 1992, 6). Half a century later, at the turn of the twentieth century, the Scottish book publisher David Bryce (1845–1923) included the Bhagavad Gita in his series of miniature books, some of which were distributed to Hindu soldiers serving in the British Army during the First World War. During the same time period several other miniatures appeared, including a copy from the Jain publisher Taraporewala (see Myrvold this volume). Several individuals have in recent years also made handwritten and printed miniature versions of the Bhagavad Gita. During a couple of weeks in March 2014, Rajendra Kantak wrote the world's smallest handwritten Bhagavad Gita (twenty-three millimeters in height, 10 millimeters in width, and ten millimeters in depth). The weight of this volume was only 1.555 grams (India Book of Records 2015). Another individual, K. Eswar Kumar, has used screen printing techniques and created three tiny Bhagavad Gitas, with the smallest measuring twelve millimeters by ten millimeters (Kannadasan 2017). A "Nano Bhagavad Gita" is sold commercially as a pendant but does not come in the form of a book. It is engraved on a single plate, and all 18 chapters are no bigger than one square centimeter, readable under a microscope (Panaji 2009).

During the last twenty years, several publishers have made small versions of the Bhagavad Gita. Some of them come in sizes that are arguably not miniatures, having a maximum measurement (height and depth) of between nine and thirteen centimeters. With those dimensions, the 700 stanzas of the Bhagavad Gita do not pose great challenges to the publishers, in the sense that the text can still have normal-sized letters, contain several stanzas per page, and include some paratexts as well. I shall limit this investigation to the editions of the Bhagavad Gita that are no bigger than three inches (seventy-six millimeters), which is the definition of a miniature book given by the Miniature Book Society (Miniature Book Society n.d.). This study focuses on four publications of the Bhagavad Gita in miniature format—three of which are Indian editions and one that is Peruvian.

Easy to carry: Miniature Bhagavad Gitas from Nightingale Press

The miniature Bhagavad Gita from Nightingale Press, or what the publisher calls the "Mini Bhagavad Gita," was launched in 2006. It first appeared in English, Hindi, and Tamil, but additional Indian languages have been added. No other publisher has produced miniature editions of the Bhagavad Gita in so many languages. Nightingale, located in Tamil Nadu, has included all the four major Dravidian languages in their translations. The miniature comes in different colors as well: blue (English, Hindi, Tamil, Malayalam), maroon (Telugu, Gujarati), and gray (Kannada). The online product description claims that it is "The World's Smallest Available Edition of the Bhagavad Gita" (Nightingale n.d.), but considering its size (fifty-nine millimeters by twenty-five millimeters by forty-five millimeters)[1] this is not the case, as we shall see below. Emphasizing that the quality is high, the product description list at Nightingale's online shop states that their miniature Bhagavad Gitas are "Hard bound," "Foil Stamped," and printed on "Premium Quality paper" (Nightingale n.d.).

In the edition published in 2013–2014, the x-height, the height of several letters like x and a, is 1.2 millimeters; this size, combined with excellent printing quality, makes this edition easy to read. "Recite the song of the lord with this handy Mini Bhagavad Gita," recommends the online product description from the publisher (Nightingale n.d.).[2] Each page contains one

1. Height and depth are the same, but the width varies slightly. I have given the width of the English edition. There are some variations between the different versions due to the width of the different letters used in the alphabets in Indian vernacular languages. The shortest is the Kannadan and has 751 pages, while the longest is the Malayalam that comes to a total of 927 pages.

2. Readability is apparently essential, but how easy is it? According to a study by Legge and Bigelow, the fastest reading occurs when the x-height—the height of letters like x and a—is 1.5 millimeters. The x-height of Nightingale's miniature is 1.2 millimeters. However, a significant decline in speed occurs when the letters are minimized to 1.09 millimeters (Legge and Bigelow 2011, 6). Consequently, Nightingale's English translation should be reasonably easy to read.

stanza in Sanskrit (Devanagari script), and the translation follows at the bottom of each page with Indian numbers for the Sanskrit text and Latin for the English. Sometimes the translation is quite long, and in those cases, it spills over onto the next page (see for example pages 132–133 and 253–254). Consequently, the book is thick (767 pages) relative to its height and width, which is thicker than many other versions of the Bhagavad Gita that have a commentary included. The width makes room for the title and the name of the publisher to be printed horizontally on the spine. First is *Bhagavad*, which can be defined as the book's "thematic title," or its "subject matter," to use the categories provided by Genette (Genette 1997, 81). It is the "The Lord" (*Bhagavan*) who is teaching. In the next line comes the "rhematic title" Gita (song), thus *The Lord's Song*. The rhematic title may be a genre description but it does not have to be (Genette 1997, 86), and the Bhagavad Gita is often referred to by its rhematic title, "The Gita." The translations into vernacular Indian languages have lengthened the title by adding one word above the main title, *Srimad*, meaning sacred or holy. It is common in India to give sacred texts the title *Srimad*. Nightingale might have one Indian and one international reader in mind. *Srimad* appears in the preface of the English translation as well but is not included on the spine of the book, suggesting that non-Indians or non-Hindus might be unfamiliar with the cultural practice of adding *Srimad*. In addition to readability, there is evidently concern for the aesthetic appeal of the book as a whole and the spine also includes some ornamentation.

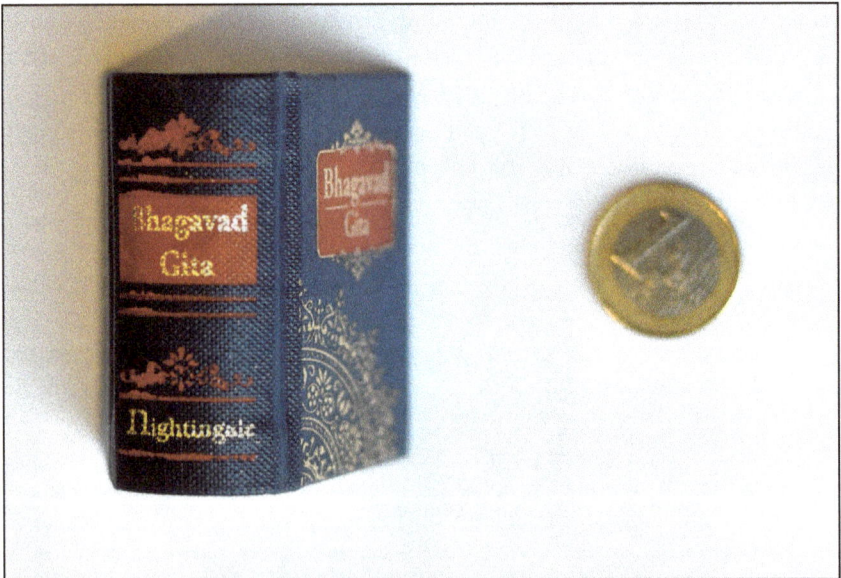

Figure 9.1: Miniature Bhagavad Gita from Nightingale Press. Photo: Asbjørn Jensen.

Nightingale's preface states that the "Srimad Bhagavad Gita" is "the essence" of the teaching in the 108 Upanishads. Undoubtedly, important philosophical teaching from the Upanishads has been included in the Bhagavad Gita, which is often emphasized in the prefaces of larger editions of the Bhagavad Gita as well (Radhakrishnan 1948; Mascaró 1962; Braarvig 1990). This wisdom is revealed by Krishna in his discourse with Arjuna, according to Nightingale. In this short preface, 63 words only, the publisher also states, "in the Vedic tradition, just the presence of this holy book is said to bring in an atmosphere of Truth, Opulence and Victory" (Bhagavad Gita 2013–2014, 2).

Nightingale is not the only publisher to point to the value of the presence of the text. In its advertisement for the Nano Bhagavad Gita, the product description of Rudraansha Export claims that "by wearing this pendant you can keep the holy sacred Hindu scripture near to your heart which gives positive energy and empowers you with some divine power" (Rudraansha Export n.d.). Some other larger editions also include the historical context of the Bhagavad Gita, which was written around 2,000 years ago, describing the circumstances surrounding its creation (see for example: van Buitenen 1981; Flood and Martin 2012). None of the miniature editions I have read contain such information and do not provide any footnotes. After a brief preface, Nightingale's version provides the contents in the form of the names of the chapters. Such a list of contents is not found in the handwritten manuscripts of the Bhagavad Gita. Some manuscripts have "intertitles" (Genette 1997, 294–318), but they are presented as a conclusion at the end of the chapters. Nightingale instead displays the intertitles at the beginning of each chapter. The standard version of Mahabharata at the Bhandarkar Oriental Institute does not contain any intertitles at all and was, among others, used in the translations by Juan Mascaró (1962) and Gavin Flood and Charles Martin (2012). As Genette writes, "intertitles are by no means absolutely required" (Genette 1997, 294).

Why publish a miniature Bhagavad Gita? A standard explanation has been the portability of miniature editions. "It will be easier for people to carry it on a daily basis," said Nightingale's national marketing manager to the Indian newspaper *The Hindu*, when the translation of Kannada was released (Kannadasan 2017). The product descriptions of other small editions of the Bhagavad Gita, such as ISKCON's "pocket edition," suggest they are "perfect for travel" (Prabhupada-books n.d.), even if this particular edition is far from being a miniature (13.3 centimeters by 10.1 centimeters). In a discussion group for Tamil Brahmins, one of the members supports not only the commentaries of Prabhupada, but also writes that it is "very handy and can be carried even during travel" (Tamil Brahmins 2010). In the interview with *The*

Hindu, Nightingale adds that the edition "was aimed at those interested in spirituality and provides guidelines for those using the book" (Kannadasan 2017).

Figure 9.2: Two drawings from Nightingale Press' English miniature Bhagavad Gita. Photo: Asbjørn Jensen.

On the last pages of the Nightingale English edition there are two illustrations without a lot of details, which fit the miniature format. The illustrations depict a seated man wearing a thread, seated women, more seated men wearing threads, a manuscript, trees, and vegetation (see Figure 9.2). According to the semiotics of Barthes, such elements belong, on the one hand, to the non-symbolic level of the illustrations. He links the word *image* to its root, imitate, and if we suspend all connotations, what is left is an "innocent" image (Barthes 1977, 42).[3] The symbolic level, on the other hand, consists of coded elements. In both illustrations of Nightingale's miniature edition of the Bhagavad Gita we can identify a Brahmin, recognizable by his sacred thread (*yajnopavitam*), who on one page is shown teaching two women, while on the next page he is sitting with four men. Both the men and the women are sitting and listening passively, with their arms crossed. The Brahmin is sitting in a slightly higher position in each scene, which illustrates the hierarchy between him and his students, regardless of whether they are male or

---

3. This is at least the case in an analysis of a photograph. An illustration is already coded but even here Barthes makes a distinction between two symbolic levels.

female. Erving Goffman writes that "high physical place symbolizing high social place" belongs to one of the elements of the "ritualization of subordination" (Goffman 1979, 40–43). Goffman labels men instructing women "function ranking" (Goffman 1979, 32). When the Brahmin teaches the men there is less contrast between him and his listeners. They are all wearing the sacred thread, and the Brahmin is holding a manuscript in his hand, and looking down. This depicts male Brahmins receiving instructions according to their class (*varna*). The drawings possibly reflect that the caste hierarchy is more strict in the south of India, particularly in Tamil Nadu, compared to the north (Fuller 2004, 93). When the Brahmin teaches the women, on the other hand, his right hand is lifted up and he appears more active than his listeners, which emphasizes the contrast between the Brahmin teacher and the women. The illustration might imply that females should have a different religious education than men, namely instruction in accordance with their female (*stri*) dharma. This teaching, or at least some of it, has to be undertaken by a male. Also, the wisdom is old, not new. The Brahmin appears to hold a handwritten manuscript, rather than a printed book, in his hand. The males are sitting close to a tree, but the females are more distant. The tree behind the males looks like a holy pipal tree (*ficus religiosa*), which would have a positive value for Hindus. Once again the males are accentuated. Although all the elements in the illustrations are innocent at the non-symbolic level, the arrangement does not belong to the things themselves but to the denotation. The denoted image of passive women, an active male, and so on, naturalizes the symbolic message; females are inferior to males and Brahmins are highest in the social hierarchy (see Barthes 1977, 45). The fact that the location is rural, devoid of all urban and modern conventions, may emphasize the naturalization of the message. The Tamil edition has nine illustrations, rather than the two found in the English version. The same Brahmin appears in all of them, in different activities. This is obviously the men's world, or rather the male Brahmins' world. In some sense it reflects the conservative gender perspective and class hierarchy found in the Bhagavad Gita, but the (conscious) motivations of the artist behind these illustrations are unknown. In one of the illustrations in the Tamil edition, the Brahmin is bending down and whispering something, possibly a mantra, in the ear of a passive female.[4] The symbolic level signified in such illustrations is "that of *ideology*" (Barthes 1977, 49). The Bhagavad Gita is conservative when it comes to social values and so are the illustrations. Both the images and the text constitute the ideology of the Gita, including

---

4. Interestingly, this illustration occurs only in the Tamil edition (2012–2013). The Gujarathi (2009–2010) and the Hindi (2012–2013) editions have six illustrations, including the two appearing in the English, the Telugu (2009–2010) and the Kannada (2009–2010) versions have no illustrations at all.

the social hierarchy of gender and classes.

So far we have examined illustrations that occur in the "peritexts" of Nightingale's miniature editions. Peritexts consist of all the texts that accompany the bound book, including the covers. The other subcategory is "epitext" which can be defined as "any elements not materially appended to the text" (Genette 2007, 344). An interesting and relevant picture is found in the epitext of Nightingale's miniature. The publisher's Facebook page contains a picture of the great movie star Amitabh Bachchan holding a copy of the miniature Bhagavad Gita (posted on December 30, 2015). There are also famous actresses, but, like the illustrations in the miniature, the publisher favors men. The next publisher also has a conservative gender perspective, but it is more indirect or hidden.

Figure 9.3: Gita Press' Miniature. Photo: Asbjørn Jensen.

A miniature for meditation by Gita Press

Toward the end of the text of the Bhagavad Gita, Krishna states: "But he who teaches this supreme secret among my devotees, giving me perfect devotion, will go to me without a doubt. There will not be another man who gives me greater joy than he, nor will there be a man dearer on earth to me than that one is" (18.68–69, translated by Miller 1986). Jaydayal Goyandka read this in the early twentieth century and felt Krishna was speaking to him. In 1923 he and some other businessmen, established Gita Press in Gorakhpur. Some years later Hanuman Prasad Poddar joined and became the leading figure together with Goyandka. By 2015 this publisher had sold seventy million copies of the Bhagavad Gita in Sanskrit and some Indian vernacular languages (Davis 2015, 154–155).

The aim of Gita Press is, according to its webpage, "to promote and spread the principles of *Sanatana Dharma*, the Hindu religion among the general public by publishing Gita [...] and other character-building books & magazines and marketing them at highly subsidised prices" (Gita Press n.d.). Gita Press' miniature costs only eight rupees (Gita Press 2014, 2), about the price of a cup of coffee on the streets in India today. None of the other miniatures examined in this study come close to that price. For instance, Nightingale's Mini Bhagavad Gita sells for 145 rupees and Khemraj's miniature (see below) costs fifty rupees. Interestingly, the dimensions (sixty-five by twelve by forty-six millimeters) seem to be the same as the miniature published by the Indian Industrial Company in Gorakhpur back in 1853. Whereas the Nightingale miniature Bhagavad Gita in English has 766 pages, the Gita Press edition is only half as thick, with 256 pages. The page number is reduced by having three to four verses on each page in Bengali, Gujarati, Oriya, or Telugu, and no Sanskrit. Instead, a separate, Sanskrit-only version is available. Unlike the Nightingale publication project, translations from Gita Press do not include English but only Indian vernacular languages. Therefore, Gita Press does not aim its publications at an international readership. The publisher also tells us that this reprint of the book is from the year 2071, according to the Hindu calendar *Vikram Samvat* (March 31, 2014 to March 20, 2015 on the Gregorian calendar). Gita Press provides only information about the year of the reprint, not the first edition, thus it is unclear when it was originally published.[5] Gita Press uses only *Vikram Samvat* for publications in Sanskrit whereas the translations into vernacular Indian languages use the Gregorian calendar. In addition to price and year, the publisher gives information about circulation figures. The copy from 2014 is the seventieth reprint and issued in 50,000 copies. The total number of the printed Bhagavad Gita is 4,428,000. This is for the Sanskrit version only, and does not include those in vernacular Indian languages.[6] Like Nightingale's miniatures, Gita Press' publication is quite easy to read. The print quality is excellent, and the letters are not too small. If we assume that the x-height is equivalent to the height of the consonants in Devanagari, we calculate it to be 1.3 millimeters, which is

---

5. *Vikram Samvat* it widely used in India as a religious calendar, but the two official calendars are the National Calendar which is *Shaka* (starting in AD 78) and the Gregorian calendar.

6. I wrote to the other publishers for information about sold copies, but only Nightingale responded with the following in an email: "We always keep such information private and confidential."

slightly larger than Nightingale's type size. The portability and availability of the scripture are also important for Gita Press as the product description on their online bookshop states: "This book is quite handy to be kept always in one's person for daily recitation" (Gita Press 2016a).

The product description on Gita Press' online shop calls this miniature edition a "Meditation Gita." The peritext is extensive, and most of it consists of mantras and an anthem. Gita Press has incorporated material from other Hindu texts; thus this peritext is also intertextual. The mantras function both as a preparation for and a conclusion to the reading of the Gita. The first page has some elements of an epigraph, both with regards to the location (the first page) and the content. An epigraph should be "more affective than intellectual," according to Genette, who quotes Stendhal (Genette 1982, 158)[7]: "The epigraph must heighten the reader's feeling, his emotion, if emotion there be, and not present a more or less philosophical opinion about the situation" (Genette 1997, 158). In the epigraph of the meditation Bhagavad Gita by Gita Press, first Shrimadbhagavad Gita is praised as the name above all names. Then follows *Tvameva*, a famous Hindu mantra (from the Pandava Gita collections). This mantra occurs on the first page of most of Gita Press' releases, and in the English publications it has the following translation: "It is You; the mother and father and both, It is You, the brother and friend both, It is You; the knowledge and riches both, It is You; all in all, O my Lord" (Goyandka 2017, 1). In India, *Shrimad* is often placed in front of the Bhagavad Gita, like in Nightingale's editions, but here it has become a part of the title in the form of a prefix, thus Shrimadbhagavad Gita.

After the publisher's peritext follows the preface in the form of mantras. Although the dominant form of a preface is "that of a discourse in prose," other variants exist as well (Genette 1997, 171). The mantras are taken from the Vaishnava tradition. They start with *nyasa*, which is then followed by *dhyanam*. The *nyasa* mantra "consists in placing divine entities on (or in) the body, in divinizing or cosmising it" (Padoux 2011, 56). The first part of the *nyasa* mantra is a preparation mantra (*karanyasa*), and comes in the form of a wreath (*malamantra*). The preparation for the mantra contains 12 parts, one for each of the body parts that are to be touched. Every phrase consists of two elements, first a verse, half of the stanza, from the Bhagavad Gita and then the body part that should be touched. The reference to the body part is not taken from the Bhagavad Gita. In principle, a Sanskrit mantra cannot be translated, but to give an example, one verse translated into in English is:

---

7. Stendhal is the pseudonym for Marie-Henri Beyle (1783–1842), which explains why there are no first names, only the surname. Bibliographies use the pseudonym rather than Beyle.

"'You grieve for those beyond grief, and you speak words of insight' [chapter 2:11] and then (touch) the navel."[8] After the preparation mantra follows the *hridayadi nyasah*, which is an inner meditation including mantras on the heart, the crown of the head, and both eyes. Having cosmisized the body, the preface of Gita Press' miniature ends with a *dhyanam*, a mental representation or visualization. Among the subjects of the visualization in this Gita Dhyanam are Krishna, Arjuna, Vyasa, and the scriptures Mahabharata and the Bhagavad Gita. The first verse is translated in the following way by some Vaishnavists: "O Bhagavad-Gita, song of the Supreme Lord Himself, You are the bestower of Arjuna's enlightenment. You have been woven into the scripture Mahabharata by the ancient sage Srila Vedavyas" (Premadharma n.d.). According to tradition, Vedavyas, or simply Vyasa, wrote the Mahabharata, including the Bhagavad Gita (Radhakrishnan 1948, 14). Vyasa is addressed three times in these mantras, and in the product description on the online shop of Gita Press, Vyasa (Vedavyas) is listed as the author for this miniature edition and all of their Bhagavad Gita publications (Gita Press, 2016a). The first of the mantras also addresses *anushtup*, the prose form used in most of the Gita. Each stanza consists of 32 syllables that are arranged into four groups (*pada*) of eight syllables each. Gita Press has in the miniature edition divided each stanza in two, that is, sixteen syllables in each line.[9] In order to gain more space for each printed line, the pages come in landscape orientation. In comparison, Nightingale's miniature (discussed above) has a letter style, and the Sanskrit text comes in quatrains, but the translation varies between five to seven lines. Some of the preface is "postludial," coming after the Gita text. According to Genette, the terminal position of the preface is "much less effective, for it can no longer perform the two main types of functions [...] holding the reader's interest and guiding him by explaining" (Genette 1997, 238). Since the terminal preface is a closing ritual text, the position is not a drawback but rather a necessity. First, comes *arati*, which is a ritual where light is waved in front of a statue of a god (Jacobsen 2003, 223). The text of the *arati* in Gita Press' miniature is nothing but a glorification of the Bhagavad Gita and begins with: "*Jaya Bhagavadgite, Jaya Bhagavadgite*" (Glory to Bhagavad Gita, Glory to Bhagavad Gita). The scripture is praised for its qualities. Finally, a ghazal (*gajalagita*), a type of light classical Hindustani music, is presented (for an example, watch Sarita Joshi singing a ghazal,

8. For the first part of the mantra, I have used Miller's translation of the Bhagavad Gita (Miller 1986). The rest of the translation is mine.

9. Some English editions appear in four lines to give the reader a certain feel of the Sanskrit prose (Flood and Martin 2012; Miller 1986). Flood and Martin has even kept the octosyllabic structure of the Sanskrit, i.e. 8 syllables for each *pada*, thus thirty-two syllables for each stanza.

Joshi 2015). It is a hymn to Krishna and the Bhagavad Gita, which addresses Arjuna, who meets God (Bhagavan), and includes some of the concepts in the Bhagavad Gita, to some extent in the form of an interpretation.

There is only one illustration in this miniature placed between the preface and the translation, and that is the logo of Gita Press. In most of the publications, it appears in color, but in this small format, it is in black and white. The logo consists of a famous motif from the Hindu tradition, Krishna and Arjuna in the chariot with four horses. Krishna is portrayed in what Ursula King defines as "The human model," where Krishna is sitting together with Arjuna in the chariot (King 1982, 154). However, the Gita Press' logo displays Krishna with a halo (gold or yellowish when the logo comes in colors). Thus, the divine aspect is fused with the human. Under the illustration comes the text: "Gita Press Gurakhpur." According to Roland Barthes, the image text operates on two levels, the non-symbolic and the symbolic. The non-symbolic, also called anchorage, helps the reader to identify the image, but this scene is one of the most famous in the Hindu tradition and needs no explanations. We are then left with the symbolic level, where the linguistic message, also called relay, is dominant and the image serves as an attribute (Barthes 1977, 38–39). The illustration gives an idea of what Gita Press is all about. The Bhagavad Gita is by far its most important publication, and we have already seen how a verse from the Bhagavad Gita inspired Jaydayal Goyandka to establish Gita Press. Strangely enough, the horses seem to be in motion although Krishna and Arjuna are sitting and talking. I have not come across this way of portraying the horses in Indian miniature drawings, and Gita Press' logo definitely belongs to the modern era. Gita Press follows the tradition of displaying the two most important figures in the Bhagavad Gita, which happen to be men. It is difficult to project a gender perspective upon Gita Press on the basis of their logo since it depicts the two most prominent persons in the Gita. However, this "Meditation Gita" from Gita Press was hardly meant for women. The exercise of such mantras belongs to the twice born (men of the three highest classes), not to females. Although ritual and social practices are changing, Gita Press has throughout its history been conservative in its approach to gender. Akshaya Mukul gives a detailed description of this in his voluminous history of Gita Press and describes how the two leading figures, Hanuman Prasad Poddar and Jaydayal Goyandka, claimed that women should not be teachers or have co-education with boys (Mukul 2015, 354–355). Even today, Gita Press publishes material written by Poddar, including the article collection *Stri Dharma Prashnottari* ("Poddar on Women's Duties").[10] Taking the ideology of Gita Press into account, it

---

10. The product description states that this is "[a] unique collection of important articles of Hanuman Prasad Poddar in question-answer form providing knowledge

does not come as a surprise that it has a Bhagavad Gita that, according to the product description, "is very useful for women, youngsters and elderly." The young and the elderly have no gender designations, but like women, are vulnerable groups that apparently require an "interpretation in a very simple language" (Gita Press, 2016b).

Amuletic Gita from 1933: Khemraj Press

Khemraj Shrikrishnadass Shri Venkateshwar Press has probably published the smallest complete and publically available Bhagavad Gita (at 37 millimeters high by twelve millimeters wide by twenty-five millimeters deep). The weight of this book is seven grams and it comes in a cardboard box weighing three grams. The size and finish are reminiscent of a matchbox. The cover of the book is made from red striped woven fabric. The printing quality of the 318 pages is not as clear as the other miniatures in this study and this, combined with small letters, makes it difficult to read. The consonants are only 0.92 millimeters in height, equivalent to an x-height with a significant reduction in reading speed. Therefore, it seems that this edition is not intended for reading, at least not in long continuous sequences. Unlike the other miniature Bhagavad Gitas it has no thread so one would need an external bookmark. Another difference compared to the other two Indian publishers (Nightingale and Gita Press) is that Khemraj has two other miniature publications: *Durga Saptashati* and *Hanuman Chalisa*. All three of the Khemraj miniatures come in Sanskrit only.

This amuletic Gita has much of the same paratexts as Gita Press' Bhagavad Gita, and the two publishers have a similar history. Khemraj was established in 1880 and, like Gita Press, founded by people from the Marwari community in Rajasthan. The two publishing houses even collaborated in the early days of Gita Press. For instance, Khemraj printed the first 13 volumes (1926–1938) of Gita Press' monthly journal *Kalyan* (Mukul 2015, 100). They mainly publish religious books and have a traditional understanding of the Hindu religion. On the front cover Shrimadbhagavad Gita is written, like the Gita Press edition, and an OM symbol is included as well (Khemraj Shrikrishnadass 1933). It has a horizontal orientation in order to have as many syllables as possible in each line. The handwritten Bhagavad Gita manuscripts may also be an inspiration since they also have a horizontal orientation.

The first page of the Khemraj miniature Bhagavad Gita starts with Gita-mahatmya ("Praise to the Gita"), and has the effect of an epigraph. It stems from the Padma Purana, and like most of the prefaces, it is not written by

---

of selfless service and moral virtuous conduct to women, mothers and girls etc." (Gita Press 2016c).

the publisher. Paradoxically, the smallest miniature has the longest peritext. The preface starts by praising the name of the god Ganesha (*Shriganeshaya Namah*). In Hinduism rituals often start with an invocation to Ganesha, and music concerts may start by addressing this god. After Ganesha, the Srimad Bhagavad Gita is praised, followed by eighty-eight stanzas from the medieval Vaishnaviya Tantrasara, a type of extract from the Upanishads. The rest of the preface is identical to the edition from Gita Press. Consequently, Khemraj also pays homage to the Gita, the prose, and the author Vyasa. According to the text, a reading of the Bhagavad Gita should be accompanied both by physical movements as well as mental exercises. Like the edition by Gita Press, Khemraj places the intertitles at the end of the chapters. Instead of a terminal preface, Khemraj ends the book with a sort of interpretation followed by the publisher's peritext. This interpretation presents the message of the Bhagavad Gita as a form of Vishishtadvaita Vedanta, and gives support to the famous philosopher Ramanuja (1017–1137), according to the tradition (Jacobsen 2003, 125). Khemraj is not the only one to take the scripture as an exponent of a particular theology. In contrast, Sarvepalli Radhakrishnan claims that the Bhagavad Gita does not give us "any arguments about its metaphysical position" (Radhakrishnan 1948, 20). On the last page, the year of publication is printed as *Samvat* 1990 and *Shak* 1855, which is more or less equivalent to 1933 according to the Gregorian calendar. The language style of the publisher's peritext is old, and in accordance with the publication year. Khemraj is not the only publisher to print new versions, but today's releases use both the *Samvat* and Gregorian calendars, no matter the language of the books.

Khemraj has included two illustrations in the book, both in black and white. Interestingly, not only the motif but also the execution as such is identical with two of the eleven illustrations in one of David Bryce's editions of a miniature Bhagavad Gita. Since the quality is not the best, it becomes difficult to identify details in this small format. One engraving shows Vishnu lying on the snake Shesha together with Lakshmi and Brahma on the cosmic ocean. Lakshmi is subordinate to Vishnu in this motif. Khemraj has published several books on Hindu goddesses, and in these editions the goddesses have no rivals. On the front covers that include both sexes, females are subordinate to men. The matchbox of the miniature Bhagavad Gita includes one illustration, which comes in colors. This motif depicts Krishna, Arjuna, the horses and the wagon. In most paintings they sit together in the wagon, but in this case Krishna is standing in front and reaching higher than both Arjuna and the horses. The divinity of Krishna is highlighted, and so is the hierarchy between god and men. Ursula King calls this "The divine model" as opposed to "The human model" (King 1982, 154), and its only Gita Press and Khemraj of the four publishers who emphasize the divinity of Krishna. The color drawing on the box is similar. Arjuna is not sitting in the wagon having trouble preparing for battle. He is down on his knees with folded hands and Krishna appears like a triumphant giant. The bow and the quiver lie on the ground, in the forefront of the drawing. The title, Shrimadbhagavad Gita, is placed between Arjuna and Krishna and the bow and the quiver, and the two men are dissociated from the weapons and the war.

Figure 9.4: Khemraj's Amuletic Gita. Photo: Asbjørn Jensen.

Similar to the ideology of Gita Press, Khemraj is conservative and the mantras given in their amuletic Gita are hardly meant for women. In fact, when it was first released in 1933, most publishers would have only men in mind for any publication, considering that the literacy rates in India were 15.6 percent for men and only 2.9 percent for women (Katiyar 2016, 51).[11] Although the numbers in 2011 were 80.9 and 64.6 percent respectively, it does not seem to have influenced Khemraj's gender perspective. Like Gita Press, it has kept a traditional view of gender, with the illustrations in the new publications portraying women as passive and subordinate to men.

Interestingly, Shaadiology, a matrimonial service company, has taken Khemraj's amuletic Gita and published it as the Silver Mini Bhagavad Gita.

---

11. These are numbers for 1931. In 1941 it had increased to 24.9 and 7.3 respectively. The literacy rate in Mumbai, where Khemraj is located, was somewhat higher.

Instead of the paper box it has been given a silver frame, thus making it decidedly the most expensive miniature (2,100 rupees). The online shop informs us that, "the price may vary based on the price of silver" (Silver Mini Bhagavad Gita 2016). The cover resembles Bryce's Gita miniature books, which came in an exclusive gold version. Instead of a magnifying glass, Shaadiology has inserted a picture of Krishna as a child with his flute. This is Gopala Krishna who acts against dharma because he transcends it (Jacobsen 2003, 110). Playing the flute, he entices the *gopis* (female shepherds). This is a motif that connects to the context of Shaadiology as a store for wedding products, since Krishna with the *gopis* has erotic elements. He does not appear as the strict Vasudeva Krishna from the Bhagavad Gita who preaches the dharma and tells Arjuna to follow his *svadharma*, which is his duty according to his warrior class. The motif is defined since only the head and the upper part of the torso are included. The title, Bhagavad Gita, does not appear on the silver box, only the illustration of Krishna and some ornamentation in silver. The product description does not give much information; it just states that the Silver Gita is "A perfect keepsake" (Silver Mini Bhagavad Gita 2016). This is different from other miniature Bhagavad Gitas that have been examined so far, where the emphasis is on readability and/or meditation. Shaadiology was launched by two young Bengali women, and their webpage reflects another attitude to gender than the publishers Nightingale, Gita Press, and Khemraj. Women are active, not only passive, and may be as tall as men when displayed as couples.[12]

Gita Nectar by Minibooks

The only non-Indian miniature edition of the Bhagavad Gita I have come across is created by Minibooks, located in Peru. In contrast to the Indian publishers, Minibooks only sells miniature books, and offers over two hundred titles. Whereas the Indian publishers only publish Hindu scriptures, Minibooks has released a series of miniatures from six world religions, much like David Bryce & Son did over a hundred years ago. The title of the series, launched in 2006, is *Extracts of the Religions*, with a second edition in 2011. The six books are all titled "néctar," thus *El Néctar de las Gita* (Minibooks 2011). In addition to Spanish, the set also comes in Italian. Except for *El*

---

12. As to the relatively size, Goffman writes that "Selective mating then enters to ensure that the very nearly every couple will exhibit a height difference in the expected direction, transforming what would otherwise be a statistical tendency into a near certitude" (Goffman 1979, 28). However, some of Goffman's gender stereotypes can be found in pictures on Shaadiology's web shop, like portraying females as unserious and the "bashful knee bend" which "seems to presuppose the goodwill of anyone in the surround who could offer harm" (Goffman 1979, 45).

Néctar de la Biblia, they are sold only in a set for twenty-five dollars, which includes a little bookcase. According to the product description, "[t]his collection presents a brilliant synthesis of the most beautiful […] educations of the Bible (Christianity), The Koran (Islam), The Bhagavad-Gita (Hinduism), Talmud (Judaism), The Dhammapa (Buddhism), and the Tao-you Ching (finished version)" (Minibooksworld 2018a). In contrast to the publishers in India, Minibooks presents the Bhagavad Gita as one sacred scripture among several others.

Figure 9.5: Silver Bhagavad Gita from Shaadiology. Photo: Asbjørn Jensen.

The *Gita Nectar* (thirty-six millimeters high by fifteen millimeters wide by twenty-seven millimeters thick) is almost as small and light as Khemraj's amuletic Gita, but does not include the entire scripture. Whereas some of the Indian editions state that the Gita gives the essence of the Upanishads or the Veda, Minibooks claims that its *Gita Nectar* provides the essence of the Gita itself. Minibooks does not neglect readability, and if a text is too long to fit its standard sizes for printing it picks selections of the text instead of making the letters smaller or the pages thinner. The Minibooks' Nectar edition has approximately the same x-height (0.85 millimeters) as Khemraj's Bhagavad Gita, but the printing quality is better, which makes it a little easier to read. The six books in the Nectar series are each about 300 pages long, and only Tao Te Ching—the shortest of these six sacred books—comes in a complete version. The Bhagavad Gita includes 192 of the total 700 stanzas, thus amounting to twenty-seven percent of the whole scripture. For comparison, the *Bible Nectar* includes approximately 0.01 percent of the Bible; from the Book of Revelation, only the first verse is included. These variations are the result of the standardization of the book dimensions, quality of paper, and the size of the letters. Most certainly this should lower the production costs. Like Gita Press, this translation does not include the Sanskrit text. Minibooks follows the tradition of many other publishers by printing miniatures from several religious scriptures and including portions rather than the complete Bhagavad Gita.

Figure 9.6: *Extracts of the Religions* from Minibooks. Photo: Asbjørn Jensen.

Minibooks' miniature includes stanzas from all the eighteen chapters of the Bhagavad Gita, but some chapters seem to contain more Nectar than others.[13] What this publication excludes is of course as interesting as what it comprises. Stanzas that might appear controversial, due to gender perspective, are omitted. This is contrary to the peritext of Prabhupada, who, in his commentary, emphasizes both female inferiority and class hierarchy.

---

13. They vary from only four stanzas (Chapters 10, 16, and 17) to 18 stanzas (Chapters 3 and 14).

The first chapter of the Bhagavad Gita consists of forty-seven stanzas, but only nine are included in Minibooks' edition. Stanza 41 is omitted: "When unrighteousness prevails, the women sin and are impure; and when the women are not pure, Krishna, there is disorder of castes, social confusion" (translation by Miller 1986). Stanza 44, which concludes the sequence of stanzas 40–44, describing the destruction of the family, is, however, included: "And have we not heard that hell is waiting for those whose familiar rituals of righteousness are no more?" (translation by Miller 1986). So, in a sense, Minibooks' edition might give the essence of the stanzas concerned with the destruction of the family. As Simon Brodbeck points out, "Kṛṣṇa locates the salvation process […] within the person's *buddhi*, that is, within the female, material pole," and points to verse 2:42 of the Bhagavad Gita: "Action is far less important than being yoked with buddhi. Seek refuge in buddhi!" (Brodbeck 2007, 163). This is subtler and requires special knowledge that Minibooks perhaps did not have. Chapter nine includes some interesting stanzas related to gender, such as: "I am the father and the mother of the universe […]" (9:17), which are also included by Minibooks. Women are also mentioned in verse 9:32: "For all those who come to me for shelter, however weak or humble or sinful they may—women or Vaishyas or Shudras—they all reach the Path supreme" (translation by Miller 1986). Minibooks has excluded this stanza, and all stanzas explicitly mentioning one of the four classes are also omitted. However, the concept of the classes, the *varna*, is included. The same goes for the *svadharma*, the individual duty, which implies a certain class. Krishna is told to adhere to his individual duty, which in this case means the *kshatriya* (warrior).

The other scriptures in the Nectar series of Minibooks also seem to downplay stanzas in which females appear to be portrayed as inferior to men. For example, *surah* 4:34 in the *Qur'an Nectar*, which states that the male is in charge of women, is omitted. The same goes for 1 Corinthians 11:3 in the miniature edition of the Bible where Paul claims that the male is the head of the woman, and 1 Corinthians 14:34 where females are supposed to be silent in gatherings. Although Minibooks has omitted gender problematic stanzas in their *Gita Nectar*, their webpage contains both problematic phrases and pictures. The short description of the book *For Him* states that: "It assembles valuable reflections about the masculine virility and his power transformer." The illustration on the cover shows a dynamic-looking man. The description of the book *For Her* reads: "The woman is the infinite source of inspiration in every sensitive man." The cover illustration displays a passive woman. Both books are under the label "The Man and the Woman" (Minibooksworld 2018b). The world is seen from a male perspective, and Minibooks' gender perspective is not consistent.

The *Gita Nectar* of Minibooks has no epigraph or preface, at least not in the form of words. The first two pages contain illustrations, one that portrays children and another depicting Krishna. The first picture of children gives rise to emotions, which is a criterion for an epigraph. The drawing of Krishna could perhaps be interpreted as a preface, but according to Genette, a preface should relate to "the subject of the text that follows or precedes it" (Genette 1997, 161). Krishna is admittedly the main character in the Bhagavad Gita, but not in the form of the flute-playing Gopala Krishna, but as Vasudeva Krishna, the social conservative who teaches Arjuna to follow his *svadharma* (the duties according to his class). The Bhagavad Gita is as silent about children as it is about Krishna playing the flute. However, children are important for Minibooks. Their homepage displays mainly pictures of children and the category "For Children and Youth," is by far the largest with its forty-seven products (Minibooksworld 2018c). In this sense, Krishna as a child fits the profile of the publisher. Apart from these two illustrations, the peritext of *Gita Nectar* consists only of the publisher's information, at the end of the book. Like Nightingale, Minibooks has paid attention to the spine of the book, and it contains the title and an OM symbol. It has a brown finish, resembling an old leather book. If historical publishers of Hindu books used Moroccan leather, today's publications of miniature Bhagavad Gita are all "vegetarians" in the sense that they do not use any leather bindings. Among Hindus, at least most Brahmins, leather is a ritual taboo. Religious beliefs affect the aesthetics of the books. Like Shaadiology, Minibooks has Krishna playing the flute on the cover, that is, once again Gopala Krishna is portrayed rather than Vasudeva Krishna. One striking difference is the use of colors. The Shaadiology cover drawing has strict divisions between the colors, for example, black and yellow. In contrast, Minibooks has transitions between the colors. Different tints of pink mingle together and gradually change to purple. In the language of structuralism, the first technique is based on binary oppositions, since the different fields have distinct colors. The drawings in Minibooks' publications, however, are characterized by the absence of binary oppositions. In a sense, this reflects the Nectar series since the six holy scriptures are portrayed as being equal. Even inside the book, the pages are a mixture of light blue and purple while other publishers in this study use white pages. On the back cover of Minibooks' edition of the Bhagavad Gita is an illustration of Vishnu, once again in close-up. It is from one of the famous motifs in India, portraying Vishnu resting on the cosmic ocean when lying on the serpent Shesha, accompanied by Lakshmi and Brahma. In this illustration one can hardly see Shesha, and Lakshmi is not present. Although she is inferior to her husband Vishnu, Lakshmi is ignored in this illustration. The only visible figure apart from Vishnu is Brahma, but in order to see him in the image one has to look carefully. However, this close-up illustration is suitable for the miniature format, since the inclusion of the whole tradition scene would make it difficult to identify the details.

Conclusion

Although the 700 stanzas of the Bhagavad Gita in Sanskrit is the same starting point for the miniature books described here (with the exception of Minibooks, who publishes selections of the text), the paratexts of the different publishers of miniature editions are quite diverse. Elements like size, preface, illustrations, and layout vary, resulting in different products. The editions may come in Sanskrit, a translation, or both. Two of the publishers offer translations in different languages and reprints with some alterations, giving rise to the variety. The study shows that some publishers have prioritized readability while others have chosen smaller amuletic versions that are more difficult to read. The physical presence of the holy Gita is considered valuable in any case, and even the tiny editions are readable. The original Sanskrit prose is also important for two Indian publishers, who have printed the text in two lines or quatrains. Although all of the editions in this study are issued in attractive hardback, some of the publishers have taken extra care of aesthetics, both with regards to the cover and the pictures. They have included the title on the book spines, which gives association to traditional and old printed books. The cover of the Silver Mini Bhagavad Gita is especially exclusive in this regard. Perhaps the most striking differences concern the prefaces of the miniature editions. The two older Indian publishers, Khemraj and Gita Press, have incorporated long prefaces in the form of mantras and texts for meditation. These reflect a particular understanding of the philosophy and religious practice of the Bhagavad Gita. The other editions do not have elaborate prefaces, and consequently do not attempt to influence the interpretation and reception of the text for the readers. However, there is one exception, namely the drawings. All the editions include distinct illustrations but, interestingly, only the editions by Gita Press and Khemraj have drawings that are directly connected to the theme of the Bhagavad Gita, that is, Krishna teaching Arjuna when he hesitates to fight the war. These two publishers also emphasize the divinity aspect of Krishna. The other publishers portray a flute-playing Krishna, who performs despite dharma and entices the shepherd girls. The war of the Gita is not a theme at all, but the illustrations instead point to innocence and childhood.

Despite all these differences in the peritexts, the publishers have quite similar attitudes when it comes to gender, except for Minibooks. The world is to a large extent seen from a male perspective. However, the gender ideology is presented in a rather indirect way. In Nightingale's miniature, the illustrations on the last pages of the book reflect a gender perspective. Although the elements are neutral—women and men sitting, men sitting, a man speaking, a manuscript, and vegetation—the arrangement and connotations are that of an ideology. The world is perceived from the viewpoint of a male Brahmin. A similar ideology is projected by most of the other publishers, if not a Brahmin then at least a male. At first glance, the miniatures from Gita Press and Khemraj seem to be devoid of any particular gender ideology. However, the peritexts include mantras and ritual prescriptions that are meant for males of the three highest classes. The epitexts and illustrations of the other publications demonstrate that Gita Press is particularly traditional when it comes to gender. In fact, the gender hierarchy and stereotypes described by Erving Goffman can to some extent be found on the webpages of all the companies. Although the homepage of Minibooks reflects much of the same gender stereotypes found at the other publishers, the Nectar miniature omits stanzas where females are described as inferior to males as well as stanzas that explicitly address the four classes. In the eyes of Minibooks, such stanzas do not form a part of the "essence of the Gita."

References

Barthes, Roland. 1977. "Rhetoric of the Image." In *Image, Music, Text*, translated by Stephen Heath, 32–51. New York: Hill and Wang.

Bhagavad Gita. 2013-2014. English translation. Sivakasi: Nightingale.

BhagavadGita. 1990. Oversatt med en innledning av Jens Braaravig [Translated with an introduction of Jens Braarvig]. Oslo: Universitetsforlaget.

Bible Nectar. 2011. Second edition. Minibookworld.

Brodbeck, Simon. 2007. "Gendered Soteriology: Marriage and the Karmayoga." In *Gender and Narrative in the Mahabharata*, edited by Simon Brodbeck and Brian Black, 144–75. Abingdon: Routledge. https://doi.org/10.4324/9780203029640

Davis, Richard H. 2015. *The Bhagavad Gita: A Biography, Lives of Great Religious Books*. Princeton, NJ: Princeton University Press.

Flood, Gavin, and Charles Martin. 2012. *The Bhagavad Gita: A New Translation*. London: W. W. Norton & Company.

Fuller, C.J. 2004. *The Camphor Flame: Popular Hinduism and Society in India*. Revised and expanded edition. Princeton, N.J: Princeton University Press.

Genette, Gérard. 1997. *Paratexts: Thresholds of Interpretation*. Translated by Jane E. Lewin and Richard Macksey. Volume 20, Seuils. Cambridge: Cambridge University Press.

Gita Nectar. 2011. Second edition. Lima: Minibookworld.

Gita Press. n.d. "An Introduction." http://Gitapress.org/english/GP_intro.htm

Gita Press. 2016a. "ShrimadbhagvadGita Tabeeji." Gorakhpur: Gita. http://Gita-pressbookshop.in/books-by-topics-subjects/shrimadbhagwadGita/shrimad-bhagvadGita-tabeeji.html

Gita Press. 2016b. "ShrimadbhagvadGita with Mahatmya, Deluxe Edition." Gorakhpur: Gita. http://Gitapressbookshop.in/shrimad-bhagvad-Gita-with-mahatmya-deluxe-edition.html

Gita Press 2016c. *Stri Dharma Prashnottari*. Gorakhpur: Gita. http://Gitapress.org/english/search_code.asp

Goffman, Erving. 1979. *Gender Advertisements*. New York: Harper & Row.

Goyandka, Jaydayal. 2017. *An Ideal Woman—Sushila*. Translated by S.N. Pandey. Gorakhpur: Gita.

India Book of Records. 2015. "Smallest Handwritten *Bhgavad* Gita." http://india-bookofrecords.in/smallest-hand-written-bhagavad-Gita-2/

Jacobsen, Knut A. 2003. *Hinduismen*. Oslo: Pax.

Joshi, Sarita. 2015. Ghazal Gita. 21 December. https://www.youtube.com/watch?v=up4Ao_-NB6Q

Kannadasan, Akila. 2017. "Small Wonder." *The Hindu*, April 17. http://www.thehindu.com/society/small-wonder-meet-k-eswar-kumar-who-prints-miniature-books/article18140258.ece

Katiyar, Shiv Prakash. 2016. "Gender Disparity in Literacy in India." *Social Change* 46 (1): 46-69. https://doi.org/10.1177/0049085715618558

King, Ursula. 1982. "The Iconography of the Bhagavad Gita." *Journal of Dharma* 7 (2): 146-163.

Legge, Gordon E., and Charles A. Bigelow. 2011. "Does Print Size Matter for Reading? A Review of Findings from Vision Science and Typography." *Journal of Vision* 11: 1–22. https://doi.org/10.1167/11.5.8

Lejeune, Philippe. 1975. *Le Pacte Autobiographique, Poétique*. Paris: Seuils.

Miniature Book Society. n.d. "What is a Miniature Book?" http://www.mbs.org/

Minibooksworld. 2018a. *Extracts of The Religions*. http://www.minibooksworld.com/product_info.php?cPath=14&products_id=86

Minibooksworld. 2018b. "For Children and Youth." http://www.minibooksworld.com/index.php?cPath=3

Minibooksworld. 2018c. "The Man and the Women." http://www.minibooksworld.com/index.php?cPath=2&osCsid=no7gf0jbsu2u26t8d8ah9v9sp2

Mukul, Akshaya. 2015. Gita *Press and the Making of Hindu India*. Noida: HarperCollins.

Nightingale. n.d. "Mini Bhagavad Gita." https://nightingaleshop.com/mini-bhagavad-Gita

Padoux, André. 2011. *Tantric Mantras: Studies on Mantrasastra*. Abingdon: Routledge. https://doi.org/10.4324/9780203814499

Panaji. 2009. "Holy Verse Etched in Tanishq Jewellery." *Navhind Times*, June 16, 2009. http://www.navhindtimes.com/story.php?story=2009061625

Prabhupada-books. n.d. "Pocket Size Donation Gita." http://www.prabhupada-books.de/pocket-Gita.html

Premadharma. n.d. "Srimad Bhagavad-Gita." https://premadharma.org/srimad-bhagavad-Gita/

Qur'an Nectar. 2011. Second edition. Minibookworld.

Rudraansha Exports. n.d. "Bhagwad Gita with Gold Platin." http://www.global-sources.com/si/AS/Rudraansha-Exports/6008832155413/pdtl/Bhagwad-Gita-Pendant/1077209084.htm

Shaadiology.com. 2016. "Silver Mini Bhagavad Gita." https://www.shaadilogy.com/index.php/wedding-store/gifting-and-favours/gifts-made-from-silver.html

Shrimadbhagavad Gita. 2014. Sanskrit. Tabeeji edition. Gorakhpur: Gita Press. Seventieth reprint.

Shrimadbhagavad Gita. 1933. Bombay: Khemraj Shrikrishnadass Shri Venkateshwar.

Silver Mini Bhagvad Gita. 2016. Kolkata: Shaadiology. https://www.shaadilogy.com/index.php/wedding-store/gifting-and-favours/gifts-made-from-silver.html

Stendhal. 1982. *Oeuvres Intimes*. Volume 2. Paris: Gallimard.

Tamil Brahmins. 2010. "Bhagavad Gita – Excellent Book." https://www.tamilbrahmins.com/showthread.php?t=3755

The Bhagavad-Gita: Krishna's Counsel in Time of War. 1986. Translated into English with an introduction by Barbara Stoler Miller. New York: Bantam Dell.

The Bhagavad Gita in the Mahabharata: Text and Translation. 1981. Chicago: University of Chicago Press.

The Bhagavad Gita. 1962. Translated by Juan Mascaró. Harmondsworth: Penguin Classics.

The Bhagavad Gita: With an Introductory Essay, Sanskrit Text, English Translation and Notes. 1948. Translated by Sarvepalli Radhakrishnan. London: Unwin Hyman Limited.

Weber, Francis J. 1992. "The ABCs of Miniature Bookdom—II." *Miniature Book Society Newsletter*, April 1992: 6–7.

10

Sutras Working in Buddha's Belly and Buddhists' Pockets: Miniature *Sutras* in Korean Buddhism

Yohan Yoo and Woncheol Yun

Yohan Yoo is Professor of Comparative Religion in the Department of Religious Studies and Associate Dean of the College of Humanities at Seoul National University.

Woncheol Yun is Professor of Buddhism in the Department of Religious Studies at Seoul National University.

Korean lay Buddhists, most of whom are unable to recite or read scriptures that are mainly written in classical Chinese, have approached and used Buddhist scriptures in non-semantic ways. They have developed various ways of repeating and possessing scriptures in order to use as well as possible the power and status of those sacred texts (Yoo 2010, 252–258). According to the pioneering study of James W. Watts (2006), scripture can be ritualized along three dimensions: the semantic, the iconic, and the performative. In the possession of scriptures and various ways of repeating them, such as reciting and copying scriptures, turning rotating sutra cases, or playing sutra CDs, it is the iconic and performative dimensions of scriptures, rather than the semantic, that are conspicuously revealed. In this chapter, we will pay particular attention to another way in which contemporary Korean lay Buddhists mobilize the sacred status and power of scriptures: how they create and utilize miniature sutras.

Miniature *sutras*, and Buddhist scriptures in general, have iconic status and sacred power that are quite autonomous from the semantic dimension of scriptures. This autonomy differs from what any text comes to possess in the process of its interpretation. Paul Ricoeur has shown that a written text can separate itself from its original semantic context, such as its author, its initial audience, and situation, and acquire a status independent of them. When what is spoken is written and becomes a text, it assumes an object-like character and is "decontextualized" from its original setting and becomes open to innumerable "recontextualizations" (Ricoeur 1995, 219). In this way, the text obtains autonomy and moreover "iconicity" (Ricoeur 1976, 42). According to Ricoeur, iconicity is not separate from the semantic dimension of the text, in that this iconicity is secured when the text breaks away from its original understanding and is interpreted in different situations and new ways. Yet Buddhist scriptures often possess an iconicity that is separate from their semantic contexts. The recontextualization of Buddhist scriptures comes about as a result of their own sacred status. Scriptures that are regarded as sacred beings perform supernatural work, which Buddhists expect to be carried out, independent of their content, not only in ritual situations but also in daily life. Miniature *sutras* of contemporary Korean Buddhism are so small that they are very difficult to read without a magnifying glass. Indeed, few lay Buddhists who possess and carry these miniature *sutras* even try to understand their content. Instead, they expect the miniature *sutras* to transform the Buddha statues in their home into the real and living Buddha, thereby bringing blessings and benefits to their lives.

It should also be noted that the scriptures' iconic status as "the word-body of the Buddha" (Seckel 1968, 114), which is often separate from their content, can perform efficacious work without extra ritual activities such as recitation. If scriptures are accepted as iconic sacred beings, then their potency lies in their very presence. As such, it can be said that the efficacy of scriptures is based on and originates from the iconic dimension. Most lay Buddhists neither understand the content of scriptures nor do they perform rituals related to the content of what is written. Instead, they make the most of the iconic dimension of scriptures by utilizing their physical forms (see Watts 2006, 142).

By investigating the example of miniature *sutras* in Korea we will demonstrate that a scripture can perform work for adherents without explicit ritual performance, as long as the scripture has iconicity. For this purpose, we will first outline the historical background to the custom of storing *sutras* in the belly of Buddha statues, which will help understand how scriptures could be equated with dharma or the Buddha himself. Then we will focus on how miniature *sutras* work efficaciously within the belly of Buddha statues and in the hands or pockets of Buddhists.

Sutras changing statues into the living Buddha

From the early stages of Indian Buddhism, Buddhist scriptures have enjoyed sacred status that is equivalent to the Buddha himself. Scriptures have been equated with dharma, the basic doctrine and teachings of the Buddha. Dharma has simultaneously occupied a very peculiar and prominent place in Buddhism. Gautama Siddhartha became the Buddha after he discovered the dharma. According to the *Nirvana Sutra*, one of the early *sutras*, the Buddha advised his disciples to take the dharma as their guide after his death. In addition, dharma is the second of the "three jewels" or refuges of Buddhists along with Buddha and *sangha*. Since cherishing and taking refuge in the three jewels is a primary criterion for being regarded as a Buddhist, it is clear that these three are important elements of Buddhism. The word dharma often designates *sutras*, the scriptural texts of the Buddha's teachings, and sometimes extends to mantras or *dharanis*, short spell-like texts thought to encapsulate various aspects of the Buddha's teachings. Furthermore, dharma is regarded as the essence of the Buddha himself. It is one of the two "bodies" that Mahayana Buddhism has distinguished in order to explain Buddha's embodiment in the scriptural traditions that recorded his teachings and in the physical form. According to Charles Willemen, "[t]he two bodies are the law-body (*dharmakaya*), which is the dharma, the essence of Buddha, and the material body (*rupakaya*), the physical aspect" (Willemen 2004, 219). The Buddha is the teacher of dharma and, at the same time, a personification of dharma.

We would like to emphasize again that *sutras* easily acquire iconic status independent of their semantic content because they are identified with dharma and therefore the Buddha. José Ignacio Cabezón correctly points out that "[Buddhist] scriptures cannot be reduced to their content or meaning, since they are put to many uses that have nothing to do with their meaning" and that "they serve as an object of worship and devotion" (Cabezón 2004, 757). The iconicity of Buddhist scriptures is founded on the religious notion that they are embodiments of dharma and the Buddha.

In the Buddhist traditions, scriptures came to be equated with relics of the Buddha and stored in stupas. In India, stupas were objects of worship because they contained relics called *sariras*, mainly ash, of a saintly person (Dallapiccola 2004, 803). With the spread of Buddhism, relics of the Buddha were laid in stupas in other countries that adopted the religion. Though it was a matter of course that the Buddha relics were limited, this practice could be widely followed because "the term 'relic' was interpreted very freely indeed, and was extended to include sacred texts (*sutras*) and spells (*dharanis*) as the word-body of the Buddha" (Seckel 1968, 114). Texts, which took various forms and were made of many different materials according to places and periods, such as birch bark, palm leaf, bamboo stalk, or paper, replaced the bodily remnants of the Buddha in stupas, effectively becoming relics themselves and making the stupas objects of worship. This practice illustrates how the iconicity of scriptures was separate from their content.

In Korea, scriptures were from the early eighth century stored in pagodas, which function as stupas in East Asia, in place of Buddha relics or symbolic substitutes such as beads and jewels. Though various *sutras* and *dharanis*, including the *Diamond Sutra, Flower Ornament Sutra, Pratityasamutpada-gatha,* and *Cundi Mantra,* were placed in pagodas, *Great Dharani Sutra of Immaculate and Pure Light* was the most common text put in pagoda reliquaries (Joo 2016, 270). Early examples of miniature *sutras* are found in the pagodas built from approximately the eighth century to the twelfth century. Pagodas frequently contained within them miniature pagodas of 5 to 10 centimeters in height, which were made of wood, metals, stone, or clay (The National Museum of Korea 1991, 112–127).[1] Some of these miniature pagodas placed in the large pagodas were furnished with a hole in which a small *dharani* paper roll was inserted (Joo 2004, 171).

The Buddha relics—understood, in a broad sense, to include *sutras, dharanis,* beads, or jewels—had been originally stored in stupas or pagodas. Gradually they came to be placed in the empty space of the Buddha statues. Korean Buddhists have believed for centuries that statues become the real Buddha and come to have sacred power if relics are stored in them. This is called the belief in *saengsin* ("the living body") (Mun 1991). As there is a high possibility that Buddha relics were installed in the *ushnisha,* the topknot appearing on top of the head of the Buddha statues, in second- and third-century Gandhara (Rhi 2004, 134–146),[2] it would seem that the relics were installed within the Buddha statues in India from quite an early period. Relics were also stored in statues in China but none dating from before the tenth century. Some scholars argue that relics including scriptures began to be stored in statues in Korea from the late eighth century; the ground of a Vairocana Buddha statue made in 776 CE bears a trace of what might have been a reliquary ("Bokjang" 2010). Around ten statues with relics, belonging to the late Goryeo dynasty period (thirteenth to fourteenth centuries), have been discovered and there are hundreds of such relic-statues belonging to the Joseon dynasty (fifteenth to nineteenth centuries) (Jeontongbulbokjang 2014, 126). Besides scriptures and relics, ceremonial items, such as the five types of incense, medicine, and grain, the five colors of thread and cloth, as well as beads and other jewels, were also stored in the statues (Jeontongbulbokjang 2014, 134–137).[3] While

1. Sometimes small pagoda images were engraved on metal plates or on the surface of the gilt bronze reliquaries (The National Museum of Korea 1991, 24, 113).

2. Buddha relics in China and Korea seem to have been sometimes stored in the heads of statues, rather than in the belly (Mun 1991). Recently, a copy of the *Mahaprajnaparamita Sutra* was found in the head of a Buddha statue in Silsangsa Temple (Namweon, South Korea). The statue is estimated to be from the late fourteenth century (Bak 2017).

3. Korean Buddhism appears to have developed its own way of storing relics distinct from that of China. Relic containers in the shape of bottles and cylinders are not seen in Chinese Buddha statues, but were commonly used in Korea.

the specific content varied, scriptures were the most important item, and were never excluded. It is clear that it was necessary to keep *sutras*—commonly *Lotus Sutra, Surangama Sutra, Diamond Sutra, Golden Light Sutra, Flower Ornament Sutra, Ksitigarbha Sutra,* and various kinds of *dharani*s written on paper – stored in the Buddha statues (Jeontongbulbokjang 2014, 118–125). The scriptures transformed the statues into "the living body" of the Buddha with their presence.

Miniature *sutras* working in Buddha's belly

The practice of storing scriptures in statues was primarily found in temples and collective places for worship. Today, however, many lay Buddhists in contemporary Korea have Buddha statues in their own homes. Though there are relatively large statues for domestic use whose height is about 60 centimeters, most are statues to be placed on desks or display cabinets and are about 20 centimeters in height. Like the small *dharani* scrolls inserted into miniature pagodas, these Buddha statues require miniature *sutras* in order to become "the living body" of the Buddha. The letters printed on the pages of these miniature books are too small to read. In addition, they are often printed in classical Chinese without Korean phonetic script or translation. It is clear that miniature *sutras* are especially made to transform the essence of the Buddha statues, and are not intended for study or recitation. They are accepted as representations of the dharma, regarded as having equivalent status to the Buddha, and make the statues become the real Buddha with power to bless and protect the possessors.

We are not arguing that Korean Buddhists do not care about the semantic dimension of scriptures. Some devout Korean lay Buddhists certainly put stress on the content of *sutras* and try to read and study them, which is proved clearly by the use of readable "mini-*sutras*" among Korean Buddhists. Korean Buddhist shops, both online and offline, sell mini-*sutras*, the purpose and usage of which can be divided into two types by size.[4] The size of the first type is 6 to 8.5 centimeters wide and 11 to 13 centimeters long containing

---

In addition, Korean Buddhists did not install items such as cloth and thread arranged in the shape of internal organs, which was a common practice in China (Jeontongbulbokjang 2014, 101–108; Lee 2016, 94).

4. The authors visited two Buddhist shops and interviewed the owners on July 22, 2017. The two shops are "Bulsimweon" and "Taeseongbulgyosa," both of which are located in Jongro-gu, Seoul, near the Jogyesa Temple, the headquarters of the Jogye Order of Korean Buddhism. The authors also consulted the catalogs of ten online Buddhist shops for this research: Buddhazone (2008), Bulgyomart (2012), Bulgyosesang (2012), Jongrobulgyosa (2012), Mahamall (1998), Moranbulgyoyongpum (2006), Sabanuri (2010), Sachalmall (2005), Sejonmall (2003), and Seonjaemall (2008).

150 to 200 pages. These scriptures are small pocket-sized books, too large to be regarded as "miniature," are easy to carry, and are made to be read. These portable *sutras* clearly involve the semantic dimension of the scriptures as well as their iconic and performative dimensions. Most books in this category consist of two parts: The first part contains *sutras* written in classical Chinese characters with Korean endings and phonetic pronunciation in Korean script. This part is intended to provide the iconic and performative dimensions of scriptures. When lay Buddhists who do not know the meaning of the Chinese scripture recite what is written by reading Korean phonetic values, they expect to have the sacred power of the *sutra*. Furthermore, they intend to enjoy the protection and blessing of the Buddha only by carrying these small books. The second part is a Korean interpretation of the classical Chinese text. Buddhists read this part to understand the teachings of the Buddha. The use of this part thus involves a semantic dimension. Many scriptures that have been popular in Korea for a long time, including the *Dhammapada*, *Lotus Sutra*, *Diamond Sutra*, *Flower Ornament Sutra*, *Heart Sutra*, *Thousand Hands Sutra*, *Avalokitesvara Sutra*, *The Sutra of the Medicine Buddha's Vows* and others, are published as pocketbooks for the laity who wants to carry and read the word-body of the Buddha at the same time.

On the other hand, there is another kind of mini-*sutras* that contains only the classical Chinese characters and their Korean transliteration, without the Korean translation. These pocketbooks are approximately of the same size, but have fewer pages in comparison to the mini-*sutras* that include translations. When using these mini-*sutras*, the semantic dimension is not present but the iconic and performative dimensions are indisputable. Lay Buddhists can easily carry and recite the part printed in Korean without understanding the meaning. In carrying these small scriptures and reciting them phonetically, Buddhists expect the scriptures to bless and protect them.

The mini-*sutras* of the second type are obviously miniatures that can involve both semantic and performative dimensions when they are used. It is almost impossible to read the smallest miniature *sutras*, which cover between 50 and 80 pages and measure just 2.3 centimeters in width and 3.3 centimeters in length. It is also very difficult to read the slightly larger books, which tend to be 3.8 centimeters wide and 5.5 centimeters long. In addition, they usually do not have Korean transliteration or translation. It is clear that they are produced neither for study nor for recitation. These two sizes of miniature *sutras* are either stored in the small Buddha statues that are kept in the home or carried by Buddhists in their pockets or bags. Inside the Buddha statues, the miniatures are believed to put life into the statues and transform them into embodiments of the real Buddha, who blesses and helps possessors in everyday life.

Figure 10.1: Miniature *sutras* (left) and readable mini-*sutras* (right). Photo by the authors.

Lay Buddhists use these miniature *sutras* in ways that differ from those of monks or nuns in two respects: First, lay Buddhists do not consider the content of the *sutras* that they place in the statue at home. Rather, the iconic status of miniature *sutras* is independent of their semantic meaning. People usually purchase miniature *sutras* that they can easily obtain, most of which are concise and therefore easily made into miniatures, such as the *Heart Sutra*, *Diamond Sutra*, *Surangama Mantras*, the chapter of "Avalokitesvara's Universal Gate" of the *Lotus Sutra*, the *Thousand Hands Sutra*, the chapter of "Samantabhadra's Conduct and Vows" of the *Flower Ornament Sutra*, and the *Avalokitesvara Sutra*. The sacred status and power of a scripture that enabled it to replace the Buddha relics and the Buddha himself were however originally related to its content. For instance, *Great Dharani Sutra of Immaculate and Pure Light*, which was one of the most popular scriptures to be put in the reliquaries of pagodas, as mentioned above, became favored by the royal family and was placed in many stupas because the text itself states that Heavenly Devas will protect the country where pagodas containing this *sutra* are built (Joo 2016, 267). This demonstrates that the iconic status and performative power of a scripture may be initially related to the semantic content and later become autonomous from it. Many Korean lay Buddhists also sometimes choose *sutras* that are known for their talismanic power, as will be explained further below.

Secondly, scriptures can perform distinctive functions as sacred beings within the Buddha statues without any specific ritual performance. Complicated rituals for installing Buddha relics or scriptures into Buddha statues were developed for Buddhist temples. As shown above, items that are stored in statues with scriptures such as incense, medicine, grain, thread, and beads, are related to temple ceremonies. Even nowadays, some people put a very small amount of grain, thread, incense, and tiny plastic beads in statues along with miniature scriptures, but they do not perform any particular rituals when installing these items in statues. Instead, the items are purchased in small pre-packed boxed sets at Buddhist shops and placed all at once into the hole at the bottom of a Buddha statue. Sometimes a small *dharani* or mandala scroll that is included for free when purchasing a statue is attached with glue at the bottom to seal the hole after the items are inserted. Though this process may be regarded as a ritual in a broad sense, there is no conscious ritual performance carried out at home. For further convenience, statues for purchase also have the scriptures or the small box pre-installed. The procedure in which scriptures and other items are stored does not appear to be important to lay Buddhists who possess the statue. Rather, the scriptures are believed to have iconicity that can activate the statues and turn them into the Buddha himself not by specific ritual performances but simply by the presence of small scriptures.

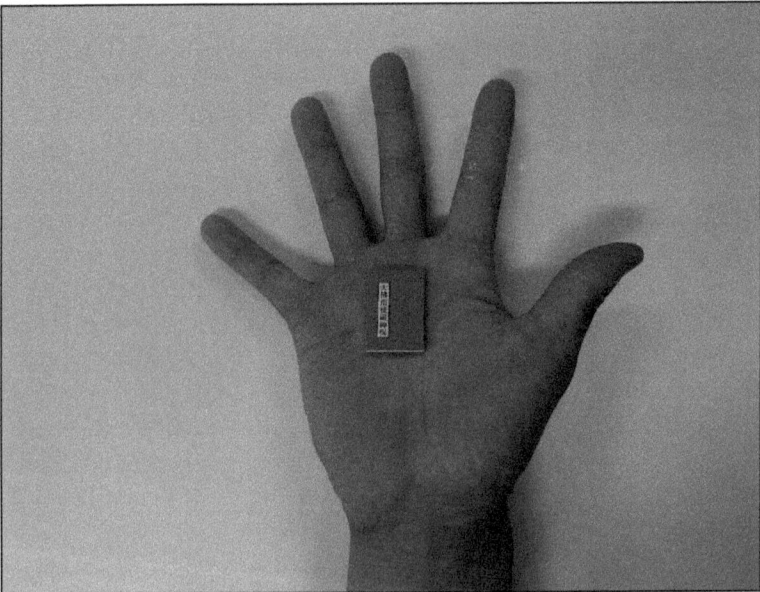

Figure 10.2: A miniature *sutra* in hand. Photo by the authors.

Sutras working in Buddhists' pockets

The power of *sutras* has been recognized and appropriated in the whole Buddhist cultural landscape. Because the dharma is considered "the protector" of people (Willemen 2004, 219), *sutras* are believed to protect their readers, listeners, and possessors. Shorter mantras and *dharanis* are more easily recited and can be efficiently used for helping Buddhists in various contexts. When these short texts are chanted, they are believed to help lay Buddhists "achieve the material blessings and protections needed for a good worldly life" (Esposito *et al.* 2015, 428). The sacred status and power of *sutras* as dharma and the Buddha are recognized and appropriated not only by the laity, to most of whom the semantic dimension of the scriptures is unavailable, but also by monks and nuns, who learn to read the *sutras* and understand their content. In all countries where Buddhism is prevalent, monks and nuns generally engage in practices and rites based on the iconic and performative dimensions of scriptures.

Figure 10.3: Items including miniature *sutras* that are stored in domestic small Buddha statues. Photo by the authors.

Though scholars of religious texts have mostly limited their research to the semantic dimension of scriptures, academics have also highlighted the performative functions of scriptures when reading, reciting, or otherwise repeating them (Graham 1987; Levering 1989). For instance, Miriam Levering explored the functions of *sutras* in a Buddhist convent in contemporary Taiwan (Levering 1989, 72–90). The Taiwanese nuns of the convent Levering observed believed that the sacred words of the scriptures recited in rituals protected people and brought benefits to them. In addition, according to Levering, the nuns recited and copied *sutras* because they believed that by doing so they could eliminate the past accumulation of negative karma (Levering 1989, 73). Other scholars have shown how certain Buddhist rituals materialize the power gained by reading or reciting *sutras*. A popular world religions textbook introduces the Buddhist ritual of making water imbued with powers of chanted *sutras*:

> In the simplest (and still most popular) universal Buddhist ritual, monks pour water into a vessel as they chant words revealed by the Buddha. Now imbued with healing powers, the liquid can be drunk or sprinkled over the bodies of those needing assistance. (Esposito, Fasching, and Lewis 2015, 446)

Figure 10.4: Inserting the box that includes miniature *sutras* into a small Buddha statue. Photo by the authors.

But it should be remembered that ritual reciting or chanting does not explain the whole non-semantic dimension of scriptures. Ritual performances are not necessarily required in order to activate the sacred power of scriptures. Scriptures can have a beneficial effect just by being held in the hands or kept in purses. In this sense, José Ignacio Cabezón likens scriptures to amulets and talismans, which are kept or worn "as a way of protecting the bearers or consumers of the text from evil or harm" (Cabezón 2004, 757). In Korea, many kinds of *sutras*, both those in book form and those with the text printed on other types of material items, are manufactured and displayed at home (Yoo 2010, 255).[5] But miniature *sutras* are the easiest to wear or carry and consequently considered to be the most effective means to protect the wearers or bearers without requiring any specific ritual performance.

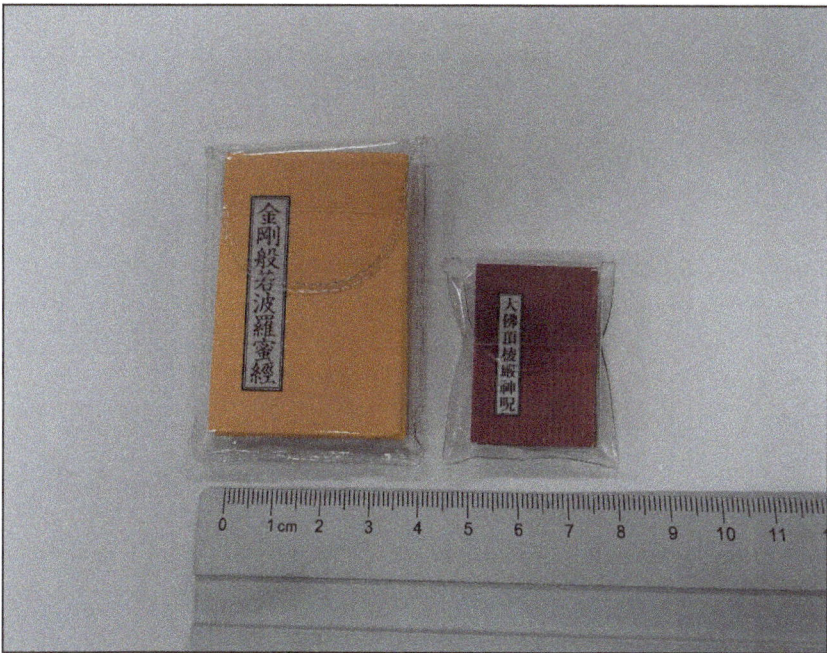

Figure 10.5: Hosinyong miniature *sutras* carried in purses or bags. Photo by the authors.

In online Buddhist shops, the miniature *sutras* that measure 2.3 by 3.3 centimeters or 3.8 by 5.5 centimeters are dubbed *bokjangyong,* which means "for storing in the Buddha statues," and *hosinyong,* meaning "for self-protection." The same tiny books that transform statues into the living Buddha are thus

5. Besides *sutras*, Korean Buddhists make and use various goods, on which some words, a few passages, or the full text of scriptures are printed or engraved, in order to gain beneficial influences from them. Buddhist shops serve customers almost every kind of everyday item upon which a passage from the *sutras* is engraved or printed, such as hand fans, stationery, tableware, tea cup sets, towels, tea cloths, wristwatches, wall clocks, mobile phone ornaments, purses, wallets, and so on (Yoo 2010, 255–257).

also believed to protect people who carry them from the evil in the world. They are usually placed in protective plastic covers and carried in purses or bags. In addition, *hosinyong* miniature *sutras* are often made into accessories to be attached to a key chain, cellphone, or the rearview mirror of a car. Wherever the bearers may go, they can be protected by the miniature *sutra*, or the word-body of the Buddha. A type of miniature *sutras* in a contemporary printed codex that can be used for this purpose is available in Buddhist shops. It is a very small book, measuring 3.5 centimeters in width and 5 centimeters in length, and has a plastic cover that looks like leather, with the pages embossed in gold. It is a real book although the letters in it are too small to read. The manufacturer of this accessory miniature book is ambitious, cramming the *Thousand Hands Sutra*, the *Heart Sutra*, the *Diamond Sutra*, "Samantabhadra's Conduct and Vows" of the *Flower Ornament Sutra*, the *Avalokitesvara Sutra*, and several prayers into the tiny tome. But as this book is fragile, more people prefer to carry a plastic replica of scriptures that measures 1.7 centimeters wide, 2.8 centimeters long, and 0.5 centimeters deep. The replica is a small box that looks like a book on which the title of a *sutra* is engraved. At the bottom of this book-shaped box there is a tiny hole in which a real text written on a small paper scroll is inserted. Concise *sutras*, like the *Diamond Sutra* or the chapter "Avalokitesvara's Universal Gate" of the *Lotus Sutra,* are used for this miniature text inside a miniature replica *sutra*. This light and strong plastic miniature is very suitable for key chains or cellphone cases.

Buddhists have thus believed that *sutras* can protect and bless their possessors and bearers. Miniature *sutras* are made to fulfill this function most effectively because they can be worn or carried very easily. The uses of these small *sutras* involve an iconic dimension since the books are too small to read and they are believed to possess powers independent of their semantic content and recitation or repetition of what is written. Even if the users do not understand their meaning and do not perform any specific rituals, the miniature *sutras* are believed to exert sacred power by being present as sacred beings.

Conclusion

From the beginning of Buddhist history, scriptures have been identified with dharma, one of the three refuges of Buddhists, and Buddhists have enjoyed the sacred status as an embodiment of the Buddha himself. This status of scriptures as sacred beings involves an iconic dimension since the scriptures are recontextualized in various situations of everyday life and rituals in which understanding of the semantic content is not given preference. Lay Buddhists especially believe the use of scriptures can be efficacious irrespective of their content and without any specific ritual performance. When a scripture,

Figure 10.6: Miniature *sutras* for key chains or cellphones. Photo by the authors.

Figure 10.7: A plastic box miniature *sutra* with a hole into which a paper scroll *sutra* is inserted. Photo by the authors.

which is an expression of dharma and therefore the Buddha himself, is stored in a Buddha statue, the statue is believed to become the living body of the Buddha. In the hands or purses of Buddhists, it is handled more like an amulet or talisman that is believed to bless them and protect them from the evil.

Though Buddhists have thought of and treated their religious scriptures as sacred beings for a long time, they also have developed various new ways of appropriating the power of scriptures more efficiently. The use of miniature *sutras* in contemporary Korea is a new means of mobilizing the power of scriptures. Because they are easy to obtain and carry, they can work within small Buddha statues on a desk at home, or can accompany users everywhere while attached to a rearview mirror, cellphone, or key chain. Though it is very difficult and sometimes impossible to read these small miniature *sutras*, for most of their users it does not matter. As long as the iconicity of a miniature *sutra* is recognized, it can work as a sacred being even if the possessors do not read or understand its content.

References

"Bokjang." 2010. In *Doopedia Doosanbaekgua* [*Doosan Encyclopedia*]. http://www.doopedia.co.kr/doopedia/master/master.do?_method= view&MAS_IDX=101013000870987

Bak, Jeongho. 2017. "A Buddhist *Sutra* Found in the Head of a Buddha Statue in Silsangsa." *Joonangilbo*. May 22. http://news.joins.com/article/21602102

Buddhazone. 2008. http://www.buddhazone.co.kr/shop/main/index.php

Bulgyosesang. 2012. http://www.bulkyosesang.co.kr/

Bulgyomart. 2012. http://www.bulkyomart.com/

Cabezón, José Ignacio. 2004. "Scripture." In *Encyclopedia of Buddhism* Volume 2, edited by Robert E. Buswell Jr., 755–758. New York: Thomson Gale.

Dallapiccola, A.L. 2004. "Stupa." In *Encyclopedia of Buddhis*, Volume 2, edited by Robert E. Buswell Jr., 803–808. New York: Thomson Gale.

Esposito, John L., Darrell J. Fasching, and Todd T. Lewis. 2015. *World Religions Today*. Fifth edition. New York: Oxford University Press.

Graham, William A. 1987. *Beyond Written Word: Oral Aspects of Scriptures in the History of Religion*. Cambridge: Cambridge University Press.

Jeontongbulbokjang mit jeomanuisikbojonhoe [Jeontongbulbokjang]. 2014. *Jeontong Bulbokjanguisik Mit Jeomanuisik* [*Traditional Rites of Storing Sacred Objects in Buddha Statues and of Drawing Eyes on them*]. Seoul: Bulgyomunhwajaeyeonguso.

Jongrobulgyosa. 2012. http://www.jongrobulkyosa.co.kr/index/index.php

Joo, Kyeong-mi. 2004. "Hanguk Bulsarijangeom-e Iseoseo *Mugujeongguangdaedaranigyeong*-ui Uiui" [Translation from Korean: The Significance of *Rasmivimalavisuddhaprabhanama-dharani-sutra* in Korean Buddhist Reliquaries]. *Journal of Buddhist Art* 2: 164–196.

Joo, Kyeong-mi. 2016. "Silla Jungdae Bulsarijangeom-ui Dayangseong-gua Munh-wasajeok Uiui" [Stylistic Multiplicity of Buddhist Reliquaries in the Middle Silla and Its Cultural Historical Meaning]. *Sogang Journal of Early Korean History* 23: 249–290.

———. 2016. "Urinara Bulbokjang-ui Teukjing" [Translation from Korean: Characteristics of Korean *Bulbokang*]. *Korean Journal of Art History* 289: 93–119.

Levering, Miriam. 1989. "Scripture and Its Reception: A Buddhist Case." In *Rethinking Scripture: Essays from a Comparative Perspective*, edited by Miriam Levering, 58–101. Albany: State University of New York Press.

Mahamall. 1998. http://www.mahamall.co.kr/

Moranbulgyoyongpum. 2006. http://moranbulkyo.co.kr/index.html

Mun, Myeongdae. 1991. "Bokjang." In *Han-guk Minjok Munhwa Daebaekgua* [*Encyclopedia of Korean Culture*]. http://encykorea.aks.ac.kr/Contents/Index

Rhi, Juhyung. 2004. "Gandhara Bulsang-gwa Sari Bongan" [Translation from Korean: The Installation of a Relic in Buddha Image of Gandhara]. *Central Asian Studies* 9: 129–159.

Ricoeur, Paul. 1976. *Interpretation Theory: Discourse and Surplus of Meaning*. Texas: Texas Christian University Press.

Ricoeur, Paul. 1995. *Figuring the Sacred: Religion, Narrative, and Imagination*. Minneapolis: Fortress.

Sabanuri. 2010. http://sabanuri.com/

Sachalmall. 2005. http://www.sachal.kr/

Seckel, Dietrich. 1968 [1964]. *The Art of Buddhism*. Translated by Ann E. Keep. New York: Greystone.

Sejonmall. 2003. http://www.sejonmall.com/FrontStore/iStartPage.phtml

Seonjaemall. 2008. http://www.seonjaemall.co.kr/

The National Museum of Korea. 1991. *Bulsarijangeom* [*The Art of Sarira Reliquary*]. Seoul: The National Museum of Korea.

Watts, James W. 2006. "The Three Dimensions of Scriptures." *Postscripts* 2: 135–159.

Willemen, Charles. 2004. "Dharma and Dharmas." In *Encyclopedia of Buddhism* Volume 1, edited by Robert E. Buswell Jr., 217–224. New York: Thomson Gale.

Yoo, Yohan. 2010. "Possession and Repetition: Ways in Which Korean Lay Buddhists Appropriate Scriptures." *Postscripts* 6: 243–259.

Index

C

www.ingramcontent.com/pod-product-compliance
Lightning Source LLC
Chambersburg PA
CBHW040254290326
41929CB00051B/3375